Settlement, Subsistence, and Society in Late Zuni Prehistory

Frontispiece.   General John A. Logan and party at Zuni Pueblo in 1882. (Photograph by Ben Wittick, courtesy of the Museum of New Mexico, Negative No. 16054.)

ANTHROPOLOGICAL PAPERS OF
THE UNIVERSITY OF ARIZONA
NUMBER 44

Settlement, Subsistence, and Society in Late Zuni Prehistory

Keith W. Kintigh

THE UNIVERSITY OF ARIZONA PRESS
TUCSON, ARIZONA
1985

About the author . . .

KEITH W. KINTIGH first participated in archaeological field work in the southwestern United States in 1973, and since then his interest in the Southwest has focused on the prehistoric period in the Zuni area of New Mexico. He has had additional field experience in Morocco and Peru. His publications cover a variety of topics, with a particular emphasis on the use of quantitative methods in archaeology. Dr. Kintigh earned a Master of Science degree in Computer Science from Stanford University in 1974, and he received a doctoral degree in Anthropology from the University of Michigan in 1982. In 1980 he was appointed Associate Archaeologist at the Arizona State Museum, University of Arizona, and in 1984 accepted a position as Assistant Professor of Anthropology at the University of California, Santa Barbara.

Cover: View of Zuni Pueblo, taken on the Wheeler Expedition, 1873. (Photograph courtesy of the Smithsonian Institution, National Anthropological Archives, Bureau of American Ethnology Collection, Negative No. 2264—B.)

THE UNIVERSITY OF ARIZONA PRESS

This book was set in 10/11 Times Roman
Manufactured in the U.S.A.

Library of Congress Cataloging in Publication Data

Kintigh, Keith W.
    Settlement, subsistence, and society in late Zuni prehistory.

    (Anthropological papers of the University of Arizona; no. 44)
    Includes index.
    1. Zuni Indians — History. 2. Zuni Indians — Antiquities.
3. Land settlement patterns — New Mexico — History.
4. New Mexico — Antiquities. I. Title. II. Series.
E99.Z9K7 1984   978.9'01   84-22769

ISBN 0-8165-0831-3

CONTENTS

FIGURES

TABLES

PREFACE

This analysis of archaeological settlement data is directed toward achieving a better understanding of the sequence of human adaptations in the Zuni area from A.D. 1250 to 1540. Results of original fieldwork are compiled with published and unpublished site information to yield a comprehensive inventory of pueblos occupied during this time interval, with the exception of some small room blocks inhabited during its first two or three decades. From an analysis of ceramic surface collections made during the fieldwork, and from a reanalysis of various museum collections, a revision of the previously published ceramic chronology is proposed and a chronology of site occupation is developed.

Within a few decades after A.D. 1250 the entire population of the Zuni area of New Mexico apparently moved from hundreds of small dispersed villages into a few large pueblos. From the time of that aggregation until the time of first Spanish contact in 1539 and 1540, people lived almost exclusively in these large towns. While no more than about 14 large pueblos were occupied at any one time, a total of 36 large, apparently planned pueblos were inhabited at one time or another during this 300-year period.

As a settlement pattern study, this research is concerned with the ways in which prehistoric settlements reflect their natural environment, and the technology and institutions of social interaction and control employed by their inhabitants (following Willey 1953: 1). Because this study relies almost entirely on data derived from archaeological survey, the range of interpretive variables that may be utilized is necessarily limited. Ceramic collections and some tree-ring dates are used to determine the contemporaneity of settlements. In addition to the artifact collections, other information available includes site size and configuration and, of course, site location and environmental context. Environmental variables of interest are the distribution of major topographic features and different landforms around each site, nearby soil types, site elevation, and the climatic variables of rainfall, temperature, and length of the growing season.

Both synchronic and diachronic analyses are required in this study. For each temporal interval, an attempt is made to understand the settlement distribution in terms of natural, technological, and social factors. While detailed reconstructions of the subsistence system cannot be made with the available data, it appears that throughout the period of interest the population relied on agriculture, with corn as the major crop.

An analysis of the modern environment reveals that extensive use of some form of water control probably was essential for any maize-based adaptation to the Zuni area. Consequently, the site locations utilized during each time interval have been analyzed with respect to their productive potential under different agricultural technologies. The results indicate that the earliest aggregated pueblos probably relied exclusively on various methods of floodwater (runoff) farming. Near the beginning of the 1300s, spring-fed irrigation was introduced and rapidly became an important part of the subsistence system. Although riverine irrigation may have begun at about the same time as spring-fed irrigation, it did not appear to be a major water-control strategy until about A.D. 1400, when spring- and river-fed irrigation agriculture became dominant.

The distribution of natural resources indicates that the protohistoric pueblos (dating after A.D. 1400) had quite uniform, economically strategic positions near irrigable land. Although most pueblos occupied prior to this time were situated on or near productive lands, other considerations must also have affected the choice of settlement location. Most of the pueblos that were poorly positioned with respect to access to fields had highly defensible locations on mesa tops, and defensive considerations also may have been a factor in the architectural layout. Most of the large, late pueblos, independent of the defensibility of their locations, had closed, high-walled perimeters.

Because of tendencies inherent in the social structures of segmentary societies, the aggregation of the inhabitants of hundreds of small villages into a dozen or so large pueblos initially resulted in a relatively high degree of social instability and a tendency of those pueblo populations to divide into factions and ultimately split apart.

While this research was not initiated with the goal of testing specific implications of hypotheses drawn from anthropological theory, I feel that an anthropologically informed description and interpretation of this evidently interesting sequence of settlement patterns not only furthers our knowledge of this prehistoric case, but, in the long term, also contributes to a more general understanding of human adaptation and cultural processes.

Throughout this monograph, the transliterations used for Zuni place names are those suggested by the Pueblo of Zuni Language Development Program; thus, Hawikku is used rather than the more common Hawikuh. Ceramic type names are not transliterated, even if they are derived from Zuni place names. Hence, the type is Pinnawa Glaze-on-white while the site is Binna:wa; the type is Matsaki Polychrome while the site is Mats'a:kya.

ACKNOWLEDGMENTS

Many people and several institutions materially aided this research. My thanks must first go to the Pueblo of Zuni and the landowners in the Ramah area who granted permission to study the ruins on their land. In this regard, I must specially thank Governor Robert E. Lewis of the Pueblo of Zuni and Mrs. Paul Davis of Ramah for their cooperation.

T. J. Ferguson, then Zuni Tribal Archaeologist and director of the Zuni Archaeology Program, provided much of the initial stimulus to undertake this research and has been a continuing source of information, insight, enthusiasm, and support. I am also grateful for his valuable comments on earlier drafts of the manuscript. During a summer at Zuni in 1979 and in continuing contact since then, I have relied on the assistance and friendship of Barbara Mills, Andrew Fowler, Barbara Holmes, and Margaret Hardin, and of other members of the Zuni Archaeology Program, including Anders Romancito, Rose Wyako, Jason Weekooty, and Terry Banteah.

As important as the fieldwork was the analysis of several museum collections. I appreciate the access so freely provided to the collections of the Museum of the American Indian, Heye Foundation; the American Museum of Natural History; Washington University; the State University of New York at Binghamton (now housed at Arizona State University); the Zuni Archaeology Program; the Peabody Museum of Harvard University; the Western Archeological Center, National Park Service; and the Arizona State Museum. Special thanks are extended to Brenda Holland of the Museum of the American Indian for her aid and interest, and to David Thomas and past curators at the American Museum of Natural History who have done a superb job of preserving Leslie Spier's marvelous collections for all these years.

Richard Woodbury has been an important source of information and inspiration. He generously provided me with notes on the Peabody Museum collection and field notes from his survey of the Zuni area. Through our discussions and letters, and by his comments on this manuscript, he has contributed far more than he knows.

Patty Jo Watson and Charles Redman have been continuing sources of patient guidance and aid since my first archaeological field season in New Mexico. In addition to her more general support, Patty Jo supplied crucial assistance in making available artifacts and information deriving from the CARP project, and in making extensive comments on drafts of this monograph.

After I joined the faculty of the University of Arizona, insights deriving from a number of discussions with Emil Haury, Paul Fish, Jeffrey Dean, and Gwinn Vivian were of particular help in developing my interpretation of the data presented here. Watson Smith provided many valuable comments and enriched my knowledge of the history of archaeology in the Zuni area. I am also grateful to Raymond Thompson for his support and interest.

The faculty and students of the University of Michigan gave generously of their time and intelligence. In particular, I would like to thank Henry Wright, John Nystuen, Jeffrey Parsons, John Speth, Vincas Steponaitis, and Robert Whallon for their special efforts on my behalf, and for reading and commenting on this manuscript.

Kathy Schreiber has been a constant source of support and archaeological insight. She aided in the fieldwork at Zuni, in the analysis of museum collections in New York, and in countless discussions of the project.

Financial assistance provided by a University of Michigan Rackham Dissertation Grant supported the fieldwork and museum research reported here, and permitted a more thorough study of museum collections than would otherwise have been possible. Raymond H. Thompson of the Arizona State Museum, University of Arizona, provided a small grant for the analysis of tree-ring samples from Atsinna. Substantial use is made of data collected by the Cibola Archaeological Research Project, which was funded by the National Science Foundation.

Carol Gifford's editing of this volume is gratefully acknowledged, as is Charles Sternberg's expert preparation of the site plans and figures included herein. A special note of appreciation is given to the fine professional staff of the University of Arizona Press, directed by Stephen Cox, whose interest in quality production has enhanced this volume.

Keith W. Kintigh

1. ZUNI PREHISTORY

The late prehistoric period in the American Southwest is characterized by dramatic changes in settlement patterns. Massive sections of the Southwest were abandoned; some populations apparently died out or moved completely away from their native regions, while others became concentrated into much smaller areas. In the Anasazi region, this abandonment and population concentration seems to have been particularly pronounced. At about A.D. 1200, Anasazi groups were dispersed over an enormous area of the Colorado Plateau and the Rio Grande River Valley. By the time of the first Spanish contact in the mid–1500s, however, the Anasazi populations were concentrated in a small fraction of this area: in the western pueblos of Zuni, Hopi, and Acoma, and in a number of pueblos along the Rio Grande.

Because the Zuni area (Fig. 1.1) was continuously occupied throughout this period of dramatic cultural change, it provides an excellent setting for the study of a sequence of apparently successful cultural adaptations and changes in settlement pattern. Although only a small portion of this area has been intensively surveyed archaeologically, it appears that all, or nearly all, of the late sites in the entire area have been identified.

During the interval between about A.D. 900 and 1300, the region experienced substantial population growth. In the early 1200s there was a large population dispersed in hundreds, if not thousands, of small- to medium-sized pueblos (with 2 to 50 rooms) spread out over an extensive area. At some time in the mid-to-late 1200s, a major shift in settlement pattern began. By 1300 virtually the entire population was concentrated in a relatively small number of large pueblos (with 200 to 1400 rooms) in the eastern part of the Zuni area. About 100 years later, around 1400, there was a dramatic shift in village location to the west, so that by the time the Spanish first arrived in 1539 and 1540, there were only six or seven pueblos spaced along the 25 km of the Zuni River just east of the Arizona-New Mexico border.

For each time period, distinguished herein on the basis of ceramic complexes, these settlement locations have been analyzed in order to infer aspects of the prehistoric agricultural technology, particularly the methods of water control and the degree to which settlement location and size seem to reflect the availability of the necessary natural resources in the vicinity. This analysis is aided by a knowledge of historic Hopi and Zuni farming practices, by the seventy-year record of the modern climate, and by an understanding of the environmental requirements of modern varieties of corn. The degree to which settlement location appears to be incompatible with agricultural self-sufficiency is used as evidence either for a location influenced by the availability of other natural resources, suggesting an interdependency among villages for subsistence items, or for social determinants of settlement location such as warfare or an advantageous location in a trading network.

This set of synchronic understandings lays the foundation for the analysis of the changes in these patterns over time. In the diachronic aspect of this study, the attempt is made to understand the changes in settlement patterns from one period to the next as evolutionary developments in technology and in mechanisms of social integration, and as responses to changes in the natural environment. Our understanding of the late prehistory of the Zuni area (briefly outlined above) indicates several obvious features of the settlement pattern sequence that demand consideration: (1) the dramatic population aggregation that occurred in the late A.D. 1200s; (2) the unusually high rate of settlement relocation within the eastern part of the study area that started during the late 1200s and continued through the 1300s (during this short interval, more than 25 large pueblos were built, inhabited, and abandoned); (3) the major settlement shift about A.D. 1400 to the lower, more uniform settlement pattern of the historic pueblos.

Dendroclimatological evidence gives an indirect record of the climatic variation through this period. The movements of settlements are analyzed with respect to the ways in which short- and long-term variability in the prehistoric climate would affect the viability of an agriculture-dependent subsistence system at a pueblo (or group of pueblos) that occupied a particular environmental situation that used a particular agricultural technology.

The great amount of construction and abandonment between about A.D. 1250 and 1400 may have resulted from social instability caused by the initial population aggregation. In a tribal society, it seems likely that a shift in community size from small pueblos housing perhaps thirty people to communities of several hundred people would strain existing mechanisms of social integration. Thus, it appears that some of the changes we observe in the settlement patterns may reflect this instability and an evolution to a more stable social structure.

The potential for understanding human adaptations and cultural processes by studying this sequence of settlement patterns is enhanced by the fact that propositions to be examined in the prehistoric case can be developed from a knowledge of the ethnographically known Pueblo Indians. Not only do the modern Zuni inhabit the area today, but they also have been exceptionally well studied ethnographically, beginning in 1879. Because a strong argument can be made for

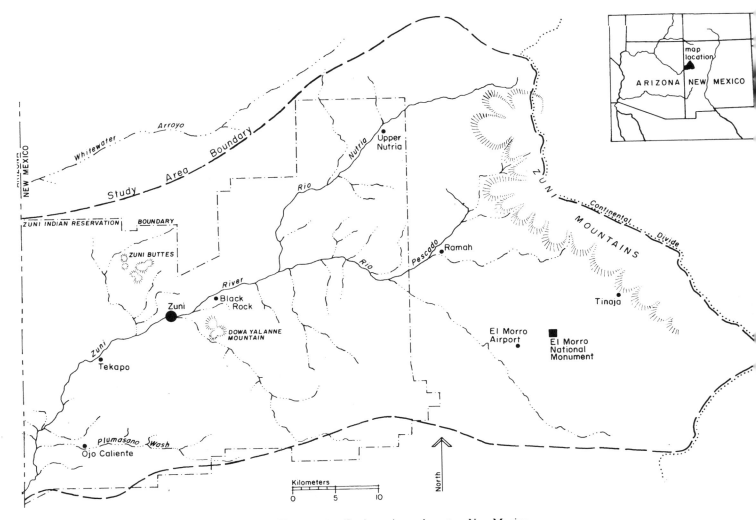

Figure 1.1.   Zuni area in northwestern New Mexico.

cultural continuity between the prehistoric groups studied and the modern Zuni, the a priori likelihood for the validity of an analogy is greater than if there were no such continuity (see Steward 1942). On the other hand, it appears that during the time period of interest both economic strategies and cultural integrative mechanisms may have undergone important changes. However apparently applicable, of course, ethnographic analogies can only be considered propositions to be rigorously examined using archaeological data (Binford 1967).

In addition to its potential for suggesting interpretive propositions, historical and ethnographic information about the Zuni offers this study an additional advantage. In many areas of the world, the reconstruction of a prehistoric economy requires the use of economic data drawn from societies that occupy substantially different natural environments. The ethnographic and ethnohistoric Zuni data provide important economic details that allow us to build environmentally and technologically plausible models of aspects of the prehistoric

subsistence system. That is, the historical and, to a lesser extent, the ethnographic pictures show a *possible* neolithic adaptation to this area (under modern climatic conditions).

PREVIOUS ARCHAEOLOGICAL WORK IN THE ZUNI AREA

A considerable amount of archaeological work has been done in the Zuni area during the last hundred years. However, due to the research interests of the investigators and the limited number of late sites, only a relatively small portion of this work has contributed substantially to our understanding of the late prehistoric period. From the time of the earliest anthropological research, the lives of the various anthropologists working at Zuni were intertwined (see also Pandey 1972) and it is helpful to review, in historical context, those people and projects that are repeatedly referenced through the remainder of this book.

Frank Hamilton Cushing was the ethnologist assigned to the Stevenson Expedition of the Bureau of Ethnology, Smithsonian Institution. As a member of this expedition he arrived at Zuni in 1879, where he stayed until 1884 (Green 1979: 5). He returned to Zuni in the summer of 1888 as the director of the Hemenway Southwestern Archaeological Expedition. Although Cushing's main contribution was ethnological, he did direct some archaeological work near Zuni. Assisted by the expedition secretary, Frederick Webb Hodge, Cushing excavated portions of the ruins of Halona:wa (Halona) and Heshot uɬa (Heshotauthla; Haury 1945: 9). Although the results of these excavations were never published in detail, Jesse Walker Fewkes (1891, 1909) published two relevant maps and, later, an article on the pottery. Excavation notes and some of the excavated material are held by the Peabody Museum of Harvard University (Green 1979: 14, 29). Some of Hodge's reports to Cushing on the progress of the excavations at Heshot uɬa still exist (Hodge 1888).

Victor Mindeleff of the Bureau of Ethnology visited Zuni in the autumn of 1881 and again in the autumn of 1885 while engaged in a study of Tusayan (Hopi area) and Cibola (Zuni area) pueblo architecture. He published superb maps and photographs of Zuni pueblo, the other historic villages, and a number of the major ruins (Mindeleff 1891). He described precisely and illustrated many features of Cibola architecture, and published a number of photographs that can be used to document the substantial deterioration of these ruins during the last century.

Adolf Bandelier, who published excellent research on the history of Zuni (1890a, 1890b, 1892b, 1981), also did early field research in the area. Under the auspices of the Archaeological Institute of America, Bandelier went to Zuni in 1883. While there, he became friends with Cushing, who accompanied him on a tour of the area. Bandelier (1892a) published a report of his investigations, and his journal of the trip has been printed more recently (Lange and Riley 1970). Unfortunately, for the most part, his descriptions of the archaeological sites do not seem particularly insightful and his drawings are not sufficiently detailed to be of much help. In 1885 he was chosen by Cushing as the historian for the Hemenway Southwestern Archaeological Expedition and in this capacity Bandelier carried out much of his extensive historical research.

Jesse Walter Fewkes took over as director of the Hemenway Southwestern Archaeological Expedition in 1889 because of Cushing's ill health (Haury 1945: 9). He visited Zuni in the summers of 1889 and 1890 (Fewkes 1891: 1) and during the second summer conducted a reconnaissance of ruins in the area (Fewkes 1891: 1, 95). As a result of this work, he published descriptions, drawings, and some imprecise maps of the ruins (Fewkes 1891).

Alfred Kroeber (1917) went to Zuni during the summers of 1915 and 1916 in order to pursue ethnological research. He became interested in the surrounding ruins and published a short but important article on his frequency seriation of surface scatters from several ruins (Kroeber 1916; see Rowe 1962: 400; Willey and Sabloff 1974: 100–101). At this early date Kroeber (1916: 21) told us:

At present five thousand sherds can tell us more than a hundred whole vessels, and the bare knowledge of the average size of room in a dozen contiguous ruins may be more indicative than the most laborious survey of two or three extensive sites.

Stimulated by Kroeber's work, Leslie Spier went to Zuni in the summer of 1916. He conducted an extensive survey of the Zuni Indian Reservation and some nearby areas, and assisted Nels C. Nelson in a survey of the Ramah–El Morro area farther to the east. The following year Spier (1917) published the descriptive results of these two surveys along with a remarkable analysis. In this pioneering study (see Taylor 1963: 379; Willey and Sabloff 1974: 101–102), Spier developed a chronology of the Zuni area ruins by ordering the proportions of different ceramic wares found in his stratigraphic trenches and random surface collections. He also discussed the evolution of architectural types that accompanied the ceramic changes and neatly laid out the settlement pattern sequence. Spier (1918, 1919) followed up questions raised in his 1916 research with two additional surveys in 1917 and 1918.

Despite the fact that Spier was working without the benefit of any prior chronological studies for the area (except for Kroeber's initial effort), his results appear to be essentially correct, even in the light of 65 years of additional work. Indeed, in many ways, the present study is modeled on Spier's and represents an attempt to refine his conclusions with respect to the late prehistoric period. The collections made by Spier remain in good condition at the American Museum of Natural History (Kintigh 1982). However, it has not been possible to locate his original field notes at either the American Museum of Natural History or the Museum of Northern Arizona, where many of his other notes reside.

Frederick Webb Hodge had his first experience at Zuni as the secretary to the Hemenway Southwestern Archaeological Expedition (at which time he met his future wife, Cushing's sister-in-law, Margaret W. Magill). As mentioned above, as a part of that expedition he aided Cushing in the excavation of Heshot uɬa. Hodge returned to Zuni in April of 1917 as the field director of the Hendricks-Hodge Expedition sponsored jointly by the Museum of the American Indian, Heye Foundation and the Smithsonian Institution. Between 1917 and 1923 the expedition undertook six seasons of excavation at Hawikku (Hawikuh; Fig. 1.2), and a more limited excavation program at Kechiba:wa (Kechipawan; Smith and others 1966: 1–3).

Although Hodge published a number of short papers concerning this work (1918a, 1918b, 1920a, 1920b, 1921a, 1921b, 1922, 1923, 1924a, 1924b, 1924c, 1926, 1952), he was never able to write an extensive report on his excavations. At Hodge's request, in 1955 Watson Smith and Richard and Nathalie Woodbury began work on an excellent report concerning Hodge's excavation of Hawikku that was published by the Museum of the American Indian, Heye Foundation (Smith and others 1966). Much of the material from Hodge's excavations remains in the Museum of the American Indian. The disposition of the other material is discussed in the introductory chapters of the 1966 volume.

Richard Woodbury carried out an archaeological reconnaissance of the Zuni area in 1953 for the purpose of examining the ceramics and selecting a ruin for more extensive work in the following summers (Woodbury 1954a,

Figure 1.2.   Frederick W. Hodge at Hawikku, 1919. (Photograph courtesy of the Museum of the American Indian, Heye Foundation, Negative No. 5819.)

1954b). During the next two seasons (1954 and 1955) he excavated a number of rooms in one corner of Atsinna, a large, 14th century ruin atop Inscription Rock in El Morro National Monument. This project was sponsored by Columbia University (with additional money from other sources) and has been reported briefly (Woodbury 1954c, 1955, 1956; Woodbury and Woodbury 1956). Sherds from the survey are in the collections of the Arizona State Museum; the excavated material is under the care of the National Park Service, Western Archeological Center, Tucson.

As a part of the project to restore the Catholic mission at Zuni, Louis R. Caywood of the National Park Service conducted excavations at the mission, which is adjacent to the older part of Zuni Pueblo. He described a variety of cultural remains and published a number of tree-ring dates that are of some importance here (Caywood 1972).

In the early 1970s, J. Ned Woodall directed a Wake Forest University project that surveyed near Ramah and excavated the Pettit Site in Togeye Canyon. A master's thesis on the architecture has been completed (Linthicum 1980) and Woodall has informed me that analysis of the Pettit Site material is still in progress.

The Cibola Archaeological Research Project (CARP), sponsored by the National Science Foundation, conducted a two-year investigation into the late 13th and early 14th century cultural dynamics of the El Morro Valley in the eastern part of the Zuni area. In the summers of 1972 and 1973, Patty Jo Watson, Steven LeBlanc, and Charles Redman directed an intensive survey of 30.7 square kilometers and limited excavation at six sites in the El Morro Valley. A provocative preliminary report on this project has been published (Watson and others 1980) and a number of specialized studies have become available (Marquardt 1974; LeBlanc 1975, 1976; Skinner 1981). Work on a final report is in progress. The

artifacts recovered by this project are now held by Washington University and Arizona State University.

The Zuni Archaeology Program (ZAP, formerly the Zuni Archaeology Contract Team and Zuni Archaeological Enterprises) was established by the Pueblo of Zuni in 1974. The program has had an ongoing research commitment to the Zuni area and has contributed greatly to our understanding of the prehistory of the area. The program has developed a valuable archive of published and unpublished manuscripts and notes, and has active site and map files that organize the large amount of settlement data available for the area. Many of their reports deal with specific sites and areas, some of which are of interest here, and additional papers have synthesized more general information concerning several important topics.

REVIEW OF ZUNI AREA PREHISTORY

Spier's eloquent summary of several aspects of Zuni area prehistory provides a setting for the remainder of this book.

> In spite of the limitations on the occupation of the Zuni region imposed by its natural resources, certain general shifts of population have taken place. While the number of localities with optimum conditions for producing food and water is strictly limited, the wide scattering of former habitations throughout the region is strong evidence for the latent possibilities of the whole. Nevertheless, the advantages of these localities are so marked that they have been the scene of repeated settlements. But the striking feature of these settlements is their transitory character. Ash heaps, as we have repeatedly stated, are a minus quantity; the fact which determined the course of this inquiry. It is certainly startling to come on ruin after ruin with long rows of rooms stretching away in straight lines or graceful curves, but with hardly a sign of ashes and broken pottery—in short, every jot of evidence pointing to a flitting occupation. The natural result has been to produce a constant movement about in the valley, a sort of milling around. It is somewhat curious to find nevertheless that the center of population has shifted from period to period (Spier 1917: 300).

A concise, well-illustrated summary of Zuni prehistory is presented by Woodbury (1979). A thorough, extensively referenced, and up-to-date review is given by Ferguson (1980). In the following summary, the discussion concerning the period from the earliest evidence of human occupation until the 13th century is drawn mainly from the latter source.

Paleo-Indian to A.D. 1250

Isolated Paleo-Indian and Archaic projectile points have been found in the area, although the closest sites dating to this period occur west of Zuni in Arizona. Recent survey by the Zuni Archaeology Program has discovered campsites and pit house villages with as many as 30 pit houses dating to the period from A.D. 700 to 900. These sites generally occur near relatively well-watered drainages. Spier found several of these ruins, which he referred to as "slab-house" sites. Some time late in this period, surface storage structures appear associated with the pit houses.

Starting about A.D. 900 there began a transition from pit houses to above-ground habitation structures (pueblos) that was completed by about 1100. Through this period there was, in general, a movement to the higher elevations of the eastern part of the area. Typical of the period from 1000 to 1125 are pueblos containing four to twelve rooms, sometimes associated with a kiva in front of the room block. The participation of the Zuni area in the Chacoan system during this time is evidenced by Village of the Great Kivas, which was excavated by Frank Roberts, Jr. (1932; see also his report on Kiatuthlanna, 1931).

From A.D. 1100 until about 1250, the typical settlements continued to be small pueblos, many of which had associated kivas. The movement to higher elevations continued and appears to have been even more pronounced after 1200. Spier found many sites from this period (which he calls "small house" sites), and he identified this settlement shift, which he graphically illustrated in maps showing site locations in successive ceramic periods (Spier 1917: 300–305).

A.D. 1250 to 1540

A dramatic shift in settlement pattern occurred late in the A.D. 1200s when the focus of occupation moved to the Ramah–El Morro region in the eastern part of the study area (see Fig. 1.1), and the scattered, small pueblos began to be replaced with large, planned pueblos. Spier refers to these large sites as the "pueblo type" and he located almost all of them that are known today. He found that these "pueblo type" sites partly overlapped the small house sites in time, but that they did not begin until the appearance of "three-color painted ware" (mainly St. Johns Polychrome) and they continued through his "Glazed Ware Series."

Ferguson notes that these large pueblos first occurred at about the same time that Chaco Canyon was finally abandoned. Woodbury (1956: 558) suggested that the settlement shift may have been caused by warfare, or by the fact that an expanding population and the increasing complexity of social organization made the large village pattern more desirable; furthermore, he suggested that an increasing agricultural surplus made this shift to larger villages possible.

This transition was also studied by Watson and others (1980; LeBlanc 1978) in the El Morro Valley, where they date this shift to about A.D. 1275. They discuss warfare and environmental change as possible causes for this settlement pattern shift. To support the case for warfare as a contributing factor in this shift, like Woodbury, they cite the apparently defensive architecture and location of many of the sites. Their excavations also revealed that several of the small pueblo rooms had been burned and hurriedly abandoned.

In addition, Watson, LeBlanc, and Redman also present an argument based on climatic variation to explain an inferred movement of population into, and then out of, the El Morro area. They argue that because the amount of rainfall and the length of the growing season are critical agricultural variables for the area, a period of warmer and drier climate would favor settlement in higher elevations such as the El Morro Valley. They reason that higher areas tend to receive greater rainfall than lower ones, and that warmer conditions would lengthen the short growing season at higher elevations to an acceptable level. Thus, the documented period of drought starting in 1276 would have encouraged migration into the El Morro Valley (see also Woodbury 1961a), and its cessation about 1300 would, correspondingly, stimulate its abandonment.

In the next settlement change, the population continued to live in large pueblos but the Ramah–El Morro Valley area was abandoned in favor of the area along the Zuni River farther to the west, where the Zuni lived at the time of Spanish contact. Again, Spier recognized this shift and saw it as accompanying a break in the ceramic sequence. In subsequent surveys in Arizona, Spier (1918, 1919) attempted to locate sites that had been occupied during this hiatus.

Ferguson (1981a: 337) and Woodbury (1956: 561) indicate that no hiatus existed but that there was continuity in settlement of the Zuni area from the time of the El Morro sites to the occupation of the six historic towns. Through a reanalysis of Spier's and Hodge's data, Watson and others (1980: 215–216) suggest that there were no gaps in the cultural sequence, although there do appear to be gaps in the archaeological record. Unfortunately, their investigations in the El Morro Valley did not provide any new evidence that bears on this question.

At present, the timing of this hiatus (if it existed) or shift of settlements downstream is not clear. Woodbury (1956: 561) believes that some of the El Morro sites were occupied until late in the 14th century, and at that point the population moved to the historic villages. In contrast, Watson and her coauthors (1980: 213) argue that the El Morro area was abandoned very early in this century, although they admit difficulty in explaining the amount of deposition at Pueblo de los Muertos if this had been the case. They argue further, as indicated above, that this abandonment might be due to the onset of a cooler and wetter climatic episode. Woodbury (1956: 561–562; 1961a: 708) made a similar argument based on climatic change concerning the movement to lower elevations, without the benefit of the recent dendroclimatological results.

Several of the pueblos inhabited after this shift were occupied up to the time of the first Spanish contact in 1539 and 1540. The locations of six of the Zuni towns in 1540 were established by Hodge (1937), mainly on the basis of historical data (although in Spier's 1917 report, this question was attacked using archaeological data). Otherwise, most work on the late sites has been on individual ruins and has not been directed to an understanding of the settlement patterns involved. Ferguson (1980: 27–28) notes that all the protohistoric sites are located on a 15 mile (24 km) stretch of the Zuni River, mostly downstream of present day Zuni, and that all are located on elevated landforms near arable land and a dependable source of water.

The Historic Period

The historic period is not of crucial concern for most aspects of this research, but some early historical data bear on the demographic questions discussed. In addition, the archaeological data collected here have some bearing on unresolved historical questions. While the historic period has received a great deal of attention in the literature (Bandelier 1890a, 1890b, 1892b, 1981; Hodge 1937; Crampton 1977; and many others cited in the aforementioned references), the brief summary presented below is intended only to introduce a few significant questions.

The first direct European contact with the Zuni occurred in 1539 (although as Henry Dobyns has pointed out, plagues of

European diseases probably came much earlier). Stimulated by stories of riches to the north, Fray Marcos de Niza headed an expedition from Mexico in search of the fabled Seven Cities of Gold. Along the way, he heard more about the famous cities (much of which was reasonably accurate) from Indians in Mexico and southern Arizona who had apparently traded with the Zuni. An advance party was led by the slave Estevan, who was a survivor of Cabeza de Vaca's ill-fated cross-country journey. This advance party reached one of the Zuñi villages at which, shortly thereafter, Estevan was killed. Some members of the party made it back to Fray Marcos de Niza, who claimed to have continued until he reached sight of the town before returning to Mexico.

There are matters of dispute in this story that are only of incidental interest to this research (see Rodack 1981: 27–39 for a review of these issues). The first question concerns the identification of the village where Estevan was killed. Bandelier (1892a: 337; 1981: 85–101) firmly believes that it was Kyaki:ma (Kiakime), while Hodge argues equally strongly that it was Hawikku (Hawikuh). Second, some historians believe that Fray Marcos never even came within sight of Zuni (Sauer in Hodge 1937: 112) while others, including Bandelier (1981), accept his story.

In any case, Fray Marcos returned to Mexico and the next year accompanied Francisco Coronado on his famous expedition. Coronado reached Hawikku (there is no dispute about the identity of this town) in July of 1540; a battle was fought, and Coronado entered the town. He was greatly disappointed not to find the extravagant riches, rumor of which drew the expedition to Zuni. Several accounts (*relaciones*) concerning Zuni resulted from Coronado's expedition (Castañeda 1966). Most mention the existence of seven towns. However, by the time the first list of town names was recorded by the Rodriguez-Chamuscado Expedition in 1581, there were only six towns listed. A further matter of dispute between Bandelier and Hodge (Hodge 1937: 56), among others, was whether there were seven towns in 1540 or whether (as Hodge believes) there were only six at that time as well.

While Zuni was visited by a number of expeditions late in the 16th century, intensive interaction with the Spanish did not start until the early 17th century. The mission at Hawikku was founded in 1629 and another was built at Halona:wa within a few years.

UNRESOLVED PROBLEMS IN THE ZUNI CULTURAL SEQUENCE

Meaningful analysis of settlement patterns is contingent on chronological control that is adequate to establish site contemporaneity. As this overview indicates, there remain important chronological problems with the late prehistoric-early historic sequence in the Zuni area.

With two exceptions, our knowledge of the period between A.D. 1250 and 1540 is extremely sketchy. Through the efforts of the Cibola Archaeological Research Project, the construction sequence within the El Morro Valley between about 1250 and 1300 is fairly well established, and the identity of six of the towns that were occupied in 1540 is reasonably secure. Thus, at both ends of the period of interest, there is reliable settlement information, but the time between 1300 and 1540 is understood only at a schematic level.

Although the settlement distribution and timing of the late 13th century transition to large pueblos is reasonably well known within the limited confines of the El Morro Valley, it is only one part of the area in which this transition occurred. The regional picture of the nature and timing of this change must be more precisely resolved. In fact, the timing of the abandonment of the El Morro Valley is open to serious debate. Watson and others argue, largely on the basis of tree-ring data, for abandonment near 1300, while Woodbury and Ferguson, based mainly on ceramic evidence, indicate that the abandonment was much later.

Although Spier identified almost all the sites that we know were occupied between A.D. 1300 and the time of the major shift in settlement location to lower elevations, the need remains to establish the contemporaneity of the many sites occupied during this time interval. The archaeological evidence is ambiguous with respect to the existence of a hiatus in occupation of the Zuni area between the prehistoric occupations of the Pescado–Ramah–El Morro areas and the protohistoric occupation of the area around modern Zuni pueblo. The sites that were occupied after the settlement shift downriver and abandoned before the Spanish *entrada* have not been adequately identified or placed in a chronological sequence with respect to the sites occupied in 1540. Finally, there remains the historical question of whether there were six or seven Zuni towns in 1540.

2. THE RESEARCH AREA AND SOURCES OF DATA

In any substantive archaeological study, it is important that the study area be of such a size that the phenomena of interest can be observed. If the research interest is in local shifts in settlement patterns, with population movements of 10 or 20 kilometers (as is the case herein), a study area of a few thousand square kilometers is probably adequate. On the other hand, phenomena such as long-distance trade can be effectively studied only over vastly larger areas.

Not only must the study area be of appropriate size, but it must be spatially located in such a way that the phenomena of interest are exposed as clearly as possible. In order to identify and understand changes in settlement strategy, the study area should be located so that only one cultural system is being observed over time rather than, for example, at the intersection of three cultural groups.

THE ZUNI AREA

For the purposes of this research, the Zuni area is defined as the approximately 3400 square kilometer area (Orr 1982: 96) drained by the New Mexico (upper) portion of the Zuni River (see Fig. 1.1). To the north, the boundary is the drainage of Whitewater Arroyo and the Puerco River. The continental divide follows the ridge of the Zuni Mountains and the northwestern edge of the barren *malpais* area of lava fields to form a "U" around the eastern part of the study area. To the south, the study area is bounded by the area drained by Venadito Draw and Jaralosa Draw. The western two-thirds of the study area is approximately coextensive with the Zuni Indian Reservation. Included in this area are all of the modern Zuni villages, the town of Ramah, and El Morro National Monument.

Although this area, to a degree, is bounded arbitrarily, it has some cultural and archaeological coherence. This land is the core of the region to which the Zuni have traditional claims (Hart 1980; Ferguson 1981a: 345, 1981b), and it includes the area that was occupied and extensively used by the Zuni at the time of Spanish contact. The continental divide to the east seems to split the distance between Zuni and Acoma both spatially and culturally.

Based largely on culture trait analyses and on stylistic studies of the ceramics, various scholars have identified the Zuni area as a coherent culture area. In the archaeological literature, the Zuni area has been included in the Zuni Province (Martin and Plog 1973: 109, 123), the Cibola stylistic area (Carlson 1970: 1–3), the Zuni district of the Little Colorado culture area (Kidder 1962: 266–279; McGregor 1965: 402), and the Cibola Branch (Gladwin 1957: 270, 283–284). Thus, the archaeological and historical

record gives ample justification for the treatment of this culture area as an entity that is never split among larger cultural divisions.

THE PERIOD OF INTEREST
A.D. 1250 TO 1540

In the mid–1200s there were hundreds or thousands of small pueblos, usually with from two to fifty rooms. The average size was probably about four rooms. Evidence available at the outset of this study indicated that sometime in the late 1200s construction of large pueblos started with the approximately concurrent abandonment of many of the smaller villages. Dates from the El Morro Valley indicate that the transition began about 1275; however, it is not clear how long the transition lasted or whether it began at different times in different places. In any case, for reasons that will be elaborated below, it seemed clear that the beginning of this transition was not prior to A.D. 1250.

Furthermore, the available evidence indicated that by at least the mid–1300s the transition was complete; there was essentially no occupation of small pueblos. From the mid–1300s to the Spanish entrada in 1539, when only six or seven pueblos were occupied, the large pueblo remained virtually the only type of habitation in the Zuni area.

Although I had hoped that this work might shed some light on the nature and causes of the transition from small to large pueblos, this was not a primary goal because it was impossible to obtain adequate data to address this problem. An understanding of that transition requires knowledge of the number of small pueblos occupied and their overall distribution. However, intensive survey of a large additional area would be required to estimate even roughly the basic demographic parameters for the dispersed occupation of the Zuni area during the mid–1200s.

The primary goal set for this research was to gain a better understanding of the rather large-scale settlement changes in the Zuni area during the period of occupation of these large pueblos. This goal seems attainable partly because it appeared that an essentially complete sample of the settlements from this period could be obtained for this large area (3400 square kilometers), so that the demographic situation within it could be reconstructed with some confidence. A few small pueblos included in this study date to the early portion of the time period under consideration (about A.D. 1250); however, they represent only a small fraction of the sites in the entire area that were occupied at that time. They were included to provide some comparative basis, both architecturally and ceramically, for the discussion of the transitional period large sites.

SOURCES OF DATA

From various documentary sources, I attempted to identify all of the sites that might fit within the scope of the research, as defined above. The available evidence suggested that all the large sites could be expected to contain Springerville Polychrome, which first appeared about A.D. 1250 (Carlson 1970: 47), or later ceramic types. Charles Redman informed me of his observation that the large sites in the El Morro Valley all had Kwakina Polychrome, a type dated to A.D. 1325 by Woodbury and Woodbury (1966), but thought by Redman to start earlier.

A search was made through the Zuni Archaeology Program site file and through a number of reports and other kinds of notes in order to find sites in the study area that were either large (more than 100 rooms) *or* had any of the late pottery types (Springerville Polychrome, Heshotauthla Black-on-red, Heshotauthla Polychrome, Kwakina Polychrome, Pinnawa Glaze-on-white, Pinnawa Red-on-white, Kechipawan Polychrome, Matsaki Brown-on-buff, or Matsaki Polychrome). Inquiries were also made to several people who might know the locations of other such sites. In this way, sites that fit within the scope of the research were identified. Furthermore, through this search the association between the late ceramic types and the architecturally large sites could be evaluated.

Not surprisingly, Spier's monograph proved to be the single most fruitful source of sites for this research, because his study area corresponded almost exactly with mine and because the large ruins were the ones he was most likely to find, either of his own accord or through information provided by local residents. However, because many of Spier's sites had not been recorded subsequently by archaeologists with modern maps, not all of them were readily located. As a result, many of the sites were not in the ZAP site file and had to be relocated.

The available information for each site located in the archival search was compiled so that maps and previous observations could be field-checked when the sites were revisited. A permit was obtained from the Tribal Council of the Pueblo of Zuni to survey and make surface collections on the Reservation, and permission was obtained to conduct the survey under the auspices of the Federal Antiquities Permit held by the Zuni Archaeology Program. A site survey recording form was developed for use in the survey, and U.S.G.S. 7½ minute quad sheets were obtained for the areas in which sites of interest were located.

The sites investigated by the CARP project were not all revisited in 1979 because, as a member of the CARP crew, I visited or worked on all of them in the summer of 1973. The recording procedures followed by CARP were similar to my own and the CARP records were available to me. All the other sites reported here were visited in 1979 or 1980 with the exception of Spier's Site 61, which was located and recorded for me by members of the Zuni Archaeology Program.

Survey Data and Field Methods

In the field, the sites were first walked over and the survey recording form was completed. The recording form included information on the provenience, environmental setting, and archaeological characteristics of the site. Available site plan maps were checked on the ground and were annotated as required. If no map of a site was available or if the available maps were inadequate, a roughly measured sketch map was drawn. Finally, each site was precisely located on a U.S.G.S. quad map.

Two kinds of ceramic collections were made in the course of the survey. At sites where areas of high sherd density were located, quantitative sector collections were made. In these collections, a 2 m radius circle was laid out over an area of high sherd density and all of the sherds that fell within the circle were collected. Usually, more than one quantitative sector collection was made if there were architecturally distinct areas of the site such as different room blocks, or a feature suggesting an architectural division of the site. In these cases, the sites were divided into loci and a quantitative collection was made for each locus.

At most sites, diagnostic collections were also made. In these collections I attempted to pick up a few examples of all ceramic types present on the site and to pick up additional sherds of temporally diagnostic types. For sites at which quantitative sector samples were also collected, the diagnostic samples were intended to augment the quantitative samples by locating sherds that were more readily identifiable and sherds of types that did not occur in the 2 m circle sectors intensively sampled. In the cases in which sites were divided into loci, diagnostic collections were made separately for each of the different areas.

A few sites had such low sherd densities that all surface sherds were collected. These collections were labeled "complete." For most analytical purposes, however, the complete collections were lumped with the quantitative collections because, in both cases, the relative proportions of the types in the collections are analytically meaningful. (These proportions are not meaningful in the case of diagnostic collections because sherds were selectively collected or ignored, based on type distinctions.)

Museum Data

Although it was possible to make collections at almost all sites under consideration, the use of museum collections was important to this study for two reasons. First, the glazed white ware and buff ware types occur on only a few sites and, as a result, they are not well known. The study of excavated collections that included many whole vessels enabled me to identify these types in collections of sherds much more reliably. Second, I wanted to use the best available data for the determination of the site chronology. For most analytical purposes, where they were available the stratigraphic samples in the museums were preferred to surface collections. I also felt that surface collections made a number of years ago might be more representative than those made today, in light of the extensive recent disturbance to some sites.

The Hawikku ceramic collections made by Hodge were studied at the Museum of the American Indian, Heye Foundation, for the purpose of better identifying the types. This collection includes over 1500 whole vessels, mostly from funerary contexts. A search was made for sherds collected from Hodge's massive plaza trench at Hawikku. This trench was 11 feet (3.3 m) wide and 75 feet (22.9 m) long and was excavated to a depth of 15 feet (4.6 m) in one foot (0.3 m) levels (see Smith and others 1966: 135–172). Apparently none of the sherds were saved. In fact, the only significant quantities of sherds in the collection were hundreds of worked sherd disks.

The Hemenway Expedition ceramic collections made by Cushing at Halona:wa and Heshot uła are housed in the Peabody Museum at Harvard University. Because Halona:wa is almost completely buried by the modern village of Zuni and no collections could be made, it was important to see whatever material was available. The Hemenway collections represent the only excavated collections from Heshot uła. As there were few buff ware sherds present on the surface I hoped to see if more diagnostically late type sherds were recovered in the excavation.

Approximately 55 whole vessels in the collection were found and tentatively related to Halona:wa or Heshot uła. At the time of my visit they had not been cataloged into the Peabody Museum collections and had only the field numbers written on the vessels. Fortunately, a partial field catalog of the materials was also available that made it possible to determine the site provenience for most vessels. In 1956 Richard B. Woodbury and Nathalie F.S. Woodbury studied this collection and the vessels were photographed for them by the Peabody Museum; they kindly provided me with their notes recording the ceramic type, vessel form, and designs, cross-referenced with Fewkes' (1909) publication of parts of the collection. I was able to correlate their notes with the appropriate vessels, and those not in the notes I recorded in a format similar to theirs. Unfortunately, most of the vessels that were either recorded by the Woodburys or listed by Fewkes could not be located at the time of my visit; of these, 42 had been on display in 1956.

The sherd collections from the American Museum of Natural History, the Zuni Archaeology Program, Washington University, and the State University of New York at Binghamton (now at Arizona State University) were subjected to the same analytical procedures (described below) as were the collections made explicitly for this research. At the American Museum of Natural History, 102 collections made by Spier and Nelson were analyzed. Spier excavated stratigraphic trenches at a number of sites. He attempted to locate these trenches in trash middens in order to get a long stratigraphic sequence. Most of these trenches were excavated in six inch (15.2 cm) levels and all sherds were kept.

In addition to the stratigraphic samples, surface collections were made by Spier and Nelson. Like the collections made especially for this study, there were both quantitative and diagnostic collections that Spier called "random" and "selected." Clearly, the latter correspond to the "diagnostic" collections referred to above. However, it is important to know whether Spier's "random" collections have properties of representativeness similar to the quantitative sector collections made for this study. While Spier is not explicit about his collection methods, it seems likely that he used the procedure followed by Kroeber at Zuni during the previous year (or one that was even more systematic):

It was immediately apparent that red, black, and patterned potsherds predominated here, as they seemed to have preponderated at Mattsakya, while white fragments had been in the majority at both Shoptluwwayala and Hattsinawa. I therefore attempted to pick up all of the sherds visible in certain spots, rather than range over the whole site and stoop only for the attractive ones. In this I may not have been altogether successful, for a red, a patterned, or a deep black fragment catches the eye more readily than either a "black" or a "white" one that ranges toward dull gray. But at least the effort was conscientious (Kroeber 1916: 8).

I have argued elsewhere (Kintigh 1982a), based on earlier tabulations of Spier's collections and on a comparison with my collections from the same sites, that Spier's collections may be considered representative and that, with some exceptions, the collections appear to be intact. In fact, the preponderance of utility wares and the small size of many sherds in his collections (which normally are found in stratigraphic and quantitative samples) led previous investigators to believe that most of the large decorated sherds had been picked out of the collection, rather than to realize that these characteristics were evidence for systematic collection procedures. It was possible to locate in the American Museum almost all of the collections relevant to this research.

The surface collections made by the Cibola Archaeological Research Project, which were in storage at Washington University and at the State University of New York at Binghamton, were collected using the same methods employed in the field research for my project. The excavated collections analyzed were all complete samples of all sherds present within an excavation level. The principal difficulty with the CARP collections was that the corrugated wares were separated from the slipped wares in the field laboratory and were not readily available for analysis, so that comparisons involving utility wares could not be made for any of those collections.

Several collections made by the Zuni Archaeology Program also were utilized in this study. Some of the surface collections were made using essentially the same methods employed here; others were complete surface collections. A few excavated samples were analyzed from the site of Halona:wa. These collections were made when water line trenches were dug to modern houses on the site and, of necessity, were stratigraphically mixed.

Ceramic Coding

The ceramic analysis for this project was oriented toward two objectives: (1) to refine the existing ceramic chronology based on associations of the ceramic types in collections, and (2) to assign each site a relative date as precisely as possible. The coding system was designed to meet these goals within the constraints imposed by the number of samples (260) and the total number of sherds to be analyzed (nearly 20,000).

Types represented in the ceramic collections span about 1000 years and, during the time period on which this study focuses, several major ceramic transitions occurred. For each separate collection the ceramic coding scheme recorded counts of different ceramic categories, including recognized ceramic types and their variants, such as matte, subglaze,

TABLE 2.1
Ceramic Categories Used in the Analysis

Ware Ceramic Category	Notes and References
White ware	
Kiatuthlana Black-on-white	Presence noted in text; counts included with unidentified white ware in Appendix.
Red Mesa Black-on-white	
Puerco Black-on-white	Includes Escavada, Gallup, and Puerco varieties.
Reserve Black-on-white	
Tularosa Black-on-white	Colton and Hargrave (1937).
Pinedale Black-on-white	Colton and Hargrave (1937).
Unidentified white ware	Plain white ware and unidentified white ware sherds.
Red ware	
Puerco Black-on-red	Carlson (1970).
Wingate types	Wingate Black-on-red and Wingate Polychrome; Carlson (1970).
St. Johns matte types	St. Johns Black-on-red and St. Johns Polychrome with matte black paint; Carlson (1970).
St. Johns subglaze types	St. Johns Black-on-red and St. Johns Polychrome with subglaze black paint; Carlson (1970).
St. Johns glaze types	St. Johns Black-on-red and St. Johns Polychrome with glazed black paint; Carlson (1970).
Springerville Polychrome	All black paint categories combined; Carlson (1970).
Pinedale Polychrome	All black paint categories combined; Carlson (1970).
Heshotauthla types	Heshotauthla Black-on-red and Heshotauthla Polychrome; all black paint categories combined; Woodbury and Woodbury (1966).
Unidentified red ware	Plain red ware, unidentified red ware, and sherds of other low frequency red ware types such as Fourmile Polychrome.
Kwakina Polychrome	Woodbury and Woodbury (1966). Subsumes Adamana Polychrome (Colton and Hargrave 1937; with black and red interior designs) and Pinnawa Polychrome (Colton and Hargrave 1937; with red slipped interior and red and white slipped exterior).
Salado polychromes	Gila Polychrome and Tonto Polychrome; Colton and Hargrave (1937).
Glazed white ware	
Pinnawa Glaze-on-white	Woodbury and Woodbury (1966).
Pinnawa Red-on-white	Woodbury and Woodbury (1966).
Kechipawan Polychrome	Woodbury and Woodbury (1966).
Unidentified cream ware	Plain sherds or sherds not identifiable by type that are apparently from a glazed white ware vessel.
Buff ware	
Matsaki types	Matsaki Brown-on-buff and Matsaki Polychrome; Woodbury and Woodbury (1966).
Unidentified buff ware	Plain sherds or sherds not identifiable by type that are apparently from a vessel of one of the Matsaki types.
Hopi buff ware	Distinguished by a very different paste than sherds of the Matsaki types.
Utility ware	
Corrugated gray ware	Colton and Hargrave (1937).
Corrugated buff ware	
Black ware	Ferguson and Mills (1982).
Historic red ware	
Hawikuh types	Hawikuh Glaze-on-red and Hawikuh Polychrome; Woodbury and Woodbury (1966).
Zuni polychromes	Ashiwi Polychrome, Kiapkwa Polychrome, and Zuni Polychrome; Harlow (1973).
Historic plain red	Plain red sherds, generally thick, that are apparently from vessels of one of the Hawikuh types or one of the Zuni polychromes.
Unidentified ware	Sherds of other wares, such as brown ware or early plain ware, or sherds not identified by ware (often burned).

and glaze paint on various White Mountain Red Wares. Some of these distinctions (such as the matte-glaze separation) were known to be chronologically sensitive; other distinctions were easily recognizable but were not known to be (or not to be) chronologically important. During the analysis, the recorded categories were combined in various ways to yield more manageable and interpretable results. The summary categories used in this presentation are listed in Table 2.1.

A micro-seriation of the sites based on a more elaborate ceramic attribute analysis was not attempted for several reasons, although it has proved fruitful for a restricted class of the ceramics considered here (Marquardt 1974; LeBlanc 1975). First the methodological assumptions could not be satisfied because of the qualitative changes that occurred in the pottery over the period of interest. Second, the available samples most probably would not have been sufficient to execute these techniques successfully, especially for some critical periods. Finally, for the period to which these techniques might best be applied, the analyses of Marquardt and LeBlanc, which include several sites considered here, provide adequate information.

ADEQUACY OF THE SURVEY DATA

Disappearance of Small Sites After A.D. 1300

After the period of transition from small to large pueblos, that is after about A.D. 1300, virtually the entire population lived in large pueblos. Only two sites occupied between 1300 and 1540 were less than an estimated 100 rooms in size—Achiya:Deyaƚa and Hambassa:wa, both originally recorded by Spier (1917).

That there were essentially no post–1300 small habitation sites or field houses may seem implausible and deserves further elaboration. Archaeologists have often ignored the rather unprepossessing small sites when faced with spectacular, huge sites in the same area. Hence, one must be cautious in evaluating negative evidence concerning small sites, especially when intuitively it seems likely that there would be many small sites such as field houses. Field houses are known from the historic period and are illustrated by Cushing (Green 1979: 277) and Stevenson (1904: 352).

To date, archaeologists have intensively surveyed on foot less than five percent of the land in the study area. Nonetheless, the amount of area that has been surveyed, particularly in apparently attractive environmental zones, is substantial. The 25 square-kilometer Yellowhouse survey area (Hunter-Anderson 1978), which included the two large pueblos of Yellowhouse and Heshot uƚa, located only two small sites (YH 94 and YH 205) at which any pottery types dating after 1300 (Kwakina Polychrome and a Heshotauthla type, respectively) were identified. Although the Yellowhouse survey had a "no collection" policy, a visit to these small sites in 1979 failed to produce sherds of these types or any other evidence of post–1300 occupation; therefore they are not included in this study. Also, the 30.7 square-kilometer Cibola Archaeological Research Project survey did not reveal any evidence of small post–1250 sites. Reports of all major surveys conducted prior to 1980 revealed no other late structures, although in a few instances, isolated late sherds have been reported.

There is one major topographic bias in the areas that have been intensively surveyed. The overwhelming portion of the surveyed area is on bottomlands or the lower portions of mesa slopes. However, information on the higher mesa slopes, mesa tops, and mountain sides is not completely lacking. The CARP survey included an environmentally stratified sample of the El Morro Valley, and in 1979 I surveyed 28 km of north-south and east-west transects across all topographic settings in the southeast portion of the Zuni

Indian Reservation (Kintigh 1980). Nonetheless, our knowledge of the mesa tops and higher mesa slope locations is much less complete than our understanding of the valleys. Although there is evidence for long use of mesa top locations, the site density there appears to be much lower, at least during the later periods of concern here.

The conclusion drawn from this evidence is that there was no substantial occupation of small sites in the late prehistoric period. There are, however, three other conclusions that might be consistent with these data. First, it is possible that there was a significant, but not extensive, occupation of small sites on the mesa tops that has simply not been found. Second, there might have been late sites on the bottomland that were impermanent and for functional reasons did not have diagnostic late pottery. Finally, smaller sites on alluvial bottomland might have been completely buried, an unlikely possibility for the eastern part of the study area because many sherd and lithic scatters, insubstantial water control features, and even small pueblos from earlier periods are found on the bottomlands (Kintigh 1980).

It must be pointed out that even if one of these three possibilities were the case, it would not substantially affect the major parts of the argument presented below, because the sites, in all likelihood, would be temporary or seasonal and the major demographic trends would not be affected.

Survey Inventory of Large, Late Sites

Because they are so obvious, and because of the amount of sheep-herding activity over most of the study area, it is likely all or nearly all of the large, late sites in the study area have been located. The sites are conspicuous, usually with dimensions over 75 m and an associated rubble mound a meter or more in height. A few sites even have large sections of standing walls more than two meters high.

Since Spier surveyed the area in 1916, only one additional large site has been found. This site, the Pescado Canyon Ruin, is situated in a forested area on a mesa top overlooking Pescado Canyon. Despite its remote location, it was known by Zuni and Anglo residents and had been reported to the Zuni Archaeology Program. Additional inquiries have not produced substantial leads concerning new sites. If there are any more, they are almost certainly on the mesa tops, which are the only areas not frequently traversed. Thus, from the time when the transition to large pueblos was complete in the late 13th or early 14th century, until the time of the Spanish entrada in 1539, it can be assumed that we have an essentially complete inventory of sites for the entire study area.

3. CERAMIC CHRONOLOGY

An understanding of the sequence of settlement patterns in the Zuni area is contingent on the assignment of reasonably accurate relative dates to the sites. In the absence of modern excavation at most sites, the chronology of settlements must be based mainly on the analysis of surface scatters and small excavated samples of temporally diagnostic pottery. By examination of observed associations of ceramic types, ceramic groups can be inferred and used as chronologic indicators for the sites.

CERAMIC COMPLEXES

The analysis of pottery in terms of ceramic complexes has a long and honorable history in Southwestern archaeology. Although Harold Colton (1946: 18) attributes the use of a similar approach to Gladwin in the early 1930s, Colton gives a clear statement of this method of analysis in his 1946 work on the Sinagua. Colton (1946: 18) defines a ceramic group as "an assemblage of contemporary, usually painted, pottery types recognized at a site of short occupation." Colton goes on to say: "For the purpose of synthesis we consider the pottery complex of a site to be made up of a ceramic group composed of decorated types and the utility pottery wares." He believed that the ceramic groups of decorated types were useful chronological indices, because they were traded over relatively large areas, while the utility ware (index ware) used at a site was indicative of the cultural group, because the cooking and storage vessels were more difficult to transport and thus more likely to be of local manufacture.

In his analysis of the ceramics from Awatovi, Watson Smith (1971: 21–22) adopted the term "ceramic group" from Colton with an additional provision: "It seems semantically legitimate to expand the meaning to include an assemblage representing a brief portion of the total period of occupation at a site of longer duration."

The following analysis is intended only to develop chronological results, not make inferences about cultural groups. However, because the utility wares are included, the term "ceramic complex" is used to refer to an association of ceramic types in an assemblage deriving from a short period of time. Because we are working mainly with surface collections from sites, some of which do have long occupations, in some cases these complexes must be somewhat hypothetical. Ideally the complexes would be composed of a set of ceramic types, vessels of which were *produced* at the same time. Of course, in the best case of excavated stratigraphic samples, the observed associations are of sherds and vessels that may have been *deposited* at about the same time. In the more common case of surface collections, the assemblages are composed of sherds deposited at some time during the occupation of the site.

Several factors obviously contribute to a divergence between the abstract production complex and the observed associations. The keeping of old pots as heirlooms and the simple fact that objects may be kept or used for a long time may result in the deposition of a sherd long after vessels of that type have ceased being produced. Even worse, from this standpoint, is the fact that, like modern Indians, the prehistoric people undoubtedly found sherds or vessels in abandoned sites and deposited them in a much later context. The Zuni were known to collect sherds from earlier sites for use as temper in new pots.

It is reasonable to assume that all ceramic samples are the result of deposition over a significant period of time. In the case of excavated samples, this period may be fairly short compared to the length of a time during which vessels of a given type were produced. However, in the case of surface collections, the types represented in a sample often come from vessels deposited during the entire period of occupation. In either case, we must be concerned about various sources of postoccupational disturbance.

Unfortunately, the prehistoric situation under consideration is rather unfavorable for the task of determining the relative dates of ceramic types or sites. There appears to be great variation in the length of occupation of sites, from perhaps only a decade or two to well over two centuries. Furthermore, the relatively high density of sites in environmentally favorable areas means that nearly all late prehistoric sites are on or near earlier sites. Finally, the general area has been relatively intensively occupied continuously for at least the last thousand years.

These factors probably all contribute to a substantial divergence between production complexes and observed surface or excavated associations, a situation that precludes an analysis based only on the presence or absence of types. For example, of the 45 sites considered here, 26 have a small number of at least one of the varieties of Puerco Black-on-white that Breternitz (1966) dates as ending in A.D. 1125. It is clear that few, if any, of these sites (some of which were inhabited in historic times) were actually occupied as early as 1125. Although most archaeologists may be willing to dismiss a small number of early sherds for the reasons discussed above, a simple presence-absence analysis cannot very well ignore such sherds. Of course, the alternative to a presence-absence analysis is a quantitative analysis in which a dismissal of one percent of the sherds might be easily justified (as in the above case).

A quantitative analysis, however, introduces another set of problems. First, there are more stringent data requirements. We must either have samples we believe are statistically representative, or we must at least be able to assess the biases of the samples. Second, we must have a general idea of the regional prevalence of the types over time because the lack of a common type has more chronological significance than the lack of a rare type. Depositional problems that may be of minor importance for a presence-absence analysis will be much more serious in a quantitative analysis. In particular, one might expect that a long occupation would skew a surface sample to overrepresent later types.

Because of these difficulties and the additional complexity of integrating data not completely comparable with respect to these concerns (quantitative surface, excavated, and diagnostic samples), no single statistical technique seems adequate for the seriation of the types or the sites. Instead, both the revised ceramic chronology proposed below and the relative dating of sites are based on the mental manipulation of the available data, using a number of heuristics for the analysis of ceramic complexes.

ANALYTICAL HEURISTICS

1. The published ceramic sequence is generally correct although the dates and the exact sequence of ceramic transitions may be substantially in error.

2. Ceramic changes occur simultaneously throughout the area under consideration. Although this assumption is probably not strictly true, the data are not at all adequate to control for this variation, and to proceed on any other assumption would probably produce a greater distortion of the actual case. It is recognized that LeBlanc (1978) has argued for an earlier introduction of glaze paint in the west (near Heshot uła) than farther to the east in the El Morro Valley. However, his conclusions are based on limited data, and are not adequate to suggest how to control for this phenomenon, if it exists.

3. Excavated stratigraphic collections are the most reliable indications of ceramic complexes, followed by surface complete and quantitative collections, and lastly by diagnostic surface collections.

4. Surface samples are biased toward an overrepresentation of late types.

5. Diagnostic samples generally overrepresent slipped and painted ceramic types and thus underrepresent utility (corrugated and black ware) types. Furthermore, rare types are overrepresented with respect to more common types.

6. Due to sampling error, small collections may lack comparatively rare types. The regional frequency distribution of the types found in controlled (quantitative or excavated) collections may be used to evaluate the comparative rarity of types.

7. Because of misidentification and variation in firing, certain types are of greater evidential value than others when found in small quantities. For example, a Kwakina Polychrome sherd would seldom be confused with any other type because different slip colors occur on the two sides. However, a sherd identified as Heshotauthla Black-on-red might actually be a St. Johns Black-on-red that received unusual firing. Such confusions can be evaluated in this study because all type identifications were done by one person and because

the identifying characteristics of the types are known.

8. Types persistently occurring in a ceramic complex that are thought, on the basis of prior evidence, to be earlier than other types in the complex may be discounted, *if* they occur in very small proportions.

9. Samples from sites known to have earlier components or to be located near earlier sites are expected to have early sherds present that are not indicative of the dating of the later component, nor important in defining complexes.

10. A later type that occurs rarely and in low proportions in a complex composed of types thought to be earlier may be discounted if the criteria distinguishing the later type from an earlier type appropriate to the complex permit easy confusion of the types, or if an unusual firing of the earlier type would cause sherds to appear similar to the later type.

11. Samples from sites that have historic shrines or that were subject to other, documentable, historic use may have late sherds that can be discounted in dating the site occupations and in identifying ceramic complexes.

Before proceeding any further, I should point out some of the pitfalls of the analysis proposed. Because there is no set sequence of analytical steps involved, it is probably not strictly replicable in all its detail. However, the procedure discussed here corresponds fairly closely to procedures used in many methodologically inexplicit, but demonstrably successful, ceramic chronologies previously developed in the Southwest and elsewhere. The most glaring problem with the method used is the possibility of creating a circular argument because of the tendency inherent in these assumptions to ignore data that do not "fit." This difficulty is mitigated by the fact that this analysis is not starting from scratch but is building on years of prior effort in developing ceramic chronologies for the area, and it takes into account a considerable amount of prior knowledge about ceramics and their likely patterns of change through time.

While such an intuitive procedure does not lead inexorably to an optimal result, neither does it allow for the justification of any a priori notion. Some solutions will be more compatible with the available data than others. Certainly one measure of the degree of compatibility is the amount of data that has to be discounted. While the stratigraphic samples are not sufficient to serve as the only basis for the construction of the chronology, they should be adequate to present strong reasons for the rejection of hypotheses that are drastically in error.

Implicit in the foregoing arguments are the reasons why a more statistically objective quantitative analysis is not appropriate. Available statistical procedures for seriation require assumptions about data comparability and representativeness. If only data that met these assumptions were used, the analysis would be relatively weak because it would be unable to incorporate an enormous amount of useful information about the ceramics contained in collections that are not strictly comparable. Indeed, many of the above heuristics suggest ways of integrating somewhat incomparable data, of assessing biases, and of using that information to arrive at a more precise result.

CERAMIC TYPES AND WARES

Woodbury and Woodbury (1966) propose type descriptions and estimated dates for the glazed red ware, glazed

Figure 3.1.   Zuni woman smoothing the surface of a jar, 1918. (Photograph courtesy of the Museum of the American Indian, Heye Foundation, Negative No. 2271.)

white ware, buff ware, and early historic types. Earlier White Mountain Red Ware types are best described by Carlson (1970). The Zuni area Cibola White Ware comprises something of a typological morass as discussed at length by Holmes and Fowler (1980: 101–110). These white ware types and the gray ware types are dated in Breternitz (1966). Harlow (1973) describes the historic Zuni matte-painted types. Ferguson and Mills (1982: 274–331) further discuss the historic types (examples are shown in Fig. 3.1), and provide the only substantial published description of Zuni Black Ware, the late utility ware called "blackware" by Kroeber (1916) and Spier (1917).

The type descriptions used in this analysis are basically those presented by the above mentioned sources (see also Colton and Hargrave 1937). From a more pragmatic standpoint, my type identifications were learned primarily in cooperation with members of the Zuni Archaeology Program and, as a consequence, should agree reasonably well with others reported by the Program.

Most researchers in the area would agree that the best ceramic chronology compiled from published sources, shown in Table 3.1, is far from adequate. That the late prehistoric ceramic chronology is relatively poor is not surprising in light of the fact that not many sites were occupied during this period and only a few of them have been intensively studied. Much of the information supporting the published dates comes from sources far from Zuni. Indeed, the above-mentioned sources repeatedly comment on the unsure bases

of their proposed dates. Furthermore, a preliminary analysis of the ceramic data presented below was sufficient to suggest that the published dates do not account adequately for the co-occurrence of ceramic types observable in the surface and excavated samples studied.

For this reason, a revised ceramic chronology is proposed in Table 3.1. This chronology is based on available knowledge from other sources and from an analysis of the associations of ceramic types in the collections studied. From the sequence of associations of ceramic types at sites (the ceramic complexes), a refined chronology is inferred. Although the revised chronology will surely be improved upon as better data become available, it now agrees with the current information from the Zuni area much better than the previously published type dates. Indeed, conclusions independently reached by Tuggle and Reid (1982) in their cross-dating of Cibola White Ware correspond well with some of the revisions suggested here.

Given the sequence of complexes described below, along with published information, it remains to assign tentative relative and absolute dates to the ceramic types. The relative dates are implied strictly by the sequence of complexes and are graphically illustrated in Table 3.1. The relative starting and ending dates for each type are arranged in order to be compatible with the ceramic complexes.

Because the evidence for the published absolute dates is slim and because few new absolute dates that bear on these questions have been obtained, the present assignment of

TABLE 3.1
Late Prehistoric Ceramic Sequence in the Zuni Area

Type Name	(Ref.)	Dates	Approximate Years A.D.
			1100 · 1200 · 1300 · 1400 · 1500 · 1600 · 1700
Puerco Black-on-white	(B)	925–1200	
		925–1125	
Reserve Black-on-white	(B)	950–1200	
		950–1125	
Tularosa Black-on-white	(B)	1175–1350	
		1100–1250	
Pinedale Black-on-white	(B)	1250–1350	
		1300–1350	
Puerco Black-on-red	(C)	1000–1200	
		1000–1200	
Wingate types	(C)	1050–1200	
		1050–1200	
St. Johns types	(C)	1175–1325	
		1175–1300	
Springerville Polychrome	(C)	1250–1325	
		1250–1300	
Heshotauthla types	(C)	1300–1500	
		1275–1400	
Kwakina Polychrome	(W)	1275–1630	
		1325–1400	
Pinnawa Glaze-on-white	(W)	1350–1630	
		1350–1450	
Pinnawa Red-on-white	(W)	1375–1630	
		1350–1450	
Kechipawan Polychrome	(W)	1375–1630	
		1375–1475	
Matsaki types	(W)	1400–1680	
		1475–1680	
Hawikuh types	(W)	1630–1680	
		1630–1680	
Zuni types	(H)	1680–1900	
		1680–1900	
Corrugated gray ware	(B)	1080–1450	
		1080–1275	
Corrugated buff ware		1300–1450	
Black ware	(F)	1375–1700	

Ceramic Complex: A | AB | B | C | D | DE | E | F | G | H | H | H | I | J

Temporal span of type: — — = proposed span, · · · = published span.

References: B, Breternitz (1966); C, Carlson (1970); F, Ferguson and Mills (1982); H, Harlow (1973); W, Woodbury and Woodbury (1966).

absolute dates must be regarded as tentative. The absolute dates proposed are shown in Table 3.1. These dates were obtained by simply fitting the published dates to the new relative sequence in an intuitively plausible way that causes minimal changes to the set of published dates.

CHRONOLOGICAL DESCRIPTION OF CERAMIC COMPLEXES

In the following paragraphs, each proposed ceramic complex is lettered and the types expected in that complex are listed. Types that might occur in a complex but are not considered diagnostic are given in parentheses in the type list.

The ceramic complexes proposed here were developed through the application of the heuristics discussed above to the ceramic data collected during this study and to published ceramic data from the area. The quantitative results of my ceramic identifications are tabulated by percent in the Appendix, using the ceramic categories listed in Table 2.1. In this tabulation, multiple collections of the same kind (diagnostic, excavated, or quantitative) from the same site often are lumped together.

Ceramic Complex A

Puerco Black-on-white, Reserve Black-on-white,
Puerco Black-on-red, Wingate Black-on-red,
Wingate Polychrome, Gray Ware

This complex is identified by the presence of one or more of the types listed above and by the absence of later types, particularly St. Johns Black-on-red or St. Johns Polychrome and Tularosa Black-on-white. Earlier types such as Red Mesa Black-on-white are usually absent. In collections with this complex, white ware sherds are generally more frequent than red ware sherds.

The complex is not strictly predicted by the published type dates. According to Breternitz, Tularosa Black-on-white might be present in this complex. A second difference is the extension in time of Puerco Black-on-white and Reserve Black-on-white to the termination date of Wingate Black-on-red and Wingate Polychrome so that these two white ware types overlap in time the introduction of St. Johns Black-on-red. Available evidence from the Zuni area does not support (nor does it absolutely contradict) the implication of the published dates that Puerco Black-on-red terminates before Wingate Black-on-red or Wingate Polychrome. Consequently, it is included in this complex.

Sites with this complex are mentioned frequently in the literature (Mills 1979: 55; Kintigh 1980: 23; Holmes and Fowler 1980: 332). This complex also corresponds to ceramic group G of the Yellowhouse study (Hunter-Anderson 1978: 32). Collections clearly showing this complex were not included in the study because this complex is indicative of a period earlier than the one considered herein. Nonetheless, it is a convenient time period with which to start the ceramic chronology. Complex A is estimated to end about A.D. 1175.

Transitional Ceramic Complex AB

Puerco Black-on-white, Reserve Black-on-white,
Tularosa Black-on-white, Puerco Black-on-red, Wingate
Black-on-red, Wingate Polychrome, St. Johns
Black-on-red, St. Johns Polychrome, Gray Ware

This complex is transitional between complex A and complex B, indicating a time during which Wingate and St. Johns, and Puerco, Reserve, and Tularosa were all produced. However, sites that were occupied during the periods of production of both complex A and B would appear to have this complex. Of course, in practice it will be difficult to distinguish mixtures of complexes A and B from complexes actually deriving from the transition period.

This complex is identified by the presence of St. Johns or Tularosa Black-on-white ceramics along with a relative abundance of the other red ware and white ware types. It seems to appear in references cited under complex A, as well as in Zier (1976: 58). Transitional complex AB is estimated to date from A.D. 1175 to 1200.

Ceramic Complex B

Tularosa Black-on-white, St. Johns Black-on-red,
St. Johns Polychrome, Gray Ware

This common complex is identified by a predominance of St. Johns and Tularosa types in the decorated pottery, and an absence of later types including Springerville Polychrome, Heshotauthla Black-on-red, Heshotauthla Polychrome, and Kwakina Polychrome. Types from complex A often appear in low proportions with complex B.

Complex B is predicted by the published type dates. However, contrary to the prediction, the Zuni area data suggest that Tularosa and the St. Johns types appear at about the same time. An examination of the published tables of type occurrences (cited in the discussion of complex A) reveals many sites that have St. Johns ceramics and no Tularosa as well as sites that have Tularosa and no St. Johns. As both of these pottery types become extremely common, it seems best, lacking better data, to assume that they appear at about the same time. It is possible that the types started approximately simultaneously in different places, or that the method used here is inadequate to detect the true sequence of their development.

St. Johns Black-on-red has been dated as starting earlier than St. Johns Polychrome. While this interpretation may well be true, the available data are not adequate to support it for the Zuni area. Fortunately, this ambiguity is not a serious problem, especially considering the difficulty of positively identifying a sherd as St. Johns Black-on-red, as opposed to a sherd of St. Johns Polychrome on which no white paint appears.

This complex is reported often in the literature and occurs in samples analyzed for this research. Complex B is also very common in the survey and excavated samples from the El Morro Valley. It corresponds to ceramic groups H and I of the Yellowhouse study and is estimated here to date from A.D. 1200 to 1250.

Ceramic Complex C

Tularosa Black-on-white, Pinedale Black-on-white,
St. Johns Black-on-red, St. Johns Polychrome,
Springerville Polychrome, Gray Ware

Complex C is identified by the appearance of either Springerville Polychrome or Pinedale Black-on-white along with the types of complex B. Late types such as Heshotauthla and Kwakina are absent. As both Springerville Polychrome and Pinedale Black-on-white are relatively rare types, complex C must be viewed as temporally overlapping with the later part of complex B rather than wholly following complex B.

Springerville Polychrome is dated by Carlson as starting later than the St. Johns types and before Kwakina Polychrome and the Heshotauthla types. The Zuni data seem to confirm this observation. Kintigh (1980: 23), Mills (1979: 55), and Holmes and Fowler (1980: 332) all report sites with Springerville Polychrome but none of these later types. Zier (1976: 58) reports one site with Pinedale Black-on-white but no later types. Several collections studied here (for example, from the Day Ranch, Box S ruins) also have Pinedale Black-on-white but no later types. No data exist to indicate whether Pinedale Black-on-white or Springerville Polychrome appears first. The best assumption, at present, is that they start about the same time.

The inclusion of Pinedale Black-on-white in this complex is at variance with dates from Breternitz (A.D. 1300 to 1350), which place the introduction of Pinedale Black-on-white after the introduction of Springerville Polychrome and the Heshotauthla types. However, his introduction date is 50 years after his termination date for Tularosa Black-on-white, with no intervening Cibola White Ware types. That scenario seems most unlikely considering the close similarity between Tularosa and Pinedale Black-on-white and the common association of the two types (about 90 percent of the sites considered in this study that have Pinedale Black-on-white also have Tularosa Black-on-white). Generally supporting the conclusions reached here, Tuggle and Reid (1982: 17) indicate that Tularosa Black-on-white spans most of the A.D. 1200s and that Pinedale Black-on-white dates from about A.D. 1300 to 1350.

Most, if not all, attributions to complex C in this study are based on the presence of Springerville Polychrome, which can be relatively easily identified by the exterior black designs on bowls. The separation of Pinedale Black-on-white from Tularosa Black-on-white, as they are found in the Zuni area, is often much more debatable. Complex C is estimated to date from A.D. 1250 to 1275.

Ceramic Complex D

Tularosa Black-on-white, (Pinedale Black-on-white),
St. Johns Black-on-red, St. Johns Polychrome,
(Springerville Polychrome), Kwakina Polychrome,
Gray Ware, Buff Corrugated

Complex D is identified by the introduction of Kwakina Polychrome to the types of complex C. While Kwakina pottery never makes up a large proportion of a collection, it is quite a bit more common than either Springerville Polychrome or Pinedale Black-on-white; it forms about 2.8 percent of all the random and complete surface collections studied here, as compared with 0.4 percent for Springerville Polychrome and 0.5 percent for Pinedale Black-on-white. Thus, Kwakina Polychrome may not appear in small collections, although it was produced at the same time as other types present in the collection.

Contrary to the sequence proposed here, Carlson dates the introduction of Kwakina Polychrome after that of the Heshotauthla types. Supporting Carlson's sequence, Mills, Zier, and Holmes and Fowler each list one site that has at least one sherd of one of the Heshotauthla types and no Kwakina Polychrome sherds. However, three sites analyzed for this study contain Kwakina Polychrome and earlier types, but no Heshotauthla ceramics (Day Ranch Ruin, the Fort Site, and Shoemaker Ranch Ruin), while only one exhibits the opposite situation. In addition, at several other sites (Box S, Heshoda Yala:wa, the Mirabal Ruin, the Lookout Site, Jack's Lake, Archeotekopa II, and the Kluckhohn Ruin) the evidence is more equivocal but seems to me to indicate an earlier introduction of Kwakina Polychrome than of the Heshotauthla types.

This apparent discrepancy may occur because the two types were introduced about the same time. More likely, however, the Heshotauthla types were indeed introduced later than Kwakina Polychrome, and evidence that seems to contradict this sequence is due to the differing overall frequencies of the two types and the possibility of misidentification or differing criteria for the identification of Heshotauthla. Heshotauthla types are twice as common as Kwakina (6 percent as opposed to 3 percent of the random and complete collections). Simply because of sampling error, then, one would expect to find sites with moderate-sized collections that have Heshotauthla types represented but no Kwakina Polychrome, *even though* Kwakina was produced during the period of occupation of the site. Also, distinguishing St. Johns sherds from Heshotauthla sherds is not always an easy task. First of all, there seems to be a continuum from St. Johns to Heshotauthla on several attributes that are used to distinguish the types: exterior white line width, degree of black paint vitrification, and slip color. The criteria used for identifying the Heshotauthla types in this analysis (including design) are probably more stringent than those used in some of the other studies cited.

At this time, an additional variety of corrugated pottery appears. The type is not formally named, but is called buff corrugated throughout this study. It looks like corrugated gray ware, except it has a definite buff or orange color. Experiments by Patricia Crown (1981: 266–267) on similar sherds from Arizona indicate that corrugated gray ware refired in an oxidizing atmosphere fires a light orange color, suggesting that the buff corrugated may only differ from gray corrugated in firing atmosphere, not in composition. In any case, this ware does have chronological significance. Although it occurs in quantities of one or two sherds on sites that seem to date as early as complex B, buff corrugated, in any significant quantities, is strongly associated with Kwakina Polychrome and later types. Complex D appears to date from A.D. 1275 to 1300.

Transitional Ceramic Complex DE

Tularosa Black-on-white, (Pinedale Black-on-white),
St. Johns Black-on-red, St. Johns Polychrome,
(Springerville Polychrome), Heshotauthla Black-on-red,
Heshotauthla Polychrome, Kwakina Polychrome,
Gray Ware, Buff Corrugated

The transitional complex between complexes D and E is identified by the presence of Heshotauthla types in relatively small proportion to St. Johns types. Kwakina Polychrome and Springerville Polychrome may or may not be present. Tularosa Black-on-white or Pinedale Black-on-white usually appears in relatively low proportion. As with transitional complex AB, it is difficult to distinguish a mixture of complexes D and E from the occurrence of the actual transitional complex DE. This complex occurs frequently in the collections studied here and probably dates from about A.D. 1300 to 1325.

Ceramic Complex E

Tularosa Black-on-white, (Pinedale Black-on-white),
Heshotauthla Black-on-red, Heshotauthla Polychrome,
Kwakina Polychrome, Gray Ware, Buff Corrugated

In complex E, the St. Johns types and Springerville Poly-chrome have terminated. White ware sherds, if they are present at all, will occur in low proportions. For this time period, the published data are sparse. The above-mentioned sources refer to a small number of sites, all of which are included in the present analysis. The published dates, how-ever, do predict this complex as it is described here, with the exception of the inclusion of Tularosa Black-on-white. Complex E is estimated to date from A.D. 1325 to 1350.

Ceramic Complex F

Heshotauthla Black-on-red, Heshotauthla Polychrome, Kwakina Polychrome, Pinnawa Glaze-on-white, Gray Ware, Buff Corrugated

Complex F is identified by the presence of Pinnawa Glaze-on-white, but the absence of Kechipawan Polychrome and Matsaki buff ware. Tularosa Black-on-white and Pinedale Black-on-white seem to have terminated by this time.

Woodbury and Woodbury (1966) suggest that Pinnawa Red-on-white was introduced at the same time as Pinnawa Glaze-on-white; however, this suggestion appears to be based mainly on the logic of an evolutionary development of pottery types. Although data from this study are not adequate to settle the question, in 10 of the 11 excavated collections containing Pinnawa Red-on-white, the type is associated with Matsaki buff ware. Because of this, and because a Kechipawan Polychrome sherd with no black glaze paint would be misidentified as Pinnawa Red-on-white, the intro-duction time of Pinnawa Red-on-white is tentatively delayed to the time of the introduction of Kechipawan Polychrome in complex G. Complex F is dated from approximately A.D. 1350 to 1375.

Ceramic Complex G

Heshotauthla Black-on-red, Heshotauthla Polychrome, Kwakina Polychrome, Pinnawa Glaze-on-white, Pinnawa Red-on-white, Kechipawan Polychrome, Gray Ware, Buff Corrugated, Black Ware

Complex G is identified by the presence of Kechipawan Polychrome and the absence of Matsaki buff ware. I tenta-tively suggest that Pinnawa Red-on-white also appears at this time, although, as discussed above, the evidence is not adequate. In the collections studied here, Pinnawa Red-on-white is almost exclusively associated with Matsaki buff ware, which is known to be later, while Pinnawa Glaze-on-white appears often on sites with earlier (as well as later) complexes. Present evidence supports the Woodburys' con-tention that Kechipawan Polychrome does start later than Pinnawa Glaze-on-white. Like Pinnawa Red-on-white, Kechipawan Polychrome is more often found on sites with later complexes than is Pinnawa Glaze-on-white.

Black ware seems to be part of an evolution from cor-rugated ware to smooth plain ware. Although corrugated gray ware and black ware differ substantially when examined in the aggregate, whole vessels from Hawikku showed cor-rugation on the upper half of a vessel and a finish that would be identified as black ware on the lower half.

Black ware seems to be introduced at about the same time or slightly later than Kechipawan Polychrome, but earlier than the Matsaki types. The main evidence for this sequence comes from the trench at Binna:wa (Pinnawa), where black ware occurs in substantial quantities (12 percent) in a com-plex G context (level M) and in even higher percentages (30 to 47 percent) in association with a small proportion of Matsaki types (1 to 2 percent). Support for an earlier intro-duction comes from sites that are primarily earlier but have evidence of postabandonment use or are in areas that have received intensive historic use: Rainbow Spring Ruin (near Ojo Caliente), Halona:wa South, Pescado West Ruin, Lower Pescado Village, and Upper Nutria Village. In these cases, it seems most reasonable to attribute the black ware to the historic period. The only other early site with black ware is Yellowhouse, where only one sherd was found. If black ware had been introduced earlier, it would be expected at many sites ending in complexes E and F, but in these contexts no black ware was found.

The existence of this complex is predicted by the published dates, except that Pinedale Black-on-white is not included here. Complex G is estimated to date from A.D. 1375 to 1400.

Ceramic Complex H

Heshotauthla Black-on-red, Heshotauthla Polychrome, Pinnawa Glaze-on-white, Pinnawa Red-on-white, Kechipawan Polychrome, Matsaki Brown-on-buff, Matsaki Polychrome, Gray Ware, Buff Corrugated, Black Ware

Complex H is identified by the presence of Matsaki buff ware and black ware in association with these earlier glaze-painted types. Of course, the historic Hawikuh glaze types must be absent.

By this point in the sequence, the task of identifying changes in ceramic complexes becomes quite difficult using Zuni area data. Only a small number of sites have these late types. Most of those that do, appear to have been occupied for quite a long time, forcing us to rely mainly on the strati-graphic evidence from a few sites.

The evidence collected in the course of this project suggests that Matsaki buff ware was introduced fairly soon after the introduction of Kechipawan Polychrome. Spier's trenches at Binna:wa and Mats'a:kya show the deepest levels contain either no Matsaki buff ware or only one sherd along with larger quantities of the glazed white ware types (see the Appendix). In higher levels, Matsaki buff ware appears in increasing proportion. All sites with Kechipawan Polychrome in substantial quantities also have considerable amounts of Matsaki buff ware.

The published dates indicate that Matsaki buff ware was introduced at the time of the termination of Pinnawa Glaze-on-white, Pinnawa Red-on-white, and Kechipawan Poly-chrome. However, many apparently transitional vessels are found in the Hawikku collection (for example, buff ware sherds with glazed paint and white ware sherds in the same style with unglazed paint), and it seems likely that there was at least some overlap between the glazed white ware types and the buff ware types. The published dates also indicate that the Heshotauthla types and Kwakina Polychrome all terminate well before the introduction of the Matsaki types.

The present evidence supports the alternate interpretation that all of these types (the Heshotauthla types, Kwakina Polychrome, Pinnawa Glaze-on-white, Pinnawa Red-on-white, and Kechipawan Polychrome) persisted well into the period of popularity of the Matsaki types. Spier's trenches at Binna:wa, Mats'a:kya, and Halona:wa North support a period of overlap of all these types with the Matsaki types, probably until the introduction of the historic Hawikuh glazes, dated to A.D. 1630. However, as the percentage of Matsaki types increases through time, the earlier glazed red ware and white ware decrease in proportion.

In the Binna:wa trench, Heshotauthla ceramics steadily decrease from 16 percent in the deepest level (M) to 2 percent in the uppermost level analyzed (D). Although the Heshotauthla types never represent more than 2 percent in the aggregated levels from the Mats'a:kya trench, unidentified red ware (mostly plain sherds, probably derived from Heshotauthla bowls) forms about 6 percent of the assemblage in the lower six levels (D–I) but only 1 percent in the upper three levels (A–C), which are dated to historic times. From this evidence it is concluded that the production of Heshotauthla ceramics rapidly declines through complex H and probably stops sometime after the abandonment of Binna:wa.

Kwakina Polychrome, Pinnawa Glaze-on-white, and Kechipawan Polychrome seem to last later than the Heshotauthla types, perhaps to the end of complex H. These types typically form less than 5 percent of an assemblage, even during complexes in which the types are relatively common. Thus, small proportions such as 2 percent must be considered potentially important. In contrast, the Heshotauthla types were much more common during their period of prevalence, often forming 10 to 20 percent of an assemblage. In this case, a long use of earlier pots could account much more easily for 2 percent of a late assemblage. Kwakina Polychrome forms 2 percent of levels K and L combined at Binna:wa, but decreases to 1 percent in level D. At Mats'a:kya it forms about 2 percent throughout the levels dated to complex H. Pinnawa Glaze-on-white forms 3 percent of level D at Binna:wa and 4 percent decreasing to 2 percent of the aggregated levels from Mats'a:kya. Kechipawan Polychrome forms 1 to 3 percent of the Binna:wa collections and 3 percent in the deepest Mats'a:kya level, decreasing to 1 percent for the aggregated higher levels.

These trends may also be seen in Hodge's trench (see Smith and others 1966, Fig. 36) in which Heshotauthla Polychrome, Kwakina Polychrome, Pinnawa Glaze-on-white, and Kechipawan Polychrome are all associated in significant proportions and with the Matsaki types.

During this same period, black ware completely replaces gray ware and corrugated buff ware, as shown in Spier's Binna:wa and Mats'a:kya trenches. The ratio of black ware to corrugated gray ware and corrugated buff ware is 0.6:1 in the deepest level of Binna:wa, but reaches 7.3:1 in the top level. At Mats'a:kya, the ratio is 0.8:1 in the deepest level but is 4.0:1 in the next two levels, 25.4:1 in the next three levels, and no corrugated is found in the top three levels.

Hopi wares and Salado polychromes both seem to appear in the area during Complex H, although these types are not considered diagnostic for this complex. Hopi sherds appear in small quantities only (never more than two in any collection unit), but they appear *only* at sites with a major occupation during complex H. Salado polychrome sherds appear only at sites with complex H components, with the exception of a single sherd at Heshoda Yala:wa and four sherds (3 percent) at Rainbow Spring Ruin. Salado polychrome sherds are infrequent, although they are more common than Hopi sherds. All the Salado vessels that have been firmly identified as to specific type are from Hawikku and are either Gila Polychrome or Tonto Polychrome.

Unfortunately, this complex lasts for a long time compared to the other complexes considered here. Temporal relations within this complex must be determined on the relative proportions of the different wares. Better definition of the ceramic changes during this complex must await additional analysis of Hodge's Hawikuh collections or excavation at one or more of the late sites.

Complex H is estimated to date from about A.D. 1400 to 1630, although these dates must be regarded as tentative.

Ceramic Complexes I and J

(I) Matsaki Brown-on-buff, Matsaki Polychrome, Hawikuh Glaze-on-red, Hawikuh Polychrome, Black Ware. (J) Zuni Polychromes, Black Ware

These historic period complexes (the Hawikuh types are dated to start in A.D. 1630) are included here because they occur in some collections studied, although they do not occur within the time period of concern for this study.

SITE DATING PROCEDURES

Only a single early site considered here (the Scribe S Site) is adequately dated by dendrochronology. A few tree-ring dates are available for the other sites investigated by the Cibola Archaeological Research Project in the El Morro Valley, and a few prehistoric dates were obtained from timbers at the mission at Zuni; unfortunately the dates are insufficient to establish either beginning or ending dates for these sites, with the noted exception.

The only other absolute dating information available is on the historic sites. Hodge (1937) has convincingly established six sites that were occupied at the time of Coronado's visit in 1540: Hawikku, Kechiba:wa, Kwa'kin'a, Halona:wa, Mats'a:kya and Kyaki:ma. The archaeological evidence presented in Chapter 4 confirms his conclusion.

Without additional excavations, most of the sites can only be relatively dated on the basis of the chronology of ceramic complexes developed above. Basically, the best available evidence was used to try to determine the complexes during which the site occupation started and finished. Once this was established, the proportions of different wares were used to relatively date sites that appeared to be occupied at about the same time.

To accomplish this, a good deal of mental filtering of the data was required. The heuristics listed at the beginning of this chapter were used to process these data in order to determine the ceramic complexes being produced at the beginning and end of the site's occupation, and thus to arrive at a proposed occupation interval for each site. For example, wherever possible, excavated collections were used in preference to quantitative surface samples. The heuristics also provided reasons for giving differential credence to certain kinds of ceramic indicators.

With the diversity of evidence available and the intricate nature of the ceramic changes taking place, it would have been unwise to try to squeeze the data into some mechanical seriation procedure. Such a procedure would not have utilized many of the more subtle bits of information available and, in any case, would not yield estimated occupation spans but only a relative ordering of the sites as points in time.

In order to simplify the analysis and presentation of the ceramic data, and also to reduce "noise" in the data, I lumped ceramically similar excavation units from a site and also lumped multiple quantitative samples from a site. There is no instance in which surface collections from various areas of a site appeared to be sufficiently different to make a strong argument for differential use of parts of a site over time.

Because sample sizes vary greatly, the ceramic data are presented in the Appendix in terms of percentages, with the sample size indicated. There are a number of legitimate ways in which the percentages could have been presented. The approach used here is to quantify each identifiable type as a percentage of the total assemblage in which it occurs.

Percentages of unidentified categories (such as unidentified red ware) are not used in the arguments for dating a specific site, unless the size of the unidentified category is substantial and the type attribution of the unidentified category can be assumed with reasonable certainty. The main case in which this is true is with buff ware. Most of the unidentified buff ware sherds are plain and polished, and are almost certainly plain pieces from Matsaki Brown-on-buff or Matsaki Polychrome vessels. The overall percentage of buff ware is considered to be of chronological importance, and hence this category is generally listed for the late sites. The unidentified white ware and red ware are used in calculating the red ware to white ware ratios, but are usually not included otherwise. In contrast, the unidentified cream category is intended for sherds that are probably Pinnawa Glaze-on-white, Pinnawa Red-on-white, or Kechipawan Polychrome. The attribution to unidentified cream is not so reliable as many of the others, and for most purposes, was not especially useful in developing the site chronology.

An alternative to this form of presentation would be to present the fraction of utility and slipped sherds, and then to present the percentage of each slipped type within all slipped types. Such a division has the advantage of controlling better for the assumed functional differences between gray ware and black ware as opposed to the slipped wares. However, most of the collections studied are either surface samples or are excavated trash deposits, which are probably not functionally differentiated. In addition, I felt that differences in these percentages might well be misleading, considering the sometimes small numbers of slipped sherds. In any case, these figures can easily be computed from the data presented.

The specific arguments for the relative dating of a particular site are given in the site descriptions in Chapter 4. In addition to the inference of the ceramic complexes represented, different indices that seem to have chronological value are used; two major examples are discussed briefly.

Leslie Spier was the first person to understand clearly the sequence of ceramic wares in the Zuni area. He recognized that during the first part of the period under consideration, decorated red ware tends to replace decorated white ware, a fact also recognized in Marquardt's (1974) microseriation study. Thus, the ratio of red ware to white ware should increase over time.

While the index does appear to be useful, it has one nonobvious limitation. During this period, white ware vessels are predominantly jar forms while the red ware vessels are mainly bowls, indicating that the red ware to white ware ratio could have a functional as well as a temporal component of variability. This problem is most acute when dealing with excavated samples from roof floors (such as the CARP Scribe S Site material) to the extent that these deposits are representative of the activities actually carried out in the rooms. Storage room floors might have had almost exclusively white ware jars, indicating an earlier time than is, in fact, warranted. In surface collections and in excavations in generalized trash deposits (which Spier tried to locate for his excavations), this problem is probably not as severe, unless contemporaneous pueblos had a dramatically different mix of functions performed within them.

The other index used is the ratio of black ware to corrugated gray ware. During complex H, black ware seems to replace gray ware as the dominant utility ware. The stratigraphic evidence for the chronological value of this indicator is strong. There is no information to suggest that this index has the same kind of defect as the red ware to white ware ratio because gray ware and black ware vessels have similar forms and, as far as we know, they were serving the same functions.

Finally, it is noteworthy that the quantitative samples had an even greater advantage over diagnostic samples than I originally anticipated. The scattering of earlier sites in the area and the heirloom effect both resulted in the presence of chronologically spurious early sherds. The quantitative samples allowed the computation of relative abundance, which made the decision of whether or not to ignore these early types in site dating *much* more reliable than any decision based on diagnostic collections alone.

4. SITE DESCRIPTIONS

The emphasis in these descriptions is on the presentation of data that are particularly relevant to understanding Zuni area settlement patterns in the late prehistoric period. The locations of the 45 sites investigated are shown in Figure 4.1. Although I have visited each of the sites except Spier 61, considerable attention is given to earlier accounts by reliable observers. In particular, Mindeleff and Spier both recorded a great deal of information on the sites when they were far better preserved than they are now. The site descriptions are presented in chronological order of site occupation, and an alphabetical listing of the numbered sites is given in Table 4.1.

SITE-SIZE ESTIMATION PROCEDURES

In order to reconstruct the prehistoric demographic changes that occurred in the Zuni area, it is necessary to determine how many people lived at each pueblo and the period of time during which each pueblo was occupied. It is obvious that neither task can be accomplished with great reliability on the basis of surface data. The procedures that were used to estimate site size are detailed below, and specific site-size estimates and idiosyncratic considerations are given with the individual site descriptions.

Assumptions

The available data are not adequate to determine absolute population estimates for the pueblos, but fortunately, for most purposes considered here, relative population estimates are sufficient. To arrive at relative population estimates requires three assumptions. (1) It is assumed that the number of rooms in use in a pueblo at a single time was proportional to the number of occupants of the pueblo at that time. (2) If no other evidence is available, it is assumed that the size of a pueblo stayed constant over its period of occupation. (3) It is assumed that a constant proportion of the number of rooms, as estimated from surface remains, was used at any one time.

With these assumptions, we can consider the number of rooms in a pueblo to be proportional to the population of the pueblo for its period of occupation. While these assumptions are rather strong and doubtless are not entirely correct, in the absence of more complete data they seem the most reasonable ones to make. Nevertheless, some consideration should be given to the justification for and consequences of these assumptions, and to some plausible alternatives.

Considerable attention has been given to the assumption of a constant of proportionality between rooms (and floor area) and people in the case of the Pueblo Indians (a review of these

data are given by Hill 1970: 75–77; see also Wiessner 1974). Hill uses a figure derived from the ethnographic Hopi data of 2.8 people per room. He notes Roberts' (1956) figure of 2.0 people per room based on ethnographic Zuni data. For the El Morro Valley population estimates, Watson and others (1980) use Casselberry's (1974) formula of one-sixth the floor area in square meters to arrive at a figure of a little less than one person per occupied room.

While the evidence indicates that there does not exist a single cross-cultural constant relating rooms to number of occupants or floor area to the number of occupants, the assumption that such a constant exists for a single time and cultural context is much easier to accept. As noted above, if we assume there is such a constant among these pueblos over the 300-year time span of interest, it is not essential to know exactly what the constant is in order to make relative population estimates.

Conversely, if the number of people per room varies widely among pueblos or changes over time in the region, this demographic reconstruction will be defective. Although there is no apparent way to test this assumption with current data, sufficient raw data are given in the reconstruction to allow computation using other assumptions. In support of this assumption it may be noted that, while there is a range of average room sizes represented in the sites considered here, room size does not seem to vary systematically over time.

The second assumption is that the number of rooms in use in a pueblo remained relatively constant through its time of occupation. Clearly, this is not generally true, even for the pueblo case. In a detailed study of architectural change, Dean (1970) dated the growth and abandonment of two pueblos over a short period of time (33 to 50 years), in contrast to the much longer occupation spans once assumed for such structures. While many of the Zuni area sites seem to be similar to Dean's Tsegi Phase sites in having a short occupation span, as far as we can tell, they are quite different in developmental pattern.

The excavations at Pueblo de los Muertos did not provide dates for the construction phases of the pueblo; however, the layout of the pueblo, as revealed by the wall bonding and abutting patterns, made it clear that major sections of the pueblo were built at one time (Marquardt 1974: 35–40; Watson and others 1980: 205–207). For example, the outside wall and outer two rows of rooms that form the 90 m square outline of the pueblo must have been built at one time. Most of the large pueblos studied here are regular in plan, suggesting a large initial building stage rather than a gradual agglomeration of rooms.

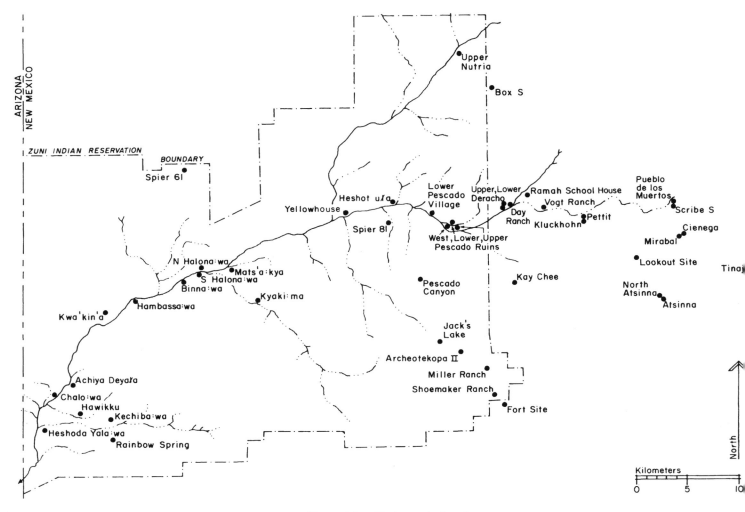

Figure 4.1.   Zuni area site locations.

An exception to this pattern is the contact period village of Hawikku where this kind of planning is not evident; rather, there seems to have been haphazard growth of the several room blocks. However, our knowledge of the earlier phases of the occupation of Hawikku is not sufficient to indicate whether there was a large initial construction phase or whether there was gradual growth, or indeed whether there might have been a planned original layout that was obscured during later growth. It should be noted that Hawikku seems to have been occupied for a much longer time than the pueblos with obvious, regular plans. Evidence of planning is not clear for several of the other contact period sites such as Halona:wa North, but, like Hawikku, they were occupied for a long period and their developmental history cannot be traced without excavation. Thus, for the sites under consideration, the most accurate assumption seems to be that major portions of the sites were built in a very short time.

The third assumption is that a constant proportion of the estimated number of rooms was occupied during the major period of occupation of the pueblo. Again, this assumption does not strictly prevail, although it is probably the most reasonable assumption to make in the absence of excavated data from the sites. This assumption in part controls for the

length of occupation. Sites with a long occupation almost certainly have a higher proportion of unused or abandoned rooms than sites with shorter occupations. However, long occupations completely obscure many rooms from the surface observations on which the estimates are based.

From their excavations, Watson and others (1980: 207) estimate that 20 percent of the rooms at Pueblo de los Muertos were abandoned while the pueblo was still occupied. On the other hand, Smith and others (1966: 12) suggest that no more than half of the Hawikku rooms were in use at any one time. (Certainly Hawikku was occupied much longer than Pueblo de los Muertos.) While the exact figure will vary from site to site, for purposes of this analysis a figure of 35 percent, midway between these two estimates, is used. Like the constant relating population to rooms, no important aspects of the conclusions are dependent on the choice of this number, as opposed to some other.

Estimating the Number of Rooms in Multiple-story Pueblos

At most sites it is difficult to estimate the total number of stories of architecture. Sites are estimated to have one, two, or three stories based on a subjective evaluation of the rubble

TABLE 4.1
Alphabetical Listing of Described Zuni Sites

Site	Description Number	Site	Description Number
Achiya:Deyaˀa	31	Lower Pescado Ruin	34
Archeotekopa II	17	Lower Pescado Village	32
Atsinna	30	Mats'a:kya	40
Binna:wa	38	Miller Ranch Ruin	2
Box S Ruin	12	Mirabal Ruin	21
Chalo:wa	43	North Atsinna Ruin	24
Cienega Site	27	Pescado Canyon Ruin	8
Day Ranch Ruin	14	Pescado West Ruin	33
Fort Site	18	Pettit Site	7
Halona:wa North	45	Pueblo de los Muertos	29
Halona:wa South	26	Rainbow Spring Ruin	36
Hambassa:wa	37	Ramah School House Ruin	23
Hawikku	39	Scribe S Site	10
Heshoda Yala:wa	11	Shoemaker Ranch Ruin	13
Heshot uˀla	35	Spier 61	3
Jack's Lake Ruin	16	Spier 81	1
Kay Chee Ruin	6	Tinaja Ruin	19
Kechiba:wa	44	Upper Deracho Ruin	4
Kluckhohn Ruin	20	Upper Nutria Village	25
Kwa'kin'a	42	Upper Pescado Ruin	28
Kyaki:ma	41	Vogt Ranch Ruin	5
Lookout Site	15	Yellowhouse	22
Lower Deracho Ruin	9		

mound height. In many cases it is not possible to determine accurately the height of the rubble mound, because it is impossible to know what constitutes the underlying terrain.

A two-story pueblo is estimated to have one-half the number of second floor rooms as ground floor rooms. A three-story pueblo is estimated to have one-half as many third story rooms as second story rooms. Thus, the total room estimate for a two-story pueblo is 1.5 times the number of ground floor rooms; a three-story pueblo is estimated to have 1.75 times the number of ground floor rooms. These factors of 1.5 and 1.75 were developed in consideration of two sources of data.

In the detailed plan of late 19th century Zuni pueblo made by Mindeleff (1891, Plate 76), the roofs are apparently shaded to show height, with higher terraces colored in a lighter shade of gray. Mindeleff (1891: 97) notes that although five levels of terraces were visible from the south side, this area of the pueblo is only three terraces high when viewed from the north. Although the distinctions are not always clear, three levels of shading can generally be distinguished. The number of outlined roof areas (which probably roughly correspond to rooms) with each color of shading was counted for Mindeleff's house numbers 1 and 4, which he believes were the oldest sections of the pueblo (Mindeleff 1891: 98, figure facing page 97). A total of 223 ground floor rooms, 126 second floor rooms (57 percent of the ground floor total), and 28 third floor rooms (17 percent of the ground floor total) are shown. When the factor of 1.75 for a three-story pueblo is applied to the 223 ground floor rooms, a total of 390 rooms is estimated in contrast to the actual total of 377 rooms.

Reconstructions of Pueblo Bonito (Judd 1964, plates 1 and 8), which is both relatively well-preserved and more similar in layout than 19th century Zuni pueblo to most of the prehistoric and protohistoric pueblos considered here, shows a much higher proportion of multiple-story room columns. The general model indicates that there is approximately the same maximum number of stories as there are concentric rows of rooms. The outermost row of rooms was four stories high; the next row in was three stories high; the next, two stories; and the last, only a single story high. This model is probably the basis for Fewkes' (1891: 127) conclusion that the Jack's Lake Ruin had five stories because it had five concentric rows of rooms. This model would suggest a 67 percent addition for the second-story rooms of a three-story pueblo and an addition of 33 percent for the third-story rooms, for a total estimate of two times the number of ground floor rooms for a three-story pueblo. For a two-story pueblo, the addition would be 50 percent for the second story rooms.

Combining these two sources of data, the 50 percent and 25 percent additions proposed for second and third story rooms, respectively, seem both reasonable and conservative. As it may well be that some of the pueblos considered here had more than three stories, an additional factor of conservatism is added.

FORMAT OF THE SITE DESCRIPTIONS

Site Identification, Bibliography, and Discussion

The sequential number and the name used here for each site is followed by a reference to its map and a list of other names for that site that have appeared in the archaeological literature. If the primary name is Zuni, the spelling preferred by the Zuni Language Development Program is used. In some cases, not all alternate spellings that appear in the historical literature (as opposed to the archaeological literature) are given. The historical synonyms are subject to somewhat more interpretation and, in any case, have been listed by Hodge (1937: 128–134). Eggan and Pandey (1979: 481) also discuss synonyms for the historic Zuni towns.

In addition to alternate names, all other known formal designations or site numbers are listed. Zuni Archaeology Program (ZAP) numbers are given for all sites. Sites to which Spier assigned numbers are so referenced, and all applicable Arizona State Museum (ASM) site numbers, all Columbia University (CU) numbers assigned by the Woodburys, and all Cibola Survey (CS) numbers from the Cibola Archaeological Research Project are listed. The Laboratory of Anthropology (LA) numbers are probably fairly complete, although no comprehensive check was made. Other site references, such as Museum of Northern Arizona numbers (NA), Zuni Indian Reservation numbers (ZIR), and Wake Forest survey numbers (WF) are recorded when available, but it is probable that not all applicable numbers are listed. These different site designations are given because they may prove useful in correlating information on sites in future research.

The bibliographic references are intended to be complete with respect to sources in the archaeological literature that present some concrete information about the site. Mere mention of the existence of the site does not necessarily warrant a citation. Probably the only exceptions to the complete citation of archaeological information are the few historic sites about which a great deal has been written, most notably Hawikku. In such cases only the major sources are listed. In the historical literature, only major sources with which I am familiar are cited; for the historic sites this list is far from comprehensive, but for all the others it is probably nearly complete.

Incidental information that does not fit into other categories is listed under Discussion. This section includes, for example, an informant's report that the site is an ancestral Zuni site, translations of site names, the relation of the site to nearby sites, major research projects that have worked on the site, relevant information concerning the discovery of the site, and any necessary discussion of the references.

Precise site locations are not presented here, in order to protect the sites, but are available in the Arizona State Museum and Zuni Archaeology Program site files.

Environmental Setting

Major nearby water sources are discussed although the hydrology of the area has changed in the last century. The combination of clear-cutting in the forests on the Zuni Mountains early in this century and overgrazing of the range since the turn of the century have resulted in increased runoff. Permanency of the water courses has changed significantly and many springs are known to have ceased flowing. Thus, the current absence of a nearby water source may not accurately reflect the prehistoric situation.

Similarly, the plant community attributions (from Lowe 1964) may not be exactly the same as the floral associations at the time the sites were occupied. Tree lines are known to change over relatively short time intervals and, in any case, juniper-pinyon woodlands often grade into grasslands and desert scrub areas. Decades of overgrazing have had dramatic effects on almost all the range land in the area (particularly lands on the reservation) and, as a result, the distinction between Great Basin desert scrub and plains grassland is not always clear. However, we know that much of the area that

was once plains grassland is now dominated by Great Basin desert scrub vegetation such as sagebrush.

Archaeological Information

Varying amounts of archaeological information are available for the different sites. Plans are provided for almost all sites and a general description of the architecture of each site is given. Most of the site plans were derived from other sources, but all were field checked, and many were substantially revised on the basis of new observations. The dimensions listed refer to the area more or less densely covered with architecture. Where relevant, the dimensions and shapes of individual room blocks are presented. Trash scatter dimensions for sites this large are probably not indicative of useful cultural information and were not recorded.

Because the type and quality of site size information varies from site to site, the specific derivation of the room count estimate for each site is described. When available, room estimates from other sources are listed for comparsion, and the total area covered by architecture or rubble mounds is listed. Average room sizes are given whenever possible.

Where useful, comments are made concerning the artifact scatters on the sites and on sources of artifactual information to which direct access was not available. For all sites, ceramic collections used in establishing the site dating are listed according to the type of collection: quantitative, excavated, or diagnostic.

Because the quality and detail of the information available varies so widely, and because the temporal placement is generally the result of a complex synthesis of the information available, an individual discussion of the estimated relative site dates (in terms of ceramic complexes) is included with each site. For all sites, percentages of the major ceramic types are listed along with the sample size. Generally, categories of unidentified wares are not listed, so that the percentages do not total 100 percent. Percentages greater than 0.5 percent are given to the nearest percent. The ceramic data are completely presented in tabular form in the Appendix. In order to make the data more comprehensible, several collections are often lumped together. However, whenever this is done, quantitative samples are lumped only with other quantitative samples and excavated levels with other levels.

Except where tree-ring dates are available, absolute dates cannot be assigned with confidence to the sites. However, approximate dates for the major site occupation span are presented with each site description. These estimated dates are based on the ceramic chronology presented in Chapter 3 (Table 3.1) and take into account the revisions to the dating of a few individual sites that are advisable based on other analyses discussed in Chapter 5. It must be emphasized that the absolute dates are only *tentative* estimates based on the available information. The sites are arranged according to the chronological order of their occupation spans.

ZUNI SITES

1. *Spier 81* (Fig. 4.2)
Identification
    Site Numbers: Spier 81, ZAP:NM:12:J3:147.
    Bibliography: Spier (1917: 237).

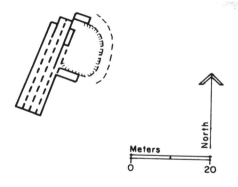

Figure 4.2.   Spier 81.

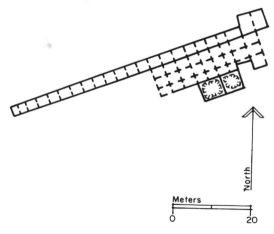

Figure 4.3.   Miller Ranch Ruin (after Kintigh 1980, map 25).

Environmental Setting
Elevation: 2060 m (6750 feet).
Exposure: East.
Landforms: The site is located at the base of the steep side of a small canyon that empties into the Pescado River Valley. There is a sandstone cliff immediately west of the site and alluvial bottomlands lie to the east. A deeply cut arroyo runs down the center of the canyon, about 50 m east of the site.
Plant Communities: The site is at the transition between the plains grassland of the canyon floor and the juniper-pinyon woodland of the canyon sides.

Archaeological Remains
Architecture: Spier's Site 81 is built of tan sandstone. The major part of the room block is rectangular and four rooms wide. East of the room block is a large kiva depression. Two small wings stick out from the main room block to form a narrow "F" framing the depression. An extensive trash scatter lies farther to the east of the room block.
Dimensions: 10 m by 26 m, with a 12 m diameter depression.
Room Estimate: Fitting the observed room size (2.5 m by 3.0 m) into the area of rooms shown on the map, I estimate a total of 39 ground floor rooms. In addition, the height of the central part of the back (western) row of rooms indicated four, two-story room columns, yielding a total estimate of 43 rooms.
Ceramic Samples: Quantitative by Kintigh; diagnostic by Kintigh.
Temporal Placement: Spier 81 is one of the two earliest sites recorded in this project (with the exception of a few early components of major late sites mentioned below). Its quantitative assemblage of 219 sherds is composed mainly of Tularosa Black-on-white (13%), Wingate types (5%), St. Johns matte (7%) and subglaze (7%) types, and gray ware (44%). The low percentages of Puerco Black-on-white (3%) and Reserve Black-on-white (1%) indicate an initial occupation of the site during the time of transitional complex AB (probably before A.D. 1200). The absence of Springerville Polychrome and glazed St. Johns types, and the relatively large amounts of Wingate pottery, suggest a termination of occupation some time during complex B (near A.D. 1250).

2. Miller Ranch Ruin (Fig. 4.3)
Identification
Site Numbers: Spier 159, ZAP:NM:13:D:41.
Bibliography: Spier (1917: 249–250), Kintigh (1980).

Discussion: This site takes its name from the ranch (identified by Spier as Miller Ranch) that is now in ruins on the canyon bottom below the site. Spier used number 159 to refer to a number of contemporaneous ruins along the edge of Miller Canyon, including this site. In this report, only the largest ruin is discussed (see Kintigh 1980 for a discussion of the other ruins).

Environmental Setting
Elevation: 2219 m (7280 feet).
Exposure: East.
Landforms: The site is located on the tip of a downsloping mesa finger. The floor of Miller Canyon is less than 100 m to the southeast of the site.
Plant Communities: The site is located in a thick juniper-pinyon woodland. A ponderosa forest is nearby in the higher country to the west, and the plains grassland of the canyon floor surrounds the site in all other directions.

Archaeological Remains
Architecture: The site is long and linear. For half its length, it is only a single room wide. It widens to two, and then four rooms, with an additional protuberance of two large square rooms with depressions inside that may be kivas.
Dimensions: 16 m by 70 m.
Room Estimate: Room sizes average 9 square meters, with a total room area of 540 square meters shown on the ZAP map. Based on a direct count, the site appears to have 60 single-story rooms.
Ceramic Samples: Quantitative by Kintigh; diagnostic by Kintigh.
Temporal Placement: Probably contemporary with Spier 81, the quantitative sample of 101 sherds from Miller Ranch Ruin consists mainly of Tularosa Black-on-white (14%), Wingate types (5%), St. Johns matte (18%) and subglaze (8%) types, and gray ware (35%). Here, the early Puerco Black-on-white (1%) is barely represented and no glazed St. Johns ceramics or later types were found. In the quantitative sample, one buff corrugated sherd was found and two brown ware sherds were in the diagnostic collection. As with Spier 81, the occupation span suggests a start during complex AB and an end late in complex B (from before A.D. 1200 to about 1250). Evidence to place Spier 81 either earlier or later than

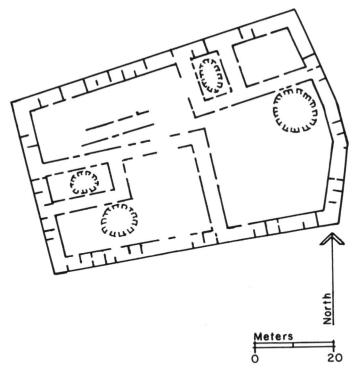

Figure 4.4.   Spier 61 (after Spier 1917, fig. 3*f*).

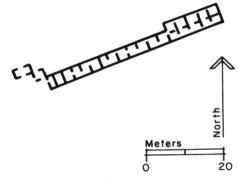

Figure 4.5.   Upper Deracho Ruin (after Spier 1917, fig. 4*a*).

Miller Ranch Ruin is contradictory. Spier 81 has a higher St. Johns subglaze to matte ratio, suggesting that it might be somewhat later. The higher red ware to white ware ratio at Spier 81 (1.7:1 versus 1.3:1) suggests the same conclusion. One sherd of Springerville Polychrome has been reported from Miller Ranch Ruin (but not seen by the author), suggesting a later date for Miller Ranch Ruin than for Spier 81, but on the basis of present evidence they are considered contemporary.

3. *Spier 61* (Fig. 4.4)

Identification
Site Numbers: Spier 61, ZAP:NM:12:X2:55, CU Z–13.
Bibliography: Spier (1917: 235, Fig. 3*f*).

Environmental Setting
Elevation: 2039 m (6690 feet).
Exposure: Open.
Landforms: The site is situated near the edge of a large open area in which Vanderwagen Draw joins Bosson Wash. About 75 m to the west of the site is a mesa, and a major arroyo is about 20 m to the south.
Plant Communities: The site is in a plains grassland community. A juniper-pinyon woodland is on top of the mesa approximately 100 m to the west.

Archaeological Remains
Architecture: Spier's Site 61 is an approximately rectangular sandstone pueblo. Spier's map and recent examinations indicate that the pueblo is generally only one room wide. In several places, linear alignments of rooms appear to protrude into the plaza formed by the rectangular outline. Two depressions in the north-northeast portion of this plaza and another in the southwest suggest the presence of kivas. A trash area is located to the south of the pueblo.

Dimensions: 50 m by 78 m.
Room Estimate: The rooms can be counted directly or easily extrapolated from Spier's map. The total count is 122 ground floor rooms. Because the site is now heavily alluviated, it is impossible to determine if the site had multiple stories. According to Spier's map, a typical room was about 3.2 m by 3.5 m, for an average area of 11.2 square meters. For present purposes I assume there was one story.
Artifacts: Surface collections were made by the Zuni Archaeology Program in 1980. Most of these collections come from the trash concentration to the south of the pueblo.
Ceramic Samples: Quantitative by ZAP (7).
Temporal Placement: Combining the seven quantitative collections at this site, the total sample is 182 sherds. Puerco Black-on-white (2%), Reserve Black-on-white (1%), and Wingate types (1%) were found in small quantities. The main part of the assemblage is composed of Tularosa Black-on-white (13%), St. Johns matte (16%) and subglaze (12%) types, and gray ware (40%). The low percentage of early types indicates a start early in complex B (probably after A.D. 1200). The high proportion of St. Johns compared with earlier types, the presence of one anomalous St. Johns glaze sherd and one Heshotauthla glaze sherd, as well as a high red ware to white ware ratio (1.8:1) indicate an occupation until late in complex B (about A.D. 1250).

4. *Upper Deracho Ruin* (Fig. 4.5)

Identification
Site Numbers: Spier 102, ZAP:NM:12:I3:111, CU R–18.
Bibliography: Spier (1917: 240, Fig. 4*a*), Fewkes (1891: 113–114).
Discussion: Fewkes does not name this site but his description of the site and its location correspond well with this site. The name comes from the property owner at the time of Spier's visit.

Environmental Setting
Elevation: 2103 m (6900 feet).
Exposure: Open.
Landforms: The site is located at the edge of a bench of a mesa slope overlooking the Lower Deracho Ruin (site 9), 15 m below and to the south.
Plant Communities: The bench on which the site is located is covered with plains grassland; however, the slopes to the northeast and south have a cover of juniper-pinyon woodland.

Archaeological Remains
Architecture: At the time of Fewkes' visit, the ruin had

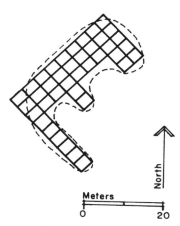

Figure 4.6.
Vogt Ranch Ruin.

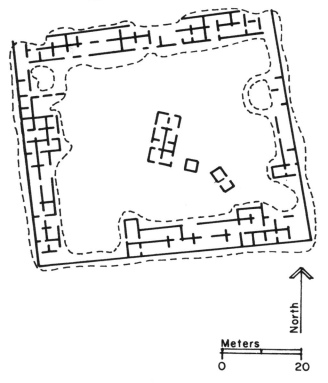

Figure 4.7. Kay Chee Ruin (after Spier 1917, fig. 4e).

standing walls. He indicates that the ruin was bracket-shaped and was 500 feet (152 m) long, which seems like an exaggeration considering the present remains. As it was in Spier's time, and as it can be seen today, the site is a small, linear room block, one or two rooms wide, on the edge of the mesa bench. Spier shows rooms about 2.6 m by 3.5 m and 2.7 m by 3.0 m. The rooms average 8.7 square meters. There are a few additional rooms on the steep slope to the south of those shown on Spier's map.

Dimensions: 3 m by 58 m.

Room Estimate: A total of 25 rooms is shown on Spier's map. An additional 5 rooms may be on the slope for a total of 30 rooms. It seems most unlikely that any of these had more than one story.

Ceramic Sample: Diagnostic by Kintigh.

Temporal Placement: Only a diagnostic collection of 19 sherds was made at the site because of the low sherd densities. The only ceramics found were Tularosa Black-on-white, St. Johns matte and subglaze types, and gray ware. Given the complete absence of earlier types, the site can only be dated sometime late in complex B (about A.D. 1225 to 1250).

5. *Vogt Ranch Ruin* (Fig. 4.6)

Identification
Site Numbers: Spier 121, ZAP:NM:12:H3:56, WF 29 Va 24.
Bibliography: Spier (1917: 243–244).
Discussion: This site is one of several small, approximately contemporaneous pueblos and cliff dwellings lining Togeye Canyon. The site is named after long-time landowners in the area.

Environmental Setting
Elevation: 2115 m (6940 feet).
Exposure: East.
Landforms: The site is on the floor of Togeye Canyon at the base of a low mesa spur. An impermanent drainage runs a few meters east of the site.
Plant Communities: The Vogt Ranch Ruin is in an area of plains grassland, although a juniper-pinyon woodland is on the mesa a short distance to the west.

Archaeological Remains
Architecture: The site has a large, roughly L-shaped rubble

mound with only a few room outlines now visible. A few meters to the southwest of the main room block is an isolated masonry room. The walls are constructed of tan sandstone.

Dimensions: 20 m by 32 m, L-shaped.

Room Estimate: The total mounded area is about 345 square meters as measured from a sketch map. Spier indicates that the pueblo is nine rooms and 106 feet (32 m) long. Based on Spier's suggested width of 24 feet (7.3 m), it is probably three rooms wide. Thus, the average room area is 8.8 square meters (2.4 m by 3.6 m). The extension on the south is probably a single row of six additional rooms. Two less-pronounced extensions give the rubble mound a contorted E shape and may add an additional six rooms, making the total ground floor room estimate 39 rooms.

Artifacts: The artifact scatter was light and no quantitative sample could be made.

Ceramic Samples: Diagnostic by Kintigh.

Temporal Placement: Only a 27-sherd diagnostic collection was made because of the low sherd densities. Tularosa Black-on-white, St. Johns matte and subglaze types, and gray ware were recovered. A single Puerco Black-on-red sherd was found, but no Wingate types, suggesting an occupation late in complex B (about A.D. 1225 to 1250).

6. *Kay Chee Ruin* (Fig. 4.7)

Identification
Site Numbers: Spier 110, ZAP:NM:12:I3:29, CU R–20.
Bibliography: Spier (1917: 242, Fig. 4e).
Discussion: The ruin is named after Kay Chee Martine, a Navajo who has lived near the site since the time of Spier's visit.

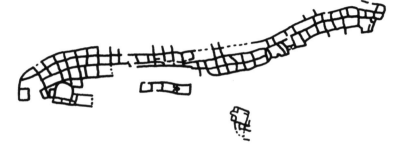

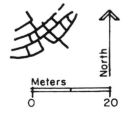

Figure 4.8.   Pettit Site
(after Linthicum 1980).

Meters
0   20

North

Environmental Setting
Elevation: 2167 m (7110 feet).
Exposure: Open.
Landforms: The site is located on a bench on a mesa side about 10 m above the floor of Kay Chee Draw. It is adjacent to a ravine that was dammed at the time of Spier's visit. The creek running down Kay Chee Draw some distance to the west has been dammed for stock tanks in several places.
Plant Communities: The site is in an open juniper-pinyon woodland with denser juniper-pinyon woodland upslope to the southwest. Plains grassland and fallow agricultural land are on the floor of the draw to the north. According to the son and daughter of the man who has lived across the draw from the site since at least 1916, their father had 28 acres under rainfall agriculture growing corn, beans, wheat, squash, oats, melons, and potatoes. They said that Kay Chee Draw, in which there is now a good deal of scrub vegetation (sagebrush and scattered junipers), was all grassland only 25 years ago.

Archaeological Remains
Architecture: The pueblo is rectangular, with two to three rows of rooms around the perimeter and a room block in the interior plaza. The depression in the room area on the western side of the pueblo (marked on Spier's map) is thought by Kay Chee Martine to be a well, although it might also be a kiva. The walls are constructed of roughly shaped, tan sandstone. Although they were reported by Spier to be still standing up to 6 feet high, no walls now stand significantly above the surface.
Dimensions: 60 m by 67 m, rectangular.
Room Estimate: A total of 156 rooms can be counted from Spier's map, with additional room areas not subdivided into rooms. A total room area of 1415 square meters is shown. Dividing this figure by the average illustrated room size of 8.3 square meters (about 2.7 m by 3.0 m), I estimate a ground floor total of 170 rooms. Based on Spier's reports of wall heights, one-half of these rooms are assumed to have two stories, yielding a total estimate of 255 rooms.
Ceramic Sample: Diagnostic by Spier.
Temporal Placement: Only Spier's diagnostic collection

of 29 sherds was available. The main ceramics recorded are Tularosa Black-on-white, St. Johns matte and subglaze types, and gray ware. One Reserve Black-on-white, one Pinedale Black-on-white, and one buff corrugated sherd were also found. The lack of early white wares and the absence of later red wares suggests an occupation late in complex B (about A.D. 1225 to 1250). Two completely anomalous sherds were found: one Pinnawa Red-on-white and one Kechipawan Polychrome. The available evidence, including the complete lack of Heshotauthla types, Kwakina Polychrome, Matsaki types, and black ware, indicate that these sherds were not associated with the major occupation of the site. In my visit to the site in 1980 (no collections were made), neither of these late types was observed.

7. *Pettit Site* (Fig. 4.8)
Identification
Site Numbers: ZAP:NM:12:H3:38, LA1571, CS190.
Bibliography: Linthicum (1980).
Discussion: This site was partially excavated by a Wake Forest University expedition directed by J. Ned Woodall. Other excavations have been conducted by Mr. and Mrs. Gordon Pettit, the owners of the land.

Environmental Setting
Elevation: 2134–2161 m (7000–7090 feet).
Exposure: Southeast and open.
Landforms: The site is located on the top and along the southeast base of a hundred-foot high sandstone butte about 100 m northwest of the Kluckhohn Ruin. An intermittent drainage runs a short distance to the southeast of the butte. South of the butte, on the far side of the Kluckhohn Ruin, is a steep ridge.
Plant Communities: Plains grassland comes up to the bottom of the butte, while the top and sides are essentially barren. A ponderosa pine forest is found on the ridge to the south.

Archaeological Remains
Architecture: The site is composed of a number of small room clusters constructed of sandstone.
Dimensions: 96 m by 7 m on mesa top; 20 m by 9 m at mesa base.

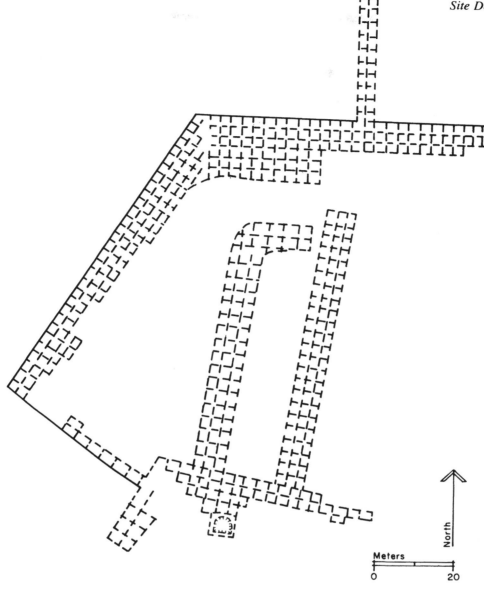

Figure 4.9. Pescado Canyon Ruin (after map by Andrew Fowler
and Barbara Mills, ZAP file, Zuni, New Mexico).

Room Estimate: According to Linthicum (1980: 3), the Pettit Site has more than 112 rooms, the majority of which are on top of a T-shaped butte. An examination of Linthicum's map suggests that there are at least 13 additional rooms, for a conservative total of 125 rooms. The average room size is about 7.2 square meters.

Artifacts: The artifact scatter is very light.

Ceramic Samples: Diagnostic by Kintigh.

Temporal Placement: Only a very small diagnostic collection (5 sherds) was made at the Pettit Site because of the low sherd densities. Only St. Johns matte types and gray ware were collected. Linthicum (1980: 54–68) indicates that Wingate Black-on-red, St. Johns Black-on-red, St. Johns Polychrome, Springerville Polychrome, Reserve Black-on-white, and Tularosa Black-on-white were present. In her analysis of painted sherds deriving from 136 vessels from 25

room floors, the overwhelming majority were St. Johns types (90%), and the remainder were Reserve Black-on-white (3%), Tularosa Black-on-white (4%), Wingate Black-on-red and Wingate Polychrome (1%), and Springerville Polychrome (1%). Some of the St. Johns is reported to have glazed decoration. With the information available, an occupation starting in complex B and lasting into complex C is indicated (from about A.D. 1225 to after A.D. 1250).

8. *Pescado Canyon Ruin* (Fig. 4.9)

Identification

Site Numbers: ZAP:NM:12:I3:140.

Bibliography: None.

Discussion: This is the only large ruin within the study area that had not been reported in print prior to the inception of this research. Inquiries to residents of the Zuni community

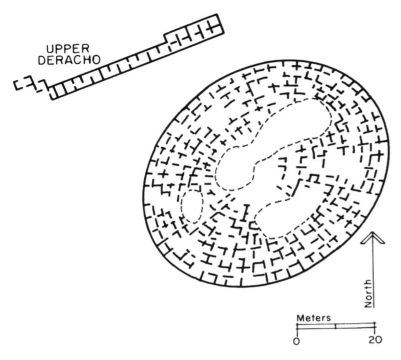

UPPER
DERACHO

Meters
0   20

North

Figure 4.10. Lower Deracho Ruin
(after Spier 1917, fig. 4*a*).

produced reports of the site, and eventually a visit to it was arranged. The site was mapped by Andrew Fowler and Barbara Mills.

Environmental Setting
Elevation: 2252 m (7390 feet).
Exposure: Open.
Landforms: The site is situated atop a mesa overlooking Pescado Canyon. Sandstone outcrops surround the site. A small seep in an arroyo bank is located about 700 m north of the site.
Plant Communities: The site is in a ponderosa pine forest. On the mesa slopes below there is a juniper-pinyon woodland, and the canyon floor has open juniper-pinyon woodland and plains grassland.

Archaeological Remains
Architecture: The site has an irregular shape formed from a composition of a number of linear room blocks from one to six rooms in width. The masonry is of well-shaped tan sandstone with a rubble core. Walls are now standing up to 2 m high, and it seems likely that the pueblo had three stories in the wider sections. A large square room on the southern end of the pueblo has a depression that may be a D-shaped or circular kiva.
Dimensions: 120 m by 160 m.
Room Estimate: The sketch map by Fowler and Mills shows 413 ground floor rooms. Multiplying by 1.75 for two additional stories gives a total estimate of 723 rooms. Room sizes measured on the sketch map and averaged within room block range from 7.0 to 8.8 square meters per room.
Ceramic Samples: Quantitative by ZAP; diagnostic by ZAP.

Temporal Placement: The quantitative collection (63 sherds) from the Pescado Canyon Ruin indicates a later occupation than at any of the sites discussed above. Tularosa Black-on-white (3%), St. Johns subglaze (13%) and glaze (22%) types, and gray ware (38%) make up virtually the entire assemblage. One Springerville Polychrome sherd was found in the diagnostic collection. This sherd, as well as the absence of matte St. Johns types and the high red ware to white ware ratio (5.4:1), indicate an occupation from late in complex B through complex C (from before A.D. 1250 to about A.D. 1275).

9. *Lower Deracho Ruin* (Fig. 4.10)

Identification
Site Numbers: Spier 101, ZAP:NM:12:I3:110, CU R–18.
Bibliography: Spier (1917: 240, Fig. 4*a*), Fewkes (1981: 113–114).
Discussion: Fewkes does not name this site but his description of the site and its location correspond well with the Lower Deracho Ruin. The name comes from the property owner at the time of Spier's visit.

Environmental Setting
Elevation: 2088 m (6850 feet).
Exposure: Southeast.
Landforms: The pueblo is located on the floor of the Ramah Valley at the base of a steep mesa slope. On a bench of this hill, only 100 m to the northwest, is a much smaller ruin, Upper Deracho Ruin (site 4). There is a depression, apparently a disused stock tank, adjacent to the site. Cebolla Creek (which now runs only intermittently) extends down the middle of the Ramah Valley about 200 m southeast of the site.
Plant Communities: The site is in an area of plains grassland; however, an open juniper-pinyon woodland is on the hillslope a few meters to the north. There is modern agricultural use of the valley bottomland near the site.

Archaeological Remains
Architecture: The pueblo forms a large oval nearly filled with rooms. Construction is of tan, shaped sandstone. The rubble mound now stands about 2 m high. Fewkes notes the presence of a large circular depression in the plain near the ruin, suggestive of a kiva or reservoir. This depression may be in or under the stock tank. He also says that there is evidence (unspecified) that building stones were taken from the ruin for the construction of the modern town of Ramah.
Dimensions: 53 m by 69 m.
Room Estimate: Spier's map shows 2504 square meters of area covered with rooms. The rooms shown on Spier's plan average 7.2 square meters in size. Dividing this room size into the total area, I obtained a ground floor room estimate of 348 rooms. If it is assumed that one-half of these rooms had second stories and that one-fourth had third stories, then the total estimate would be 609 rooms.
Ceramic Samples: Quantitative by Kintigh; diagnostic by Kintigh.
Temporal Placement: A quantitative sample of 96 sherds from Lower Deracho Ruin had mainly Reserve Black-on-white (2%), Tularosa Black-on-white (2%), St. Johns matte

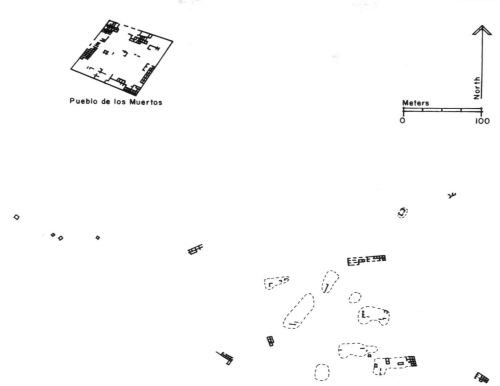

Figure 4.11.   Scribe S Site (after Watson and others 1980, fig. 2).

(2%) and subglaze (6%) types, with a preponderance of gray ware (73%). One Springerville Polychrome sherd (1%) was found. The red ware to white rare ratio was high (4.2:1). The site occupation span appears to be about the same as for the Pettit Site, the Scribe S Site, and the Pescado Canyon Ruin, from late in complex B through complex C (from before A.D. 1250 to about 1275).

10. *Scribe S Site* (Fig. 4.11)

Identification
Site Numbers: ZAP:NM:12:G3:4, 7, 9, 11, 12, 14, 22, 23, 24, 25, 26 (no ZAP site numbers have been assigned to CS 44 and CS 80); CS4, 7, 9, 11, 12, 14, 39, 40, 41, 42, 43, 44, 80.

Bibliography: Watson and others (1980: 203–209, Fig. 2), Marquardt (1974: 58–63), LeBlanc (1978).

Discussion: This site was not noted by Spier, although he recorded the large ruin, Pueblo de los Muertos, which is only about 300 m distant. To my knowledge, the Scribe S Site was first recorded in the 1930s in a survey of the El Morro National Monument area. This site consists of a cluster of about 15 room blocks on a ridge. While each might be considered a single site, they all appear to be contemporaneous and, as a group, probably constituted a prehistoric community.

A total of 26 rooms in the Scribe S Site was excavated by the Cibola Archaeological Research Project in 1972 and 1973 (Watson and others 1980). A number of the rooms were burned and then abandoned. Many tree-ring dates were obtained during these excavations (shown graphically by Watson and others 1980: 207). Cutting dates range from

about A.D. 1210 to 1276, with the majority between 1250 and 1276.

Environmental Setting
Elevation: 2231 m (7320 feet).

Exposure: Open, southeast.

Landforms: The Scribe S Site is located on the top and the southern slope of a ridge in the foothills of the Zuni Mountains. The mountains rise to over 2680 m (8800 feet) to the northeast of the site. About 500 m to the northwest is the opening of Muerto Canyon, down which flows a stream fed by Muerto Spring at the base of the mountains. The site overlooks the broad floor of the El Morro Valley to the south. El Morro rock is visible on the opposite side of the valley from the site.

Plant Communities: The ridge on which the site is located has a cover of open juniper-pinyon woodland. Plains grassland covers the floor of the El Morro Valley south of the site. A ponderosa pine forest is on the Zuni Mountains to the north.

Archaeological Remains
Architecture: The site consists of about 15 room blocks in an area about 350 m by 400 m on the ridge. The complete outlines of all these room blocks are not apparent, but several have been wall-trenched and most of them seem to be rectangular, L-shaped, or C-shaped. They range in size from just a few rooms to about 60 rooms. The walls are constructed of tan sandstone.

Dimensions: Area containing architecture is about 350 m by 400 m.

Room Estimate: Watson and her colleagues estimate that there was a total of 410 rooms in the Scribe S Site. Most of these rooms were ground floor rooms.

Ceramic Samples: Quantitative by CARP; excavated by CARP (5).

Temporal Placement: According to tree-ring data mentioned above, the major construction occurred between A.D. 1250 and 1275. The site appears to have been abandoned about 1276.

The five excavated CARP samples analyzed form a sample of 219 sherds. (Because the corrugated pottery was not available for analysis, the percentages that follow are not directly comparable to other samples that include gray ware.) Puerco Black-on-white (0.5%, 1 sherd) and Reserve Black-on-white (1%) were found in very low percentages. Tularosa Black-on-white (16%), Pinedale Black-on-white (6%), and St. Johns matte (18%) and subglaze (43%) types make up the remainder of the assemblage. The quantities of Pinedale Black-on-white, the dominance of the subglaze variant of St. Johns, and a high (3.3:1) red ware to white ware ratio indicate an occupation late in complex B (starting before A.D. 1250).

The CARP quantitative collection of 239 sherds, exclusive of gray ware, suggests about the same dates. The main difference is that Wingate (2%) and Springerville (0.4%, 1 sherd) also appear. Because it is a surface collection, the quantitative sample is the result of activity over a larger area of the site and is probably more representative of the site as a whole. Thus, the ending date for the site is extended into complex C (about A.D. 1275).

11. *Heshoda Yala:wa* (Fig. 4.12)
(Heccotayala)

Identification
Site Numbers: Spier 4, ZAP:AZ:15:H:16.
Bibliography: Spier (1917: 219, 221, Fig. 3*b*).
Discussion: Spier gives a translation of this Zuni name as "ruin + mountain."

Environmental Setting
Elevation: 1875 m (6150 feet).
Exposure: Open.
Landforms: Heshoda Yala:wa is on a bluff overlooking the Zuni River Valley near the mouth of Plumasano Wash. Plumasano Wash, which drains the Ojo Caliente springs, is 600 m north of the site and was probably the nearest permanent source of water.
Plant Communities: The country surrounding the site is an open juniper woodland. The river valley below the site is plains grassland.

Archaeological Remains
Architecture: The site is a rectangular rubble mound, about 1 m high, around a central plaza. Many wall outlines are still visible, and in most places the pueblo appears to be about two rooms wide with an opening to the plaza on the east. The plaza has two large circular depressions that may indicate subterranean kivas.
Dimensions: 62 m by 80 m.
Room Estimate: Based on a count of rooms on Spier's map, I estimate 150 ground floor rooms. The height of the rubble mound suggests that there was only one story to the

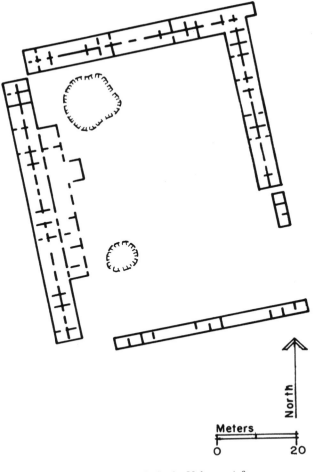

Figure 4.12.   Heshoda Yala:wa (after Spier 1917, fig. 3*b*).

pueblo. Room sizes average about 9.1 square meters, with most rooms about 2.9 m by 3.1 m.

Artifacts: The artifact scatter was light and most of the artifacts were found in the plaza.

Ceramic Samples: Quantitative by Spier, Kintigh; diagnostic by Spier, Kintigh.

Temporal Placement: Two quantitative samples, one made by Spier and one by me, totaling 396 sherds, were used. The percentages vary somewhat between the two collections so they are presented separately. The core assemblage of complex B is well represented in both collections: Tularosa Black-on-white (9%, 4% for Spier), matte St. Johns types (18%, 3%), gray ware (43%, 58%), and buff corrugated (6%, 0.3%). Pinedale Black-on-white (1%, absent), St. Johns subglaze types (1%, 1%), and Kwakina Polychrome (1%, 1%) also occur. The red ware to white ware ratio in my collection is 1.6:1.

In addition, Spier's quantitative sample shows a substantial complement of earlier ceramics: Puerco Black-on-white (6%), Reserve Black-on-white (3%), Puerco Black-on-red (1%), and Wingate types (5%), as well as one brown ware (0.3%) and one (0.3%) Pinnawa Glaze-on-white sherd. Spier's red ware to white ware ratio is 1.1:1.

My diagnostic collection did contain some Wingate pottery (3 sherds) and a substantial complement of later ceramics:

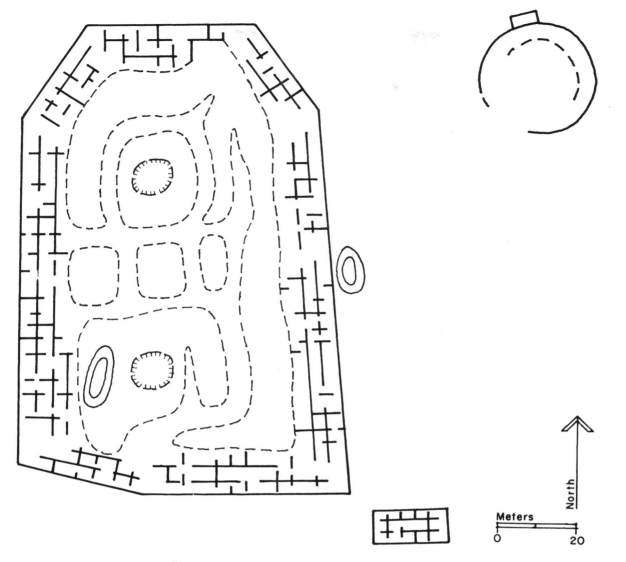

Figure 4.13.   Box S Ruin (after Spier 1917, fig. 5e).

Heshotauthla types (3), Kwakina Polychrome (4), Pinnawa Red-on-white (1), a Matsaki type (1), unidentified buff ware (5), and black ware (25). A single Salado polychrome sherd was also identified. Spier's diagnostic collection produced more Heshotauthla pottery (4 sherds), Kwakina Polychrome (9), and an additional Pinnawa Glaze-on-white sherd. Spier also found a single sherd of early Red Mesa Black-on-white.

This assemblage presents a perplexing situation. The architectual remains and trash associated with the site do not seem sufficient to allow for any occupation of great length. The Red Mesa Black-on-white, Puerco Black-on-white, Reserve Black-on-white, Puerco Black-on-red, and Wingate Black-on-red suggest an early component at the site, early in complex A, or even earlier. The Tularosa Black-on-white and dominance of matte St. Johns types over the subglaze variants indicate a complex B component. However, the large amount of Kwakina Polychrome, considering its usual frequency, and the frequency of other late types, indicate that these later types were associated with the major habitation, extending the dates of that major occupation from late in complex B to early in D. Finally, some reuse of the site during complexes G or H is indicated by the glazed white ware, buff ware, and black ware. This late reuse may be

associated with the peculiar stone features on the western side of the pueblo. Although the location fits better with the late settlement pattern of complexes G and H (as discussed in Chapter 8), the diagnostic samples tend to indicate that the major occupation of the site was the middle one from complex B to D (probably from before A.D. 1250 to after 1275).

12. *Box S Ruin* (Fig. 4.13)
(Heshodan Imk'osk'wa, Heshota In Kuosh,
Heccotaimkoskwia, Heshota Im-kuosh-kuin,
Mim-kuosh kuin)

Identification
Site Numbers: Spier 97, ZAP:NM:12:Z2:46, LA5538, CS187, CS188.
Bibliography: Bandelier (1892a: 329, 340), Spier (1917: 240, Fig. 5c), Amsden (1934a: 2), Marshall and others (1979: 325).
Discussion: Amsden notes that both Acoma and Zuni claim this site as ancestral.

Environmental Setting
Elevation: 2106 m (6910 feet).
Exposure: Open.

Landforms: The Box S Ruin is situated on the floor of Blind Canyon Draw at the juncture of two drainages (one of which is now eroding away the site). It is located just to the west of an opening in a hogback that has plentiful sandstone outcrops.

Plant Communities: The site is in an area of plains grassland, although juniper-pinyon woodland and ponderosa pine forests are not too distant.

Archaeological Remains

Architecture: Spier's map appears to be more accurate than any map made subsequently. However, his map of this site is at a different scale from most of the rest of his maps, and the room outlines shown may represent multiple rooms. He depicts the main pueblo as having a six-sided irregular (but roughly rectangular) outline with several tiers of rooms along the perimeter and several room blocks in the interior of the pueblo. Interior features of the pueblo suggest the presence of kivas. The Museum of New Mexico survey form indicates that a particularly deep depression in the southwest corner of the pueblo interior may be a walk-in well or a great kiva. The site is constructed of red sandstone masonry. The height of the rubble mound suggests a multiple-story structure. Across one of the drainages to the east of the pueblo there is a feature about 27 m in diameter that appears to be a great kiva. At least one room appears to have been built along the outside of the kiva.

Dimensions: 90 m by 115 m.

Room Estimate: Spier shows about 225 individual rooms, and a significant area of rooms in which he does not show individual outlines. The room area of the Box S Ruin as illustrated in Spier's map is 3804 square meters. The rooms outlined average 14.1 square meters per room. Dividing the total area by this figure provides an estimate of 270 ground floor rooms. Multiplying by 1.75 for second and third stories produces a total estimate of 473 rooms.

Artifacts: Bandelier notes glazed pottery from the Box S Ruin, although very little has been collected recently.

Ceramic Samples: Excavated by Spier (5); diagnostic by Spier, CARP.

Temporal Placement: Five excavated collections from successive six-inch (15.2 cm) levels of Spier's stratigraphic trench have sample sizes from 13 to 38 sherds, with a total of 134 sherds. Dominant are Tularosa Black-on-white (13%); St. Johns matte (3%), subglaze (16%), and glaze (1%) types; and gray ware (40%). Additional ceramics identified are Reserve Black-on-white (1%), Pinedale Black-on-white (1%), Wingate types (1%), Heshotauthla types (1%), and Kwakina Polychrome (1%). Puerco Black-on-white is also found in the diagnostic collections. Interestingly, the only Wingate sherds (2) were found in the deepest level, perhaps indicating an earlier site beneath the large pueblo as is found at several other sites of this period. Otherwise, the levels do not seem to show a recognizable chronological sequence. The red ware to white ware ratio is 1.3:1. The occupation probably began late in complex B and lasted into complex D (probably from before A.D. 1250 to after A.D. 1275). This attribution ignores the single Heshotauthla sherd.

13. *Shoemaker Ranch Ruin* (Fig. 4.14)

Identification

Site Numbers: Spier 156, ZAP:NM:13:D:102,

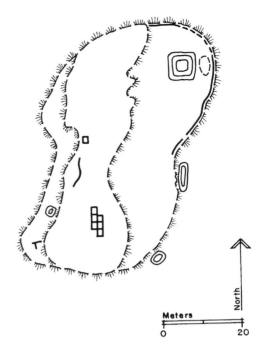

Figure 4.14.   Shoemaker Ranch Ruin (after map in ZAP file, Zuni, New Mexico).

NM M:2:1(ASM).

Bibliography: Spier (1917: 249).

Discussion: The site is named for the nearby ranch house (now in ruins) that was identified by Spier as the Shoemaker ranch house.

Environmental Setting

Elevation: 2274 m (7460 feet).

Exposure: Open.

Landforms: The site is located on several terraces of an elevated mesa point. All around the ruin are steep mesa slopes, and Shoemaker Canyon extends below to the south. The pueblo had a commanding view of the surrounding area and was in an apparently good defensive position.

Plant Communities: The site is in a juniper-pinyon woodland with an area of plains grassland on the canyon bottom below.

Archaeological Remains

Architecture: The site is composed of a number of distinct room clusters. There is a wall with an opening along the eastern edge of a lower terrace that today (and probably prehistorically as well) provides the easiest access to the site. A depression, possibly indicative of a kiva, is associated with the largest rubble mound in the northeast corner of the site.

Dimensions: Scattered room blocks in a 32 m by 60 m area (according to Spier, 30 m by 46 m).

Room Estimate: There appear to be about 17 rooms spread out on this mesa point. There is no evidence for rooms more than a single story high.

Ceramic Samples: Quantitative by Kintigh; diagnostic by Kintigh (4).

Temporal Placement: The four diagnostic samples were collected in different areas of this disaggregated site; also, I made a single quantitative collection of 42 sherds. The major ceramics represented are Tularosa Black-on-white (10%),

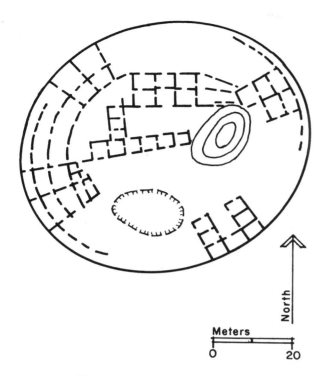

Figure 4.15.   Day Ranch Ruin
(after Spier 1917, fig. 4b).

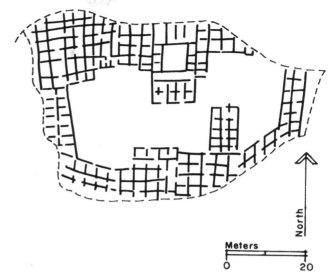

Figure 4.16.   Lookout Site (after
CARP field notes, St. Louis,
Missouri).

St. Johns matte (12%) and subglaze (14%) types, and gray ware (48%). A single sherd of Pinedale Black-on-white (2%) was found in the quantitative collection and the red ware to white ware ratio is 1.75:1. The diagnostic collections also yielded small quantities of Reserve Black-on-white, Wingate types, glazed St. Johns types, Springerville Polychrome, Pinedale Polychrome, and Kwakina Polychrome. The occupation probably started late in complex B and lasted into complex D (from before A.D. 1250 to after 1275).

14. *Day Ranch Ruin* (Fig. 4.15)

Identification
Site Numbers: Spier 104, ZAP:NM:12:Z2:82, CU R–19.
Bibliography: Spier (1917: 242, Fig. 4b).
Discussion: The site is named after the landowner at the time of Spier's visit.

Environmental Setting
Elevation: 2091 m (6860 feet).
Exposure: Open.
Landforms: The site is on the floor of the Ramah Valley about 800 m upstream (east-northeast) of the Deracho sites. It is located immediately across Cebolla Creek from a small spur of 120 m high Antenna Hill.
Plant Communities: The site is located in an area of plains grassland. There is a good deal of modern agricultural use of the valley bottom areas near the site. Juniper-pinyon woodland grades into ponderosa pine forest on the hill southeast of the site.

Archaeological Remains
Architecture: The Day Ranch Ruin forms a large oval similar to Lower Deracho Ruin. It has a couple of substantial depressions. The areas shown by Spier to have visible room outlines are the highest parts of the interior of the pueblo. The rubble mound formed by the site is 2 m to 3 m high around the outside wall. The visible walls are constructed of roughly shaped sandstone.
Dimensions: 62 m by 73 m.
Room Estimate: The room area shown by Spier is 3284 square meters. The walls Spier shows on his map seem to be outlining multiple rooms. Using a conservative figure of 10 square meters per room (found at the similar Jack's Lake Ruin), a reasonable ground floor room estimate is 328 rooms. Adding second and third stories, the total estimate may be 574 rooms.
Ceramic Samples: Quantitative by Kintigh; excavated by Spier (13); diagnostic by Spier, Kintigh.
Temporal Placement: Spier excavated 13 levels, each 6 inches (15.2 cm) deep, in a single trench. These collections, which include 548 sherds, do not show marked chronological changes, although Reserve Black-on-white is more common in the lower levels. The latest diagnostic sherd, one of Kwakina Polychrome (0.2%), occurred in the fifth level (from the top). The main ceramics are Tularosa Black-on-white (3%), Pinedale Black-on-white (3%), St. Johns matte (5%) and subglaze (12%) types, and gray ware (57%). Occurring in low percentages are Reserve Black-on-white (1%), St. Johns glaze (1%), Pinedale Polychrome (0.2%), and buff corrugated (0.2%). The red ware to white ware ratio is 2.1:1. Relying on the one Kwakina Polychrome sherd and the relatively common matte St. Johns pottery, I suggest an occupation span through complexes C and D (from about A.D. 1250 to 1300).

15. *Lookout Site* (Figs. 4.16, 4.17)
(Gigantes, Hole-in-the-Rock)

Identification
Site Numbers: Spier 146, ZAP:NM:12:H3:13, LA1551, NM G:15:5(ASM), CS 146, CU R–3, El Morro 34 (Reed).
Bibliography: Spier (1917: 247–248), Woodbury (1954b: 4), Watson and others (1980: 213).

Figure 4.17.   View of the El Morro Valley through the hole in the rock at the Lookout Site.

Discussion: The names Lookout and Hole-in the Rock derive from a hole cut in a sheer sandstone cliff to the north of the site. Of the two, it appears that the Lookout name appeared first and is adopted for this study. Spier's name (Gigantes) is problematic because the sandstone pillars bearing the name, Los Gigantes, are attached to a different mesa just north of the one on which the Lookout Site is located. Furthermore, another site that is referred to as Los Gigantes (Marshall and others 1979: 325) is on the mesa to the north.

Environmental Setting
Elevation: 2271 m (7450 feet).
Exposure: South.
Landforms: The ruin is perched on a shelf that is partly formed by talus. To the north is a sheer natural sandstone wall only a few meters thick. The mesa on which the site is located forms part of the southwestern edge of the El Morro Valley. The land to the southwest is a steeply sloping area between fingers of the back of the mesa.
Plant Communities: Southwest of the site is a ponderosa pine forest. A juniper-pinyon woodland covers the mesa slopes on the other side of the cliff to the north. An open juniper-pinyon woodland and plains grassland cover the El Morro Valley floor even farther to the north.

Archaeological Remains
Architecture: The ruin is an irregular collection of room blocks that seem to surround two plazas. (Woodbury also noted the plazas, although they are not mentioned in the CARP field notes.) The masonry is roughly shaped tan sandstone. A person-sized hole through the sandstone cliff at the north edge of the site affords a view of a large part of the El Morro Valley (Fig. 4.17), including the areas of Pueblo de los Muertos, the Cienega Site, and the Mirabal Ruin. Unfortunately, no adequate map of the ruin exists.
Dimensions: 48 m by 70 m irregular (Spier records 38 m by 52 m).
Room Estimate: Any room estimate for this site involves a great deal of guesswork, because no thorough investigation has been made. Watson and her colleagues estimate 300 total

rooms, while Woodbury suggests 100 rooms. My estimate, based on the approximately 1615 square meters that seem to be covered with rooms, is 200 ground floor rooms (or about 8 square meters per room). Of these, probably half were two-story for a total of 300 rooms.
Ceramic Samples: Excavated by Spier (8); diagnostic by Spier, CARP.
Temporal Placement: Spier's excavated collections from successive 6-inch (15.2 cm) levels yielded 598 sherds. The most common ceramics are Tularosa Black-on-white (7%), St. Johns matte (8%) and subglaze (21%) types, and gray ware (43%). No earlier types are evident in the excavated collections. Later types do occur in small quantities: St. Johns glaze (1%), Springerville Polychrome (0.2%), Kwakina Polychrome (0.2%), Pinnawa Glaze-on-white (0.2%), and buff corrugated (0.2%). The single Pinnawa Glaze-on-white sherd (from the fourth level) is difficult to understand in the absence of the other types we would expect to find associated with it. The most likely possibility is that the sherd was misidentified and it is actually one of the Kwakina Polychrome variants that has glaze paint on a white band of exterior slip, appearing as glaze-on-white on both sides. The red ware to white ware ratio is 3.7:1. The levels of the trench do not show a marked chronological progression.

Additional ceramics found in the diagnostic surface collections are Puerco Black-on-white, Reserve Black-on-white, Pinedale Black-on-white, Pinedale Polychrome, Heshotauthla types (19 sherds), Pinnawa Glaze-on-white (6), Pinnawa Red-on-white (5), and Matsaki types (9). Obviously the surface collections indicate a substantially later site than the excavations suggest. It is possible that the trench went into an exclusively early area. The more likely explanations are that the site was revisited as a shrine and pots were deposited, or that it was reused in a minor way because of its value as a lookout. Relying on the excavated collection to date the major habitation, an occupation through complexes C and D is indicated (from about A.D. 1250 to 1300).

16. *Jack's Lake Ruin* (**Fig. 4.18**)
(Archeotekopa I, Soldado – Lower Ruin)

Identification
Site Numbers: Spier 162, ZAP:NM:12:I3:21.
Bibliography: Fewkes (1891: 119–121), Spier (1917: 250–251), L. Robertson (1983).
Discussion: This site is named for the modern stock tank (Jack's Lake) that now backs up water around its eastern half, almost up to its edge. It is in the upper part of Knife Hill Canyon. The Zuni told Fewkes that the ruin had been inhabited by their ancestors.

Environmental Setting
Elevation: 2225 m (7300 feet).
Exposure: Open.
Landforms: The site is located on sloping ground on the southern edge of Knife Hill Canyon. The canyon floor lies directly north and west of the ruin. A sandstone outcrop is on the same hillslope as the site, only a few meters distant.
Plant Communities: The site is in an area of plains grassland that grades into juniper-pinyon woodland south of the site. Higher up and a short distance farther to the south is a ponderosa pine forest.

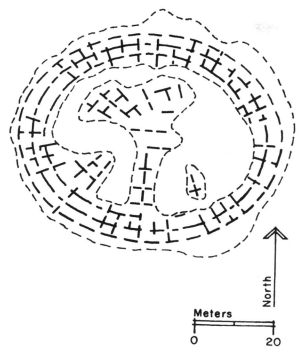

North

Meters

0   20

Figure 4.18. Jack's Lake Ruin (after Spier 1917, fig. 5*b*).

Archaeological Remains

Architecture: The site is oval and forms a rubble mound about 2 m high. Substantial relief in the interior of the ruin suggests interior room blocks, kivas, and plaza areas. At the time of Fewkes' observation the entire outside wall was intact and he could find no openings in it. He indicates that it attained the height of 15 feet (4.5 m), suggesting at least three stories (Fewkes indicates there were five stories, but this seems to be based on his supposition that if there were rooms five-deep along the perimeter of the site, then there must have been five stories). Spier notes that at the time of his visit, the outer wall was 5 to 10 feet high (1.5 m to 3 m), and that the ruin was two or possibly three stories high.

Dimensions: 55 m by 65 m, oval.

Room Estimate: Room sizes shown by Spier average 10 square meters. The total area of rubble mound was 1829 square meters. An approximate count from Spier's map is 140 rooms. Based on the earlier descriptions, I assume that the pueblo was three stories high in places and I estimate a total of 245 rooms (140 times 1.75).

Ceramic Samples: Quantitative by Kintigh (2); diagnostic by Kintigh (2).

Temporal Placement: Quantitative samples totaling 236 sherds were taken from two areas of the site. The major ceramics represented are: Tularosa Black-on-white (5%); St. Johns matte (3%), subglaze (8%), and glaze (2%) types; and gray ware (57%). The only earlier type represented is Reserve Black-on-white (0.4%, 1 sherd). Later types include Springerville Polychrome (0.4%), Kwakina Polychrome (0.4%), and buff corrugated (0.4%). The red ware to white ware ratio is 2.5:1. Two sherds of Heshotauthla types turned up in the diagnostic collections. The suggested occupation is through complexes C and D (from about A.D. 1250 to 1300). The two quantitative samples were similar except that the latest sherds came from Locus 2, the southern part of the site.

17. *Archeotekopa II* (Fig. 4.19)
(Soldado – Upper Ruin)

Identification

Site Numbers: Spier 161, ZAP:NM:13:D:103.

Bibliography: Fewkes (1891: 122–126, with architectural sketches), Spier (1917: 250, Fig. 5*e*), L. Robertson (1983).

Discussion: This name was given to the ruin by Fewkes after his transliteration of the Zuni name for the canyon (Achiya:Dek'yapbow:a or Attciatekyapoa), meaning "knife + hill." The Zuni told Fewkes that the pueblo had been inhabited by their ancestors. In Spier's time Knife Hill Canyon, in which this site lies, was apparently called Soldado Canyon.

Environmental Setting

Elevation: 2256 m (7400 feet).

Exposure: East.

Landforms: This ruin is in the upper end of Knife Hill Canyon. It extends from the creek running down the middle of the canyon to the treeline on the western side of the canyon. A modern stock tank backs up water nearly to the edge of the site. The land slopes up gradually west of the site, and more steeply on the opposite side of the canyon.

Plant Communities: The site is located in a small juniper-pinyon woodland community that lies between the plains grassland of the canyon floor and the ponderosa pine forest of the higher country west of the site and across the canyon to the east.

Archaeological Remains

Architecture: The site bears some similarity to the Kluckhohn Ruin in its architectural configuration. It consists of an irregular circular part that merges with a larger rectangular section to the west. It is difficult to determine the underlying terrain, but the rubble mound seems to range from 1 m to 2 m in height. When Spier and Fewkes visited the ruin it was in better condition than it is today; three-story sections of wall were visible to Fewkes, and both he and Spier noted a dramatic narrowing of the walls between the first and second stories.

Dimensions: The circular section is 99 m in diameter; the rectangular section is 98 m by 107 m.

Room Estimate: Spier's map is misleading; because of the scale of the map, in many places he apparently shows the outline of only every other room. The total room area is about 8072 square meters, while the total area covered by rubble mound is about 8504 square meters. From his map, the average room size appears to be about 32 square meters, which is much larger than has been observed at any other site in the area. A room size one-fourth that, 8 square meters, corresponding to the every-other-wall hypothesis, is much more reasonable. To be conservative, however, I assume a size of 10 square meters per room (as observed at the nearby Jack's Lake Ruin), yielding a ground-floor room estimate of 807 rooms. Given the documentary evidence for a three-story pueblo, the total estimate is 1412 rooms.

Ceramic Samples: Quantitative by Kintigh (2); excavated by Spier (11); diagnostic by Spier, Kintigh (2).

Temporal Placement: Spier excavated two trenches, one in the rectangular part of the site and one in the circular part, collecting 11 samples with 491 sherds. Overall, they are

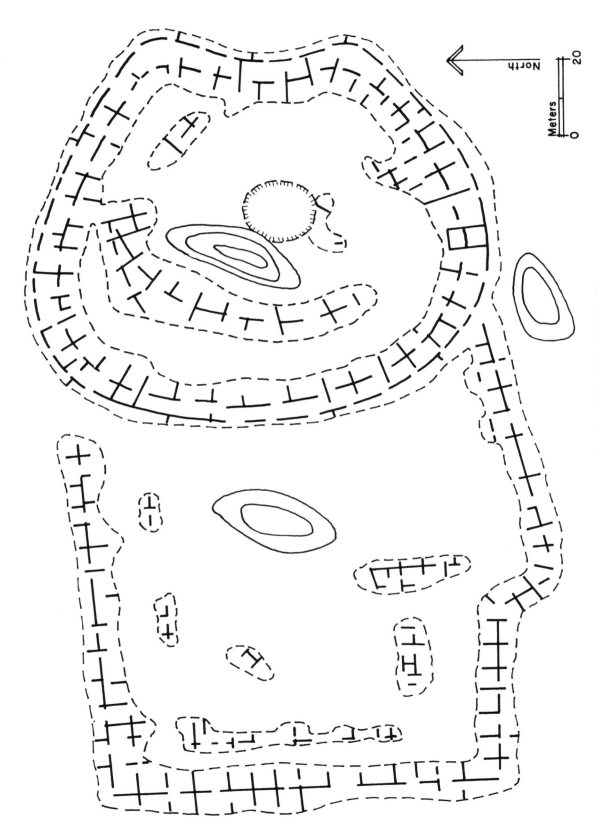

North

Meters
0 ___ 20

Figure 4.19.   Archeotekopa II (after Spier 1917, fig. 5e).

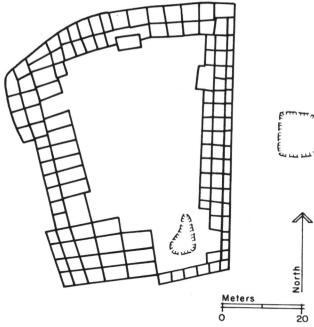

Figure 4.20. Fort Site (after map by Ferguson and Gagner, ZAP file, Zuni, New Mexico).

quite similar in composition; dominant are: Tularosa Black-on-white (14%), St. Johns matte (6%) and subglaze (18%) types, and gray ware (43%). Five earlier Reserve Black-on-white (1%) sherds and one sherd (0.2%) of a Wingate type were identified. Later ceramics are Pinedale Black-on-white (1%), glazed St. Johns types (1%), Springerville Polychrome (1%), Pinedale Polychrome (0.2%), one of the Heshotauthla types (0.2%), Kwakina Polychrome (1%), and buff corrugated (2%). The red ware to white ware ratio is 1.8:1. The only additional type found in the diagnostic collections was Pinnawa Red-on-white (1 sherd) that could be a misclassified variant of Kwakina Polychrome with a white exterior band. Again, an occupation through complexes C and D is suggested (from A.D. 1250 to 1300).

18. *Fort Site* (Fig. 4.20)
(Crockett)

Identification
Site Numbers: Spier 154, ZAP:NM:13:D:101, NM M:2:2(ASM), CU C–3.
Bibliography: Spier (1917: 249, Fig. 4f), Woodbury 1954b: 3).

Environmental Setting
Elevation: 2289 m (7510 feet).
Exposure: Open.
Landforms: The site is perched on top of a mesa with a commanding view of Shoemaker Canyon to the north. Shoemaker Ranch Ruin is visible across the canyon. Investigators commonly remark on the good defensive location of the ruin.
Plant Communities: The site is located in a juniper-pinyon woodland with scattered ponderosa pine. A plains grassland covers the floor of Shoemaker Canyon below the site. Sandstone outcrops are present in the immediate vicinity of the site.

Archaeological Remains
Architecture: The ruin is rectangular with one curved end. Two to four tiers of rooms surround a plaza. Roughly shaped, well-laid sandstone walls still stand 2 m high in places, with second-story beam holes visible. A circular depression that may have served as a reservoir is cut into the bedrock within the site. A depression, probably indicative of a kiva, is located in the southeast corner of the interior plaza.
Dimensions: 46 m by 69 m, rectangular.
Room Estimate: The total room area of the Fort Site is 1672 square meters. The Zuni Archaeology Program map (drawn in 1977) shows 123 ground floor rooms. Spier's map depicts 144 ground floor rooms. Using the 144-room figure, and assuming that half had second stories, I obtain a total estimate of 216 rooms. On the ZAP map, the average room size is 13.6 square meters, but Spier's map indicates a smaller average room size.
Ceramic Sample: Diagnostic by Spier.
Temporal Placement: Spier's diagnostic collection of 36 sherds is the only sample available. The dominant ceramics are Tularosa Black-on-white, St. Johns subglaze types, Springerville Polychrome, and gray ware. One sherd each of Reserve Black-on-white, Pinedale Black-on-white, and Kwakina Polychrome were identified. The occupation range indicated is from complex C through complex D (from A.D. 1250 to 1300).

19. *Tinaja Ruin* (Fig. 4.21)
(Pueblo Tinaja, Pueblito)

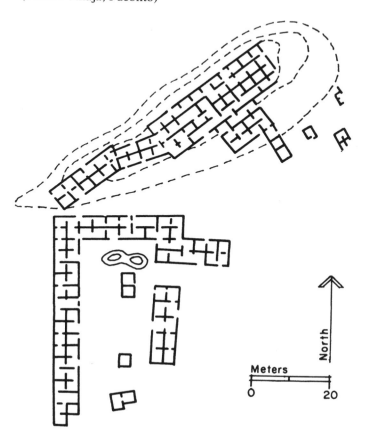

Figure 4.21. Tinaja Ruin (after Spier 1917, fig. 5a).

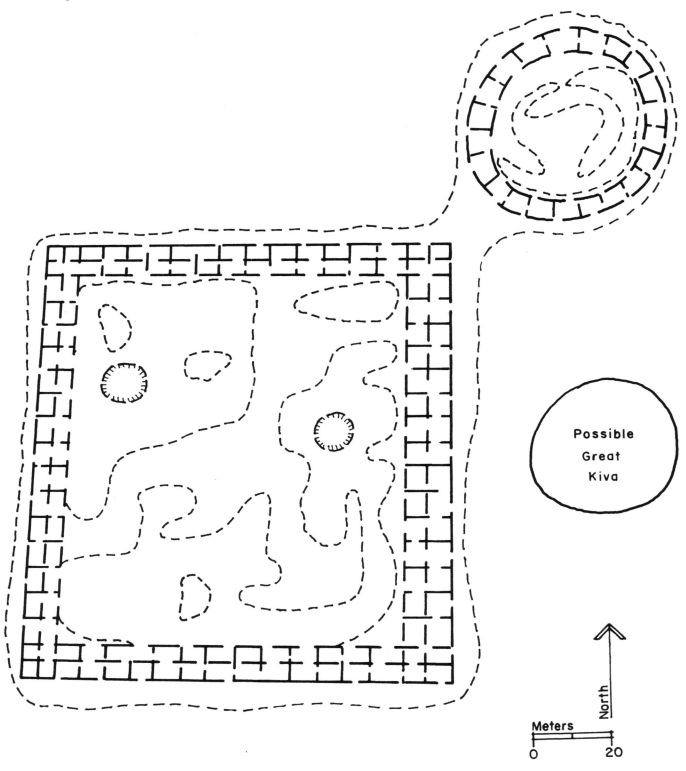

Figure 4.22.   Kluckhohn Ruin (after Spier 1917, fig. 5f).

Identification

Site Numbers: Spier 144, ZAP:NM:12:G3:99, LA427, NM G:16:1(ASM), CS 144, CU T–20.

Bibliography: Spier (1917: 247, Fig. 5a), Woodbury (1954b: 4), Marquardt (1974: 55–56, Fig. 2–8), Watson and others (1980: 213).

Discussion: The site name derives from the name of the ruined Mexican town of Tinaja located about 1.7 km to the north-northwest. Limited excavations were carried out by the Cibola Archaeological Research Project at the Tinaja Ruin.

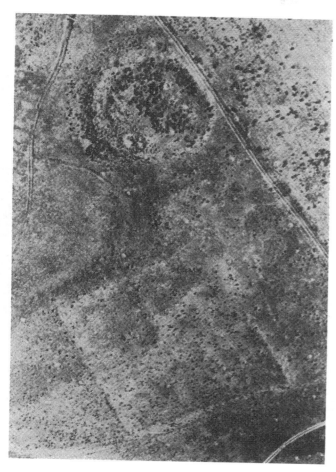

Figure 4.23. Aerial view of the Kluckhohn Ruin. (Photograph by Charles Redman.)

Environmental Setting

Elevation: 2240 m (7350 feet).

Exposure: Open.

Landforms: The Tinaja Ruin covers the top of a small butte and spreads along the valley floor to the south. Two springs are marked on the U.S.G.S. quad map at distances of 1.7 km north and 1.9 km northwest of the site. The ruin is only a few hundred meters southwest of the base of the Zuni Mountains. Sandstone outcrops are plentiful on the site.

Plant Communities: The site is in a plains grassland community. A ponderosa pine forest covers the slopes of the Zuni Mountains.

Archaeological Remains

Architecture: A room block two to four rooms wide covers the top of the eccentric-shaped butte. An L-shaped room block and scattered rooms and room clusters are spread out to the south on the valley floor. The masonry was of tan sandstone and was exceptionally well shaped and laid. Watson and her colleagues note the presence of water catchment basins in the outcrop boulders on the site and indicate that some walls were stone robbed. They also note that one excavated room that had burned was a store room; other excavated rooms were empty. A possible seep is indicated by Marquardt (1974: 57).

Dimensions: 19 m by 66 m, linear on the butte top; 45 m by 55 m, L-shaped on the valley floor.

Room Estimate: Watson and others (1980: 209) estimate a total of 211 rooms. Spier's map shows 163 ground floor rooms with a total area of 1537 square meters. Spier notes room sizes of about 6.5 square meters (probably interior area), while the average from his map is calculated as 9.4 square meters including walls. The rubble height does not suggest multiple stories, so an estimate of 163 rooms is used.

Ceramic Samples: Excavated by CARP (3).

Temporal Placement: Three excavated CARP collections were analyzed. The surface and first level of one unit (two samples, 144 sherds total) had earlier ceramics than the other unit: Tularosa Black-on-white (6%); St. Johns matte (2%), subglaze (40%), and glaze (1%) types; Pinedale Polychrome (1%); and Kwakina Polychrome (3%). Gray ware and buff corrugated were present but were not available for quantitative analysis. The other excavated sample (153 sherds) from level four in a different excavation showed: Tularosa Black-on-white (18%); St. Johns matte (7%), subglaze (35%), and glaze (2%) types; as well as Heshotauthla types (5%). The units had red ware to white ware ratios of 7.2:1 and 2.8:1 respectively. This suggests an occupation starting during complex D and lasting into transitional complex DE. However, Marquardt's (1974) more detailed analysis (discussed in Chapter 5) indicates that the occupation was through complexes C and D (about A.D. 1250 to 1300).

Tree-ring cutting dates from Tinaja (Watson and others 1980: 207) are A.D. 1270 and 1284, and several noncutting dates range from about 1230 to 1270.

20. *Kluckhohn Ruin* (Figs. 4.22, 4.23)
(Cebollita 1 and 2, Pipkin's Ruin, Figure 8 Ruin, Togeye Canyon Ruin)

Identification

Site Numbers: Spier 138, ZAP:NM:12:H3:45, LA424, NM G:15:11(ASM), CS 138, CU R–4.

Bibliography: Fewkes (1891: 114–116, with plan sketch), Spier (1917: 244–245, Fig. 5*f*), Watson and others (1980: 213).

Discussion: The site was owned by Clyde Kluckhohn and is named after him.

Environmental Setting

Elevation: 2137 m (7010 feet).

Exposure: Open.

Landforms: The site is on the floor of Togeye Canyon where it widens to join the much larger El Morro Valley. It is next to an intermittent drainage that has been dammed to form a stock tank. About 100 m northwest of the site is a 30 m high sandstone butte with the Pettit Site on its top and spread out along its southeastern base. South of the site is a steep ridge slope.

Plant Communities: The Kluckhohn Ruin is in an area of plains grassland with ponderosa forest on the ridge to the south.

Archaeological Remains

Architecture: The ruin has a large rectangular section joined to a smaller circular part by a rubble mound. The site is on a natural slope so that it is difficult to judge the true height of the rubble mound, although it is certainly 2 m high in

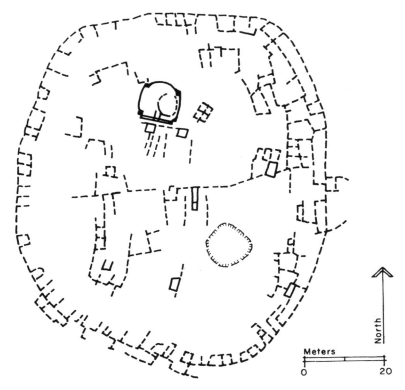

Figure 4.24.   Mirabal Ruin (after Watson and others 1980, fig. 6).

places. For the most part, the circular section seems to be filled with rooms, and the square section has an internal relief that is difficult to interpret. The construction is mainly of red sandstone masonry. On a Museum of New Mexico survey map, a great kiva was noted outside and west of the rectangular ruin.

Dimensions: Rectangular part is 107 m by 114 m; circular part has a diameter of 55 m.

Room Estimate: The mound area shown by Spier is 10,464 square meters. Of this, about 7614 square meters of rubble are within the exterior walls (that is, neglecting the connecting "causeway" and mounded areas outside the exterior walls). For comparison, the entire interior area of the two sections together (again neglecting the "causeway") is 14,574 square meters (some of which Spier does not show as covered with rubble). No room outlines are shown on Spier's plan nor are any distinctly visible today. For lack of a better procedure, I divided the interior rubble area by 10 square meters per room (derived from contemporaneous Jack's Lake Ruin) for a ground floor room estimate of 761 rooms. Multiplying this by 1.5 for two projected stories, the total is 1142 rooms. This compares well with the 1100 rooms projected by Watson and others (without explanation).

Artifacts: The artifact scatter is surprisingly light, considering the size of the site.

Ceramic Samples: Diagnostic by Spier (2).

Temporal Placement: Unfortunately the only collections available for this site are two diagnostic collections made by Spier. Ceramics found in quantity are Tularosa Black-on-white, subglaze St. Johns types, and Heshotauthla types. Reserve Black-on-white, St. Johns matte types, Springerville Polychrome, Pinedale Polychrome, and Kwakina Poly-

chrome occur in smaller quantities. The occupation appears to be slightly later than those of the sites discussed above, from complex C or D to early in transitional complex DE (probably from some time after A.D. 1250 to after 1300).

21. *Mirabal Ruin (Fig. 4.24)*

Identification

Site Numbers: Spier 141, ZAP:NM:12:G3:97, LA426, CS 141, CU T–28.

Bibliography: Spier (1917: 245–247, Fig. 4g), Marquardt (1974: 49–55, Fig. 2–6), Watson and others (1980: 211, Fig. 6).

Discussion: The site is only about 300 m southwest of the Cienega Site. It is named after Sylvester Mirabal, the rancher who now owns the property. Excavations were conducted at this site by the Cibola Archaeological Research Project.

Environmental Setting

Elevation: 2198 m (7210 feet).

Exposure: Open.

Landforms: The Mirabal Ruin is located in the broad central portion of the floor of the El Morro Valley. A basalt outcrop is on the valley floor near the site. The base of the Zuni Mountains is about 3 km northeast of the site. Inscription Rock (El Morro), along the southern edge of the valley, is located about 5 km south of the Mirabal Ruin.

Plant Communities: The site is located in an area of plains grassland. The nearest woodland and forest communities are on a hill 2 km east of the site, and in the Zuni Mountains to the north.

Archaeological Remains

Architecture: Like the Cienega Site, the Mirabal Ruin is oval and built primarily of basalt. However, the Mirabal Ruin rubble mound is only about 1.5 m high, a difference that may be due to a shorter occupation with less rebuilding than at the Cienega Site. Perhaps the most interesting architectural feature of the Mirabal Ruin is the long east-west wall that seems to have divided the pueblo in half. A large kiva (11 m across) was located in the northern part of the interior of the site. The kiva had been remodeled and made smaller before abandonment.

Dimensions: 77 m by 92 m, oval.

Room Estimate: Marquardt (1974: 51) conservatively guesses that 300 ground floor rooms were present. Although the table in Watson and others (1980: 209) does not separately identify the room estimates for the Cienega Site and Mirabal Ruin, I believe the estimate of 700 rooms applies to the Mirabal site. Spier's map (which conforms reasonably well to the map presented by Watson and others) shows an average room size of 8.8 square meters. His total room area is 4354 square meters, which, divided by 8.8 square meters per room, yields 495 ground floor rooms. Adding one-half of that figure for second story rooms gives a total count of 743 rooms, the estimate used for this analysis.

Ceramic Samples: Excavated by CARP (4); diagnostic by CARP.

Temporal Placement: Four excavated CARP collections are available. Two samples are from levels 1 and 5 from one excavation. The other two are from level 8 from each of two different excavations. As with the other CARP samples, counts for the corrugated wares are missing.

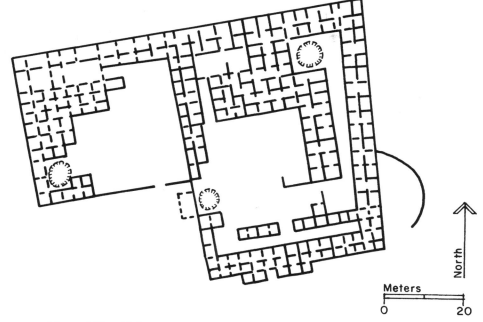

Figure 4.25. Yellowhouse (after Spier 1917, fig. 3*e*; Hunter-Anderson 1978: 80).

All four samples are similar in composition, except that Kwakina Polychrome occurs in both levels 1 and 5 of the first-mentioned samples and in neither of the Level 8 samples. The absence of Kwakina Polychrome from these deeper levels may indicate that they are earlier deposits. The deeper two samples (51 sherds total) have Tularosa Black-on-white (4%), St. Johns matte (4%) and subglaze (55%) types, as well as a single sherd of Puerco Black-on-white (2%). The red ware to white ware ratio is 3.2:1.

The levels closer to the surface (130 sherds total) include mainly Tularosa Black-on-white (5%); St. Johns matte (8%), subglaze (45%), and glaze (2%) types; and Kwakina Polychrome (5%). A single Pinnawa Glaze-on-white sherd is also recorded that may be a misidentified Kwakina Polychrome sherd. A single Reserve Black-on-white was also found. In the later levels the red ware to white ware ratio is 8.3:1. The CARP surface collection included only two additional types that are expectable with this assemblage, Springerville Polychrome and Pinedale Polychrome.

The deeper levels suggest a start of occupation in complex C. The appearance of Kwakina Polychrome in significant quantities indicates that occupation terminated near the end of complex D. However, Marquardt's (1974) analysis (discussed in Chapter 5) indicates that the site is better dated from late in complex C through complex DE (from after A.D. 1250 to about 1325).

Tree-ring dates reported by Watson and others (1980: 207) show one cutting date of A.D. 1260 and a cluster of four cutting dates between 1279 and 1286.

22. *Yellowhouse* (Fig. 4.25)
(Heshoda Łupts'inna, Heccota Luptsinna, Heshota Thluc-tzinan, Hesh-o-ta-sop-si-na)

Identification
Site Numbers: Spier 71, ZAP:NM:J3:99,
NM G:14:2(ASM), YH170.

Bibliography: Simpson (1964: 117, original edition 1850), Fewkes (1891: 112), Bandelier (1892a: 333), Spier (1917: 236), Hunter-Anderson (1978: 79–82, Fig. 7).

Discussion: Spier gives the translation of the Zuni name as "ruin + yellow."

Environmental Setting
Elevation: 2012 m (6600 feet).
Exposure: Open.
Landforms: Yellowhouse is located on a low hill just north of a bend in the Pescado River. A lava flow is exposed in a number of places in the Pescado River Valley, and a basalt outcrop is exposed in the river bank about 20 m south of the site. A sandstone outcrop appears about 50 m west of the site.
Plant Communities: The site is located in an area of plains grassland. A sparse juniper-pinyon woodland is on the side of a hill about 200 m south of the site.

Archaeological Remains
Architecture: Yellowhouse is in the shape of a block L. The construction is of shaped and unshaped sandstone and basalt masonry. The rubble mound rises well over 2 m from the native land surface. Two trash concentrations are found east of the site. Several depressions appear on the site but from surface evidence it cannot be determined if they represent kivas or are simply areas that did not contain rooms.
Dimensions: 66 m by 83 m, L-shaped.
Room Estimate: Spier's map of Yellowhouse does not appear to show accurately the number of rooms at the site. His map indicates about 145 ground floor rooms. Yellowhouse was mapped by the Office of Contract Archaeology of the University of New Mexico. Presumably based on this map, Hunter-Anderson (1978) suggests that the site had about 400 rooms. This map, included in Hunter-Anderson's report, shows 243 ground floor rooms with a total room area

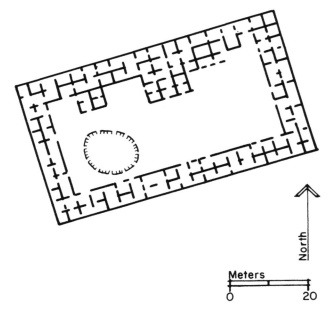

Figure 4.26. Ramah School House Ruin (after Spier 1917, fig. 4*e*).

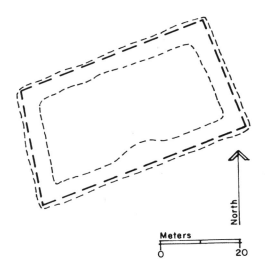

Figure 4.27. North Atsinna Ruin.

of 2522 square meters, 10.4 square meters per room. Assuming one-half two-story and one-fourth three-story room columns, an estimate of 425 rooms is obtained.

Artifacts: The artifact scatter at the site is light, and most of the sherds are rather small. The site is visible at the intersection of two state highways and as a result has been subject to extensive collection.

Ceramic Samples: Quantitative by Spier; diagnostic by Kintigh (4).

Temporal Placement: Spier's quantitative sample of 195 sherds shows an assemblage of mainly Tularosa Black-on-white (13%), St. Johns matte (3%) and subglaze (7%) types, Heshotauthla types (4%), gray ware (42%), and buff corrugated (4%). Other types in the quantitative sample were Puerco Black-on-white (1%), Reserve Black-on-white (2%), Pinedale Black-on-white (1%), and Kwakina Polychrome (1%). The only other ceramics found in the diagnostic samples were Springerville Polychrome (2 sherds) and black ware (1). The red ware to white ware ratio is 1.6:1. Thus, overall indications are for an occupation of complex D through transitional complex DE (from about A.D. 1275 to 1325).

23. *Ramah School House Ruin* (Fig. 4.26)

Identification

Site Numbers: Spier 111, ZAP:NM:12:A3:17, CU R–21.

Bibliography: Spier (1917: 242, Fig. 4*c*).

Discussion: Little remains of this pueblo because of development of the town of Ramah. Several houses have been built into the site and probably only small portions remain undisturbed.

Environmental Setting

Elevation: 2099 m (6885 feet).

Exposure: Open.

Landforms: The site is on the floor of the Ramah Valley,

about 200 m southeast of Cebolla Creek, which is now fed by Ramah Reservoir. A 260 m high mesa is about 400 m to the east.

Plant Communities: Deciduous riparian vegetation now covers the site. A plains grassland area is about 100 m west of the site and a juniper-pinyon woodland is on the mesa slopes to the east.

Archaeological Remains

Architecture: The only available information is Spier's map, which shows a rectangular pueblo two to four rooms wide around the perimeter. A depression is shown in the southwest corner of the interior plaza.

Dimensions: 37 m by 66 m, rectangular.

Room Estimate: Spier's map indicates a total of 124 rooms with an average size of 9.0 square meters. A total of 1143 square meters is covered by rooms. Spier indicates that part of the pueblo had been two stories high, so the total estimate is 186 rooms.

Artifacts: With extensive searching I could find only a few gray ware and plain red ware sherds.

Ceramic Sample: Diagnostic by Spier.

Temporal Placement: The only available sample is a diagnostic collection made by Spier. Ceramics present include Tularosa Black-on-white, St. Johns matte and subglaze types, Heshotauthla types, Kwakina Polychrome, and gray ware, indicating an occupation from complex D through DE (from about A.D. 1275 to 1325).

24. *North Atsinna Ruin* (Fig. 4.27)

(Heshota Yasht-ok)

Identification

Site Numbers: Spier 148, ZAP:NM:12:G3:100, LA 430, NM G:15:7(ASM), CS 148, CU T–21.

Bibliography: Simpson (1964: 128–132, original edition 1850), Fewkes (1891: 117), Bandelier (1892a: 328–329), Spier (1917: 248), Amsden (1934a: 1), Woodbury (1954c, 1955), Watson and others (1980: 212).

Discussion: This site is one of two large ruins on top of the famous Inscription Rock (El Morro), now a part of El Morro

National Monument. Bandelier lists the Zuni name (above) and reports that the Zuni told Cushing that this and the other site on El Morro (Atsinna) were ancestral Zuni towns. Woodbury's informal name for this site has been adopted (see the discussion under the site Atsinna). In 1955 Woodbury put one test trench into this site.

Environmental Setting
Elevation: 2268 m (7440 feet).
Exposure: Open.
Landforms: The site is located on the northern peninsula of El Morro. On the east side of the rock, about 300 m away, is a deep shaded pool fed by runoff. The floor of the El Morro Valley lies directly below North Atsinna. To the east and west the mesa drops off sharply within a few hundred meters of the site, while to the south it slopes down more gently.
Plant Communities: The mesa top, on which the site is located, is covered with plains grassland. The lower slopes of the mesa have a juniper-pinyon woodland cover. The El Morro Valley floor below also has a plains grassland community.

Archaeological Remains
Architecture: The ruin is rectangular. Parts of the north wall still stand over a meter high. The wall is constructed of well-shaped tan sandstone. According to Spier's description, the north, east, and west sides are two or three rooms wide with the exterior wall the highest.
Dimensions: 30 m by 52 m, rectangular.
Room Estimate: Without explanation, Watson and others (1980) estimate a total of 165 rooms for this pueblo. Spier's description implies that there are about 125 ground floor rooms, if it is assumed that the rooms were about 3 m long and were an average of two and one-half tiers deep around the ruin. If the exterior tier of 55 rooms had a second story, a total estimate of 180 rooms is obtained.
Ceramic Samples: Excavated by CARP (2).
Temporal Placement: Two excavated CARP collections were available from this site. They did not show a chronological sequence and are lumped for present purposes (210 sherds). The ceramics found were: Tularosa Black-on-white (4%); Pinedale Black-on-white (0.5%); St. Johns matte (7%), subglaze (32%), and glaze (0.5%) types; Pinedale Polychrome (1%); Heshotauthla types (5%); and Kwakina Polychrome (2%). Gray ware was present, but was not available for analysis. The red ware to white ware ratio was 11.1:1. The occupation appears to have been from complex D through transitional complex DE (from about A.D. 1275 to 1325).

25. *Upper Nutria Village* (Figs. 4.28, 4.29)
Identification
Site Numbers: ZAP:NM:12:S2:60.
Bibliography: Mindeleff (1891: 94–95, Plates 67, 68, Fig. 17).
Discussion: As at Lower Pescado Village, a prehistoric ruin lies beneath the historic Zuni farming village of Nutria. The modern village has been almost completely abandoned, and today it is difficult to discern even the room configuration shown by Mindeleff.

Environmental Setting
Elevation: 2079 m (6820 feet).

Exposure: Open.
Landforms: The site occupies a low finger of a butte (Mexican Hill) and stretches out northwest onto the Rio Nutria valley floor. Sandstone outcrops occur on the site. About 350 m east of the ruin is one section of a 120 m high hogback. The Rio Nutria, which passes about 100 m northwest of the site, flows through a gap in the hogback 1 km northeast of the site. A major spring, Nutria Spring, lies another kilometer upstream.
Plant Communities: The site is in an area of plains grassland, and a deciduous riparian community lies along the Rio Nutria. Juniper-pinyon woodland covers the nearby mesas.

Archaeological Remains
Architecture: The major part of the historic village is a C-shaped series of three room blocks with another two room blocks in the opening of the C. On the hill to the east of this section of the site are several isolated room clusters. Mindeleff reports that a curved section of the outer wall of the C-shaped section is ancient masonry. This observation, added to the fact that the entire area seems to be mounded a meter or two above the surrounding valley floor, suggests that the prehistoric site occupied about the same area and probably provided the foundation walls for many of the major walls of the historic village.
Dimensions: 65 m by 85 m, semicircular with detached front room block.
Room Estimate: About 60 rooms are depicted on the plan of the village made by Mindeleff in the 1880s. The mound configuration and the walls Mindeleff identifies as "ancient" suggest that the historic village followed the general outline of the prehistoric ruin. Considering the size of the mound and the layout of sites contemporary to the prehistoric pueblo, it seems reasonable to assume that it had at least twice as many rooms as the historic village. Adding half for the second floor rooms to the estimate of 120 ground floor rooms, I obtained a total of 180 rooms. However, this estimate must be considered tentative.
Ceramic Samples: Quantitative by Kintigh (3); diagnostic by ZAP.
Temporal Placement: Surface scatter was very light at Upper Nutria Village, largely because of the overburden of the historic village and the absence of any major ground disturbance. Three quantitative samples yielded a total of only 36 sherds. The ceramics present were St. Johns types (8%), Heshotauthla types (3%), unidentified buff ware (39%), gray ware (22%), black ware (6%), and historic Zuni wares (3%). A ZAP diagnostic collection yielded, in addition, two sherds each of Tularosa Black-on-white and Pinedale Black-on-white, as well as more St. Johns (3 sherds) and Heshotauthla (1).

Although this assemblage provides scanty evidence, an occupation from late in complex D to early in complex E is suggested (from after A.D. 1275 to some time after 1325). As mentioned, the site has a late historic component.

26. *Halona:wa South*
(Halona, Halonawan, Hallonawa)
Identification
Site Numbers: Spier 39, ZAP:NM:12:K3:172.

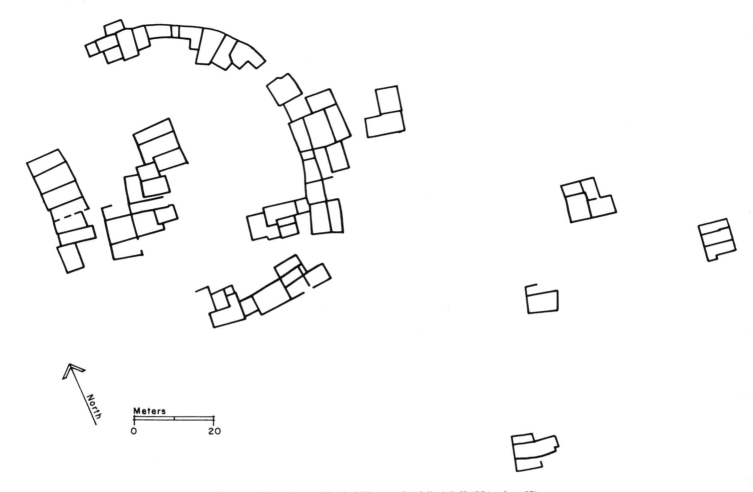

North

Meters

0   20

Figure 4.28.   Upper Nutria Village (after Mindeleff 1981, plate 68).

Bibliography: Cushing (1886, Plate 2), Mindeleff (1891: 88, Plate 57), Fewkes (1891: 101–105, with site plan; 1909), Bandelier (1892a: 337), Kroeber (1917: 200–204, map 9), Spier (1917: 227), Hodge (1937), B. Robertson (1980: 23–30), Ferguson (1981a), Ferguson and Mills (1982), Upham (1982).

Discussion: The name Halona:wa is used to refer both to modern Zuni Pueblo on the north side of the river and to the ruin and modern settlement immediately opposite on the south side of the river (see Kroeber's discussion and the one given by Ferguson 1981a: 348). In the archaeological literature, Halona:wa (or other transliterations thereof) is generally used to refer explicitly to the ruins on the south side of the river. However, in the historical literature this name refers to the 16th and 17th century Zuni village in the area, without differentiating on which side of the river it is located. In order to avoid this confusion, the name Halona:wa South refers to the *ruin* on the south side of the river and Halona:wa North refers to the *ruin* on the north side without any a priori assumptions as to their periods of occupation.

Parts of the site of Halona:wa South were excavated by the Hemenway expedition in 1888. The expedition house was built on part of the site. Although Fewkes notes the presence

of a few Zuni houses on the south side of the river, there was apparently little settlement there at the turn of the century. The name Halona means "red ant place" (Eggan and Pandey 1979: 481).

Environmental Setting

Elevation: 2050 m (6725 feet).
Exposure: Open.
Landforms: Halona:wa South is located on a low flat hill on the south bank of Zuni River. The prehistoric site is well raised from the river, although modern structures have been built right on the floodplain.
Plant Communities: The site is in an area of plains grassland. Until recently, substantial agriculture was practiced in the immediate area of the ruin.

Archaeological Remains

Architecture: The site is completely buried today, and virtually no surface manifestations of the pueblo are visible. Bandelier (in Lange and Riley 1970: 53) wrote in his 1883 journal that there was a substantial ruin but that nothing was left of which a ground plan could be drawn. The Hemenway Expedition excavations, as illustrated by Fewkes, show 25 rooms in a solid block. Mindeleff's plate shows the rubble

Figure 4.29.   Upper Nutria Village about 1895. (Photograph by Ben Wittick, courtesy of the School of American Research Collections, Museum of New Mexico, Negative No. 16423.)

mound with the Hemenway excavations open. From this photograph it is clear that the pueblo had been a fairly large one and it appears that it was roughly rectangular. The field catalog indicates that many rooms were excavated, although no complete field map could be found.

Dimensions: Not available.

Room Estimate: No good room estimate can be made because the ruin is now almost completely covered or obliterated. A comparison of Fewkes' map of a portion of the site with Mindeleff's photograph suggests that the ruin was substantial. An estimate of 250 ground floor rooms and 375 total rooms is far from reliable, but is probably a reasonable guess of the site size.

Artifacts: Because of the intensive modern occupation of the area, prehistoric sherds are sparse on the surface. However, recent (1978) water line trenches provided excavated artifact samples.

Ceramic Samples: Excavated by Spier (3), ZAP (4).

Temporal Placement: Two sets of excavated samples were analyzed from Halona:wa South. The best controlled are probably those collected by Spier. These three samples were taken at a depth of 0 to 18 inches (0 cm to 45.7 cm) in one spot, 24 to 42 inches (61.0 cm to 106.7 cm) in another, and 54 to 66 inches (137.2 cm to 167.6 cm) in a third spot (unlike the sequential stratigraphic levels of the rest of Spier's exca-

vated samples). In any case, the collections do not show a chronological progression and are lumped into a single sample of 223 sherds. The major ceramics represented were Reserve Black-on-white (4%), Tularosa Black-on-white (8%), St. Johns types (17%), Heshotauthla types (3%), and gray ware (49%). Other ceramics in evidence are Puerco Black-on-white (0.4%, 1 sherd), Wingate types (1%), Springerville Polychrome (0.4%), Pinedale Polychrome (0.4%), Kwakina Polychrome (1%), Pinnawa Red-on-white (1%, 2 sherds), and black ware (0.4%). The ZAP water line trenches add Pinedale Black-on-white, Pinnawa Glaze-on-white (2 sherds), Matsaki types (2 sherds), buff corrugated (4 sherds).

The low frequencies of Puerco Black-on-white and Wingate types probably derive from earlier sites in the area. The collections discussed thus far indicate that the main occupation may have been early in complexes D and DE, considering the high ratio of St. Johns to Heshotauthla. However, several whole vessels of Heshotauthla types but only a few vessels of St. Johns types were found in the Hemenway collections from the site. Pinnawa Glaze-on-white vessels and a single Salado polychrome vessel from Halona:wa were also found in that collection. It appears that the Hemenway excavations may have been in a later part of the site than the others discussed here. Thus, the occupation of the main ruin seems

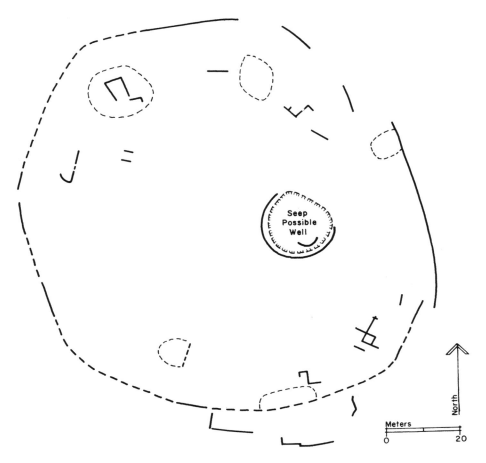

Figure 4.30.   Cienega Site (after Watson and others 1980, fig. 5).

to run from complex D to early in complex F (from after A.D. 1275 to after 1325). For comparison, B. Robertson (1980) dates the site from A.D. 1250 to 1350, which corresponds fairly closely to the dates implied by the complex D to F interval.

27. *Cienega Site* (Fig. 4.30)
(Sandy Corner Ruin)

Identification

Site Numbers: Spier 140, ZAP:NM:12:G3:96, LA425, NM G:15:6(ASM), CS 140, CU T–4.

Bibliography: Spier (1917: 245), Marquardt (1974: 47–49, Fig. 2–5), Watson and others (1980: 209–211, Fig. 5).

Discussion: This site was wall-trenched and several rooms were excavated by the Cibola Archaeological Research Project. The site is so-named because of the spring or seep at its center. (*Cienega* is the Spanish word for a marshy area.)

Environmental Setting

Elevation: 2201 m (7220 feet).

Exposure: Open.

Landforms: The Cienega Site is located in the broad central portion of the floor of the El Morro Valley. The ruin is built around a seep or well in the plaza area. A basalt outcrop is on the valley floor near the site. The base of the Zuni Mountains is about 3 km northeast, and Inscription Rock (El Morro) is located about 5 km south of the Cienega Site.

Plant Communities: The site is located in an area of plains grassland. The nearest woodland and forest communities are on a hill 2 km east of the site, and in the Zuni Mountains to the north.

Archaeological Remains

Architecture: The ruin is visible as an apparently oval rubble mound that rises 4 m from the valley floor. The most conspicuous feature is the seep, which is ringed by a masonry wall. Spier notes that the ruin may conform to natural features and, by implication, may not be as high as it appears. However, a floor was found at a depth of 3 m below the present surface (not at the highest part of the rubble mound; Marquardt 1974: 49) and it appears that most, if not all, of the height of the mound is due to human activity. Watson and others (1980: 209) believe that the ruin that is apparent today was built on top of an 85 m diameter earlier ruin.

Dimensions: 107 m by 137 m, oval.

Room Estimate: From the size of the mound, it is apparent that an enormous volume of rock was moved to build this pueblo. However, the basalt construction makes the determination of room outlines from the surface impossible. Marquardt (1974: 47) guesses that 200 rooms might be present below the surface. It is not clear from their table, but it appears that Watson and others estimate a total of 500 rooms for the Cienega Site, the figure used in this analysis for lack of superior data.

Ceramic Samples: Excavated by CARP (4); diagnostic by Spier.

Temporal Placement: Four levels excavated in one unit by the CARP project serve as the major source of data. Levels 1 and 2 are similar and are lumped together (86 sherds) and levels 10 and 12 are lumped together (129 sherds). As with the other CARP collections, the gray ware was not available for study and hence is not included in the counts or percentages. Considerable time depth is revealed through these excavations, although it is not altogether apparent whether separate temporal components or a single long occupation are demonstrated.

The deep levels have Tularosa Black-on-white (2%), Pinedale Black-on-white (2%), St. Johns matte (15%) and subglaze (40%) types, and Kwakina Polychrome (2%), indicating a start of the occupation in complex D. Marquardt's (1974) analysis (discussed in Chapter 5) indicates a start in complex C (after A.D. 1250). The earliest samples are probably associated with a smaller earlier structure, as suggested by Watson and others (1980), probably moving the start of the major occupation to transitional complex DE.

The top two levels have Tularosa Black-on-white (2%), St. Johns subglaze (26%) and glaze (2%) types, Heshotauthla types (59%), Kwakina Polychrome (3%), and Pinnawa Glaze-on-white (1%). This assemblage indicates an end of occupation early in complex F, or, if the Pinnawa Glaze-on-white sherd is ignored, complex E. However, with the high percentage of Heshotauthla types, the occurrence of Pinnawa Glaze-on-white is likely, so the major occupation of the site is dated from late in complex D through complex F (from after A.D. 1275 to about A.D. 1375). The red ware to white ware ratios were 11.4:1 (deep levels) and 12.7:1.

The diagnostic collection made by Spier does not change the ceramic picture substantially; Springerville Polychrome is added, as is a single Matsaki sherd (perhaps a misfired white ware sherd).

28. *Upper Pescado Ruin* (Fig. 4.31)

Identification
Site Numbers: Spier 86, ZAP:NM:12:I3:8, LA9108, ZIR 20.

Bibliography: Simpson (1964: 123–124, original edition 1850), Whipple (1856, Pt. 1: 65), Bandelier (1892a: 333), Spier (1917: 238), Dodge and Ferguson (1976: 27–32).

Environmental Setting
Elevation: 2067 m (6780 feet).

Exposure: Open.

Landforms: The site lies on a basalt flow, from the base of which (directly below the north wall of the site) flows Upper Pescado Spring. Sandstone outcrops are on the mesa slopes about 250 m north of the site.

Plant Communities: The site is in an area of plains grassland, although areas around the site are now used for irrigation agriculture. A riparian community occurs about 200 m west of the site. Juniper-pinyon woodlands are on the mesas to the north.

Archaeological Remains
Architecture: The pueblo is an irregular shape, open to the

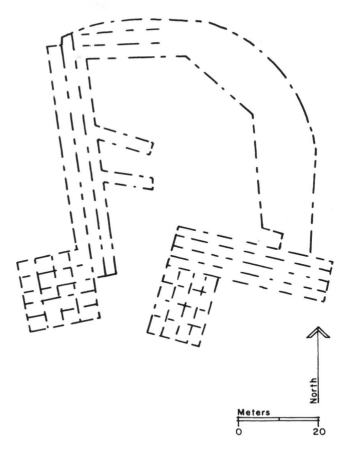

Figure 4.31. Upper Pescado Ruin (after Dodge and Ferguson 1976, map 9).

south. It has both straight and curved sections. To a certain extent, the shape of the pueblo on the north may be determined by the underlying landform. A road has been built across the site so some of the central features are now obscured. In most places, the perimeter of the ruin seems to be four or five rooms wide. A square projection of solid rooms extends off the southwest corner of the site. There are at least two lines of rooms extending from the perimeter into the interior of the site. The rubble mound is 1 m to 2 m high.

Dimensions: 76 m by 84 m.

Room Estimate: As with Pescado West and Lower Pescado, the room estimate is based on the total room area as measured off a field-revised version of the map by Dodge and Ferguson. It is estimated that rooms covered 2700 square meters of the site. Using the Jack's Lake Ruin figure of 10 square meters per room, 270 ground floor rooms are estimated. Adding one-half second story rooms yields a total of 405 rooms. On a site survey form from the Museum of New Mexico, 1500 rooms were estimated for this pueblo.

Artifacts: Dodge and Ferguson note a 230 square meter trash deposit south and east of the site.

Ceramic Samples: Quantitative by Kintigh, ZAP (10).

Temporal Placement: The 10 quantitative samples (1003 sherds) from the Zuni Archaeology Program seem to drastically underrepresent gray ware (6%) and buff corrugated

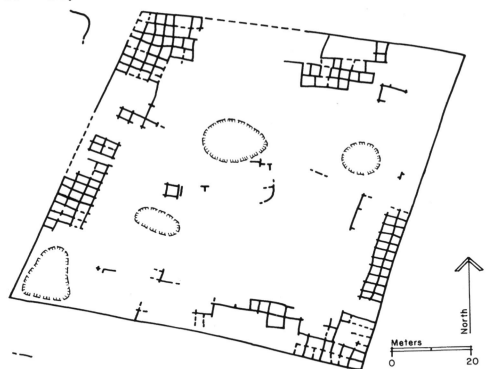

Figure 4.32. Pueblo de los Muertos (after Watson and others 1980, fig. 4).

Meters

North

0　　　20

(3%), as is the case with the other ZAP samples at the Pescado sites. (In my 51-sherd quantitative sample, gray ware equals 37 percent and buff corrugated 35 percent of the samples.) Therefore, these utility wares are ignored in the following percentages, making a revised total of 908 sherds in the ZAP collections.

The ZAP sample is composed mainly of Tularosa Black-on-white (15%), Pinedale Black-on-white (3%), St. Johns types (27%), Heshotauthla types (12%), and Kwakina Poly-chrome (2%). Two Pinnawa Glaze-on-white sherds were found in my quantitative sample. An occupation through complexes DE and E and into F is indicated (from about A.D. 1300 to after 1350).

29. *Pueblo de los Muertos* (Fig. 4.32)
(Possibly the Candelaria Ruin)

Identification

Site Numbers: Spier 139, ZAP:NM:12:B3:20, LA1585, CS 139, CU T–27.

Bibliography: Spier (1917: 245, Fig. 4d), Marquardt (1974: 35–47, Fig. 2–2), Watson and others (1980: 205–209, Fig. 4).

Discussion: A number of rooms were excavated at Pueblo de los Muertos by the Cibola Archaeological Research Project. (It should be noted that the scale on the figure presented by Watson and others in 1980 is incorrect; it should read 0–5–10–15–20, not 0–5–10–20–30.)

Environmental Setting

Elevation: 2219 m (7280 feet).

Exposure: Open.

Landforms: The pueblo is built on high ground at the mouth of Muerto Canyon. A creek, fed by Muerto Spring (about 1.5 km northeast of the site), runs down the canyon a short distance west of the ruin. The site is at the base of the

Zuni Mountains on the northern edge of the broad floor of the El Morro Valley.

Plant Communities: Pueblo de los Muertos is located near the ecotone between three different plant communities. On the ridges to the southeast is a juniper-pinyon woodland. To the north is the ponderosa pine forest that covers the Zuni Mountains. To the south and southwest is the plains grassland of the El Morro Valley floor.

Archaeological Remains

Architecture: The ruin is large and square, with an im-pressive rubble mound nearly 3 m high. The rooms are of tan, shaped sandstone. One kiva was located by the excavation and more may be present. Wall trenching by the CARP project revealed the building sequence for most of the ruin. The outer two tiers of rooms were laid out and constructed as a unit. A short time later, the third tier was added on sterile soil, and finally the fourth tier was added on top of plaza trash. A deep trench in the plaza revealed what was probably a wall of a much smaller earlier site. A trash midden is south of the ruin. Adjacent to the pueblo on the west, near an opening in the perimeter wall, Watson and her colleagues found a low masonry wall following the slope contour on the arroyo bank.

Dimensions: 84 m by 94 m, square (Spier's measurement was 260 feet, about 79 m, square).

Room Estimate: The room size distribution at Pueblo de los Muertos is illustrated by Marquardt (1974: 44). The average room size is 5.6 square meters. A total number of ground floor rooms is not given by Watson and others, but it would appear to be about 470 rooms. They estimate a total of 740 rooms.

Because this is the only site Spier mapped for which there is now better overall architectural information, it is useful to compare the CARP estimates with the estimates that can be

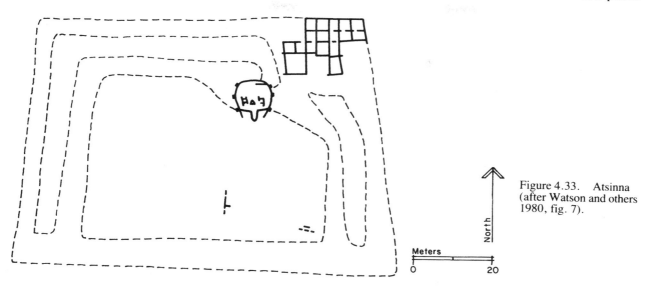

Figure 4.33. Atsinna (after Watson and others 1980, fig. 7).

made using only Spier's data. The average room size shown by Spier is 6.4 square meters (close to the 5.6 square-meter measurement by Marquardt). Dividing Spier's size estimate into Spier's total room area of 3266 square meters, a ground floor estimate of 510 rooms is obtained. A direct count of the rooms shown by Spier yields a ground floor total of 503 rooms (compared with a total of 470 on the map presented by Watson and others, and an estimate of at least 500 by Marquardt, 1974: 43). Multiplying 503 by 1.75 for a three-story pueblo gives a total estimate of 880 rooms (compared with Watson and others' 740; however, it should be noted that they do not have good data on the number of stories per room column). Marquardt (1974: 43) suggests that the outer two tiers were at least two stories high. The estimate of 880 rooms is used in this analysis in order that the data from this site can be reasonably compared with estimates from the many other sites that Spier mapped.

Ceramic Samples: Excavated by CARP (3).

Temporal Placement: Tree-ring dates from Pueblo de los Muertos (Watson and others 1980: 207) include two cutting dates between A.D. 1280 and 1290, and 25 other dates between 1200 and 1290, mostly clustered between 1260 and 1290.

Three excavated levels from a CARP plaza trench, Levels 2, 7, and 11, show a clear chronological progression. (Corrugated wares were not available for inclusion in these counts.) The deepest level (48 sherds) has no Heshotauthla pottery and shows a complex D assemblage: Pinedale Black-on-white (4%), St. Johns types (54%), and Kwakina Polychrome (2%). The middle level (33 sherds) has Tularosa Black-on-white (3%), St. Johns types (45%), Heshotauthla types (6%), Kwakina Polychrome (6%), and an anomalous Matsaki sherd (perhaps a misfired white ware sherd). This level is easily placed early in transitional complex DE. The top level (185 sherds) is clearly a complex F assemblage. The main ceramics represented are St. Johns types (13%), Heshotauthla types (43%), Kwakina Polychrome (4%), and Pinnawa Glaze-on-white (3%). Pinedale Black-on-white (1%) was found, as was another anomalous Matsaki sherd. Considering the relatively high percentage of Pinnawa Glaze-on-white, an occupation from some time in complex D

until late in complex F is indicated (from about A.D. 1275 to about 1375).

If, as has been suggested, the middle level is associated with the major construction of the pueblo, the main occupation may start in complex DE (about A.D. 1300), with the earlier occupation relating to an earlier (buried) structure.

30. *Atsinna* (Fig. 4.33)
(Heshota Yasht-ok)

Identification
  Site Numbers: Spier 149, ZAP:NM:G3:121, LA99, NM G:15:1(ASM), CS 149, CU T–2, El Morro 1 (Reed).
  Bibliography: Simpson (1964: 128–132, with figure; original edition 1850), Whipple (1856, Pt. 1: 63, Pt. 3: 21, Plate 7), Bandelier (1892a: 328–329), Fewkes (1891: 117–119), Spier (1917: 248), Amsden (1934a: 1, 1934b: 2), Woodbury (1954b, 1954c, 1955, 1956, 1979: 469), Woodbury and Woodbury (1956), Marquardt (1974: 56–58, Fig. 2–9), Watson and others (1980: 211–212, Fig. 7).
  Discussion: Simpson gives a detailed description of the ruin, including the location of the circular kiva. Bandelier reports that this was an ancestral Zuni pueblo. Woodbury excavated 12 rooms at this site in 1954 and 1955; some of his excavations were stabilized by the National Park Service. The name Atsinna ("where pictures are on the rock") was given by Woodbury as suggested by his Zuni workmen. The Cibola Archaeological Research Project did a limited amount of additional testing at the site.

Environmental Setting
  Elevation: 2265 m (7430 feet).
  Exposure: Open.
  Landforms: The site is on the southern peninsula of El Morro. At the base of the east side of the rock, about 200 m away, is a deep shaded pool fed by runoff (which is sometimes incorrectly identified as a spring). The floor of the El Morro Valley lies directly below and north of El Morro. To the east and west the mesa drops off sharply within a few hundred meters of the site, while to the south it slopes down more gently. The location certainly would be defensively advantageous.

Plant Communities: The mesa top where Atsinna is located is covered with plains grassland. The lower slopes of the mesa have a juniper-pinyon woodland cover. The El Morro Valley floor below also has a plains grassland community.

Archaeological Remains

Architecture: The site is generally rectangular and it had three to five tiers of rooms surrounding a central plaza. The exterior wall of this rectangle was heavy and well made; however, excavations revealed that rooms had been added on the outside. In Woodbury's excavations in the northwest corner of the pueblo, two kivas were found: one square, and one round (9 m diameter). Excavation in three tiers of rooms in the north wall revealed that only the southernmost rooms (that is, those toward the plaza) had hearths and benches. Five of the domestic rooms dug had stone paving on the floor. In addition, wall painting on plaster was revealed in one room. Plaza trenches uncovered 2.5 m of trash as well as earlier walls. Trash mounds were also found to the southeast and southwest of the ruin. Woodbury indicates that the refuse remaining in the rooms showed the pueblo had been abandoned gradually. Woodbury and Fewkes note the bedrock basins and pools on top of the rock. Woodbury (1956: 559) trenched one of three similar depressions south of the ruin and found a reservoir 7.5 m in diameter and 1 m deep. Woodbury's deepest stratigraphic trench in the plaza revealed walls with an entirely different orientation, suggesting an earlier ruin on the spot, a situation reminiscent of Pueblo de los Muertos, the Cienega Site, and Heshot uɬa.

Dimensions: 64 m by 91 m, rectangular.

Room Estimate: Woodbury's excavated rooms have an average area of about 9.3 square meters. Watson and others suggest an estimate of 750 rooms total. In 1956 Woodbury estimated 500 to 1000 rooms, and in 1979 (p. 469) he reiterated 1000 rooms, indicating that the pueblo had been three stories tall. Assuming 500 ground floor rooms with half bearing second stories and one-fourth third-story rooms, a conservative total of 875 rooms is obtained.

Ceramic Samples: Excavated by CARP (2).

Temporal Placement: Two samples excavated by CARP are included in this analysis. Because a chronological sequence does not show in these samples (from Levels 2 and 7 of an excavation unit), they are lumped for a total sample of 272 sherds. As with the other CARP samples, utility wares are not included. The major ceramics represented are St. Johns types (8%), Heshotauthla types (43%), and Kwakina Polychrome (4%). Small percentages of Puerco Black-on-white (0.4%), Tularosa Black-on-white (2%), Pinedale Black-on-white (2%), and Pinnawa Glaze-on-white (0.4%) are found. The Woodburys (1966: 316, 319, 321) also report excavated quantities of Pinnawa Red-on-white and Kechipawan Polychrome. The major occupation seems to start during transitional complex DE and last through complex F and into complex G (from about A.D. 1300 to 1400). The walls beneath the plaza suggest an earlier component, perhaps lasting through complex D (starting about A.D. 1275).

Watson and others have two tree-ring cutting dates of A.D. 1285 and 1288 and a selection of 11 earlier noncutting dates between 1240 and 1290. Tree-ring samples excavated by Woodbury and dated for this study produced a cutting date of 1274 and noncutting dates of 1177, 1200, 1229, 1231, 1249,

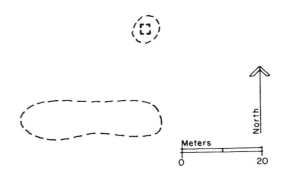

Figure 4.34.   Achiya:Deyaɫa

1266, 1273, 1277, 1296, 1299, 1300, 1312 (2), and 1349. Thus, the tree-ring evidence suggests that Atsinna may have been built about 1275 and occupied until at least 1350.

31. *Achiya:Deyaɫa* (Fig. 4.34)

(Acenntelowa)

Identification

Site Numbers: Spier 30, ZAP:NM:13:A:9.

Bibliography: Spier (1917: 225).

Discussion: Spier gives a translation of the Zuni name as "ruin + crooked."

Environmental Setting

Elevation: 1878 m (6160 feet).

Exposure: Open.

Landforms: The site is on top of a low ridge extending west into the Zuni River Valley. The river lies about 400 m to the west. Spier reports that during his field work there was cultivation in the delta formed where the adjacent arroyo empties into the Zuni River.

Plant Communities: The site is in an area of plains grassland and desert scrub. Up the ridge slope to the northeast there are scattered junipers.

Archaeological Remains

Architecture: This site consists only of a row of contiguous rooms and a single isolated room. The masonry is mainly tannish gray sandstone.

Dimensions: 9 m by 36 m and 6 m by 7 m.

Room Estimate: Spier says that there are four contiguous rooms and one isolated room. These figures are consistent with the observable surface remains, for a total of 5 rooms.

Artifacts: The sherd scatter on this ruin was light. All observable sherds were collected.

Ceramic Samples: Quantitative by Kintigh.

Temporal Placement: A complete surface collection of the site, yielding 35 sherds, was made in 1979. The types found indicate an unbelievably long time range for this rather insubstantial site. The ceramics found are Tularosa Black-on-white (3%), St. Johns types (6%), Heshotauthla types (17%), Kwakina Polychrome (14%), Pinnawa Glaze-on-white (3%), Matsaki types (6%), and gray ware (26%). Ignoring the Matsaki, an occupation span from transitional complex DE to early complex F is indicated (from after A.D. 1300 to some time after 1350). The proximity of the site to Hawikku may have resulted in a postabandonment deposition of Matsaki types. Had there been substantial occupation during the time Matsaki was produced, black ware would be expected.

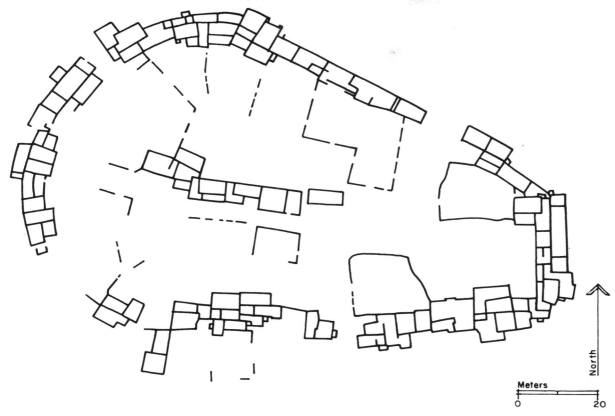

Figure 4.35. Lower Pescado Village (after Mindeleff 1981, plate 69).

32. *Lower Pescado Village* (Fig. 4.35)
(Heshoda Ts'in'a, Hesh-o-ta-tzina)

Identification
   Site Numbers: ZAP:NM:12:I3:109.
   Bibliography: Mindeleff (1891: 95–96, Plates 69–72, Fig. 18), Fewkes (1891: 103), Holmes and Fowler (1980: 56–58, 225–232).
   Discussion: The prehistoric site of Lower Pescado Village lies beneath one of the historic Zuni farming villages. As with several other sites, the extent of the prehistoric ruin cannot be determined from surface evidence. The Zuni name of the village means ''marked house'' in reference to pictographs in one of the nearby ruins (Eggan and Pandey 1979: 481).

Environmental Setting
   Elevation: 2048 m (6720 feet).
   Exposure: Open.
   Landforms: The site is on a rise adjacent to the Rio Pescado. Although its present height above the valley floor is significant, it cannot be determined how much of this elevation is natural and how much is a cultural deposit. The southwestern portion of the site, which is eroding into the river, shows a substantial depth of cultural material. The site is located in approximately the middle of the river valley, with mesas a few hundred meters to the north and south.
   Plant Communities: The site is in an area of plains grassland. There is modern agricultural use of the area adjacent to the site. A riparian community also exists along the river near

the site. Juniper-pinyon woodland covers the mesa sides and tops, a few hundred meters distant.

Archaeological Remains
   Architecture: The modern village is egg-shaped. Mindeleff was able to locate several sections of ancient masonry, leading him to believe that the historic village followed the outlines of the ancient ruin. The depth of the cultural deposits visible in the edge of the river bank suggests a substantial prehistoric site. The rubble mound is 2 m to 3 m in height.
   Dimensions: 105 m by 150 m (for the modern village, and probably for the prehistoric ruin as well).
   Room Estimate: As nearly as can be determined from the roof outlines, Mindeleff's plan of the historic village shows about 120 ground floor rooms. The mound configuration and the walls Mindeleff identifies as ''ancient'' suggest that the historic village followed the general outline of the prehistoric ruin. Considering the size of the mound and the layout of sites contemporaneous with the prehistoric village, I assume that it had at least twice as many rooms as the historic site. The height of the mound indicates multiple story structures. Thus, assuming one-half second-story and one-fourth third-story rooms, a rough estimate of 420 rooms is derived. This compares well with the observation by Holmes and Fowler that this site is comparable in size to Yellowhouse, estimated to have 425 rooms.
   Artifacts: The surface artifact scatter is light. However, because the southern edge of the site is eroding into the Pescado River, artifacts are plentiful in the river cut and on the river bed below.

Ceramic Samples: Quantitative by Kintigh; diagnostic by Kintigh (4).

Temporal Placement: A quantitative sample of 42 sherds was obtained from the bank of the river that intersects the site. The main constituents of the assemblage are Tularosa Black-on-white (5%), St. Johns types (5%), Heshotauthla types (14%), gray ware (14%), and buff corrugated (17%). Red Mesa Black-on-white (2%), Kwakina Polychrome (2%), and historic Zuni ware (2%) were also represented with one sherd each. Four diagnostic collections on the sparse site surface yielded, in addition, Puerco Black-on-white (2 sherds), Pinedale Black-on-white (3), Springerville Polychrome (1), Pinedale Polychrome (2), Pinnawa Glaze-on-white (1), Matsaki types (3), and black ware (1). In the quantitative sample the red ware to white rare ratio was 2.7:1.

These data suggest an early component at the site, probably prior to complex A. The major site construction may have started in transitional complex DE (note the low incidence of white wares), with the major site occupation probably lasting until complex F (from after A.D. 1300 to some time after 1350). The site was re-occupied in late historic times as one of the Zuni farming villages.

33. *Pescado West Ruin* (Fig. 4.36)

Identification

Site Numbers: Spier 84, ZAP:NM:12:I3:4, ZIR 16.

Bibliography: Simpson (1964: 123–124, original edition 1850), Whipple (1856, Pt. 1: 65), Bandelier (1892a: 333), Spier (1917: 238), Dodge and Ferguson (1976: 17–20).

Discussion: Pescado West is one of three sites in the vicinity of two major springs located along the Rio Pescado. Lower Pescado Ruin is about 50 m east and Upper Pescado Ruin is about 600 m east. All three ruins were identified to Simpson as ancestral Zuni villages.

Environmental Setting

Elevation: 2060 m (6760 feet).

Exposure: Open.

Landforms: The site is on the floor of the Rio Pescado Valley about 40 m west of Lower Pescado Spring, a large permanent spring that supplies water for modern farming. In the area of the spring is a basalt outcrop. Sandstone is available from the mesa slopes about 500 m northeast of the site.

Plant Communities: Pescado West is in an area of plains grassland, adjacent to the riparian zone along the stream that flows next to the site. Juniper-pinyon woodland covers the mesa sides and tops.

Archaeological Remains

Architecture: The site is an irregular oval constructed of basalt and tan sandstone. The rubble mound formed by the pueblo's outside wall is 2 m to 3 m high in many places. The site appears to have had an oval perimeter, two to three rooms wide, with a major room block as many as 5 rooms wide cutting across the interior. Stones from the pueblo have been taken for the construction of modern farm houses.

Dimensions: 66 m by 84 m, oval (Spier indicates 150 feet by 215 feet, 46 m by 66 m).

Room Estimate: It is estimated that 2540 square meters were completely covered by rooms, based on measurements

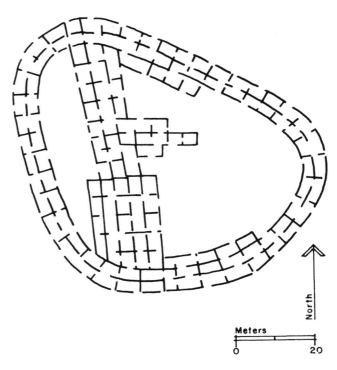

Figure 4.36.   Pescado West Ruin (after Dodge and Ferguson 1976, map 5).

from a map revised in the field from the one presented by Dodge and Ferguson (1976: 19). Room outlines could not be determined, so an average (conservative) room size of 10 square meters per room was used. (This room size was observed at the architecturally similar and approximately contemporaneous Jack's Lake Ruin.) Thus, a ground floor estimate of 254 rooms is obtained. Using the factor of 1.75 for a three-story pueblo, the total estimate is 445 rooms.

Artifacts: Dodge and Ferguson note a large artifact scatter south of the ruin and indicate that a water line trench north of the site revealed deep trash deposits.

Ceramic Samples: Quantitative by Kintigh, ZAP (5).

Temporal Placement: My quantitative collection of 75 sherds from Pescado West yielded mainly St. Johns types (3%), Heshotauthla types (15%), Kwakina Polychrome (3%), gray ware (35%), and buff corrugated (27%). One Puerco Black-on-white sherd and one Kechipawan Polychrome sherd were also found. The red ware to white ware ratio is 25.0:1.

The five ZAP quantitative samples had low percentages of gray ware (3%) and buff corrugated (3%). It is assumed that these wares were not systematically collected and they are ignored in computing the percentages that follow. Based on a sample of 733 sherds, the main ceramics represented were Tularosa Black-on-white (8%), St. Johns types (21%), Heshotauthla types (23%), and Kwakina Polychrome (6%). Incidental quantities of Reserve Black-on-white (0.3%), Pinedale Black-on-white (1%), Pinedale Polychrome (2%), Pinnawa Glaze-on-white (0.3%), a Matsaki sherd (0.1%), black ware (1%), and historic Zuni ware (0.4%) were found.

Historic use of the site is evidenced by the Zuni ware. It seems best to conclude that the single Matsaki sherd out of 733 collected indicates only a later prehistoric use of the area. Although the glazed white wares are relatively infrequent (5

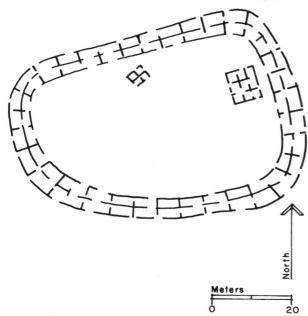

Figure 4.37. Lower Pescado Ruin (after Dodge and Ferguson 1976, map 7).

sherds total), their occurrence in association with a large amount of Heshotauthla is evidence that both types are probably associated with the main occupation of the site. The presence of significant quantities of St. Johns types indicates that the site (or an earlier component in the same location) started its occupation in transitional complex DE or the beginning of complex E (after A.D. 1300). Habitation appears to have ended in complex F or G depending on how much significance is given to the single Kechipawan sherd. For present purposes, I conclude that the occupation ended during complex F (after A.D. 1350).

34. *Lower Pescado Ruin* (Fig. 4.37)

Identification

Site Numbers: Spier 85, ZAP:NM:12:I3:6.

Bibliography: Simpson (1964: 123–124, original edition 1850), Whipple (1856, Pt. 1: 65), Bandelier (1892a: 333), Spier (1917: 238), Dodge and Ferguson (1976: 21–24), Banteah (1979).

Environmental Setting

Elevation: 2060 m (6760 feet).

Exposure: Open.

Landforms: Lower Pescado Ruin is immediately adjacent to a major spring and the stream that drains the spring into the Rio Pescado. Basalt is available at the spring and sandstone is available on the mesa slopes about 400 m northeast of the site.

Plant Communities: The site is in an area of plains grassland with a riparian zone along the stream. Juniper-pinyon woodland covers the mesa slopes and tops.

Archaeological Remains

Architecture: The pueblo was constructed of tan sandstone and basalt. The rubble mound rises about 2 m above the valley floor. It appears to have two or more rows of rooms following the irregular ovoid perimeter of the pueblo. Two

detached room blocks are in the interior of the ruin.

Dimensions: 50 m by 72 m, oval.

Room Estimate: Using the map by Dodge and Ferguson as a base, I determined the area that appeared to be covered with rooms from a field inspection. This area was estimated to be 1200 square meters. Using the 10 square meters per room found at the Jack's Lake Ruin, the estimate is 120 ground floor rooms. Judging from the height of the rubble mound, I assumed half second-story rooms for a total of 180 rooms.

Ceramic Samples: Quantitative by Kintigh, ZAP (3).

Temporal Placement: As with the other ZAP Pescado collections, in these three samples (673 sherds), gray ware (5%) and buff corrugated (5%) are drastically underrepresented, compared to my quantitative sample of 70 sherds in which gray ware makes up 39 percent and buff corrugated 31 percent. Thus, these wares are ignored in computing percentages, reducing the sample to 600 sherds.

The major ceramics in the ZAP assemblage are Tularosa Black-on-white (5%), St. Johns types (4%), Heshotauthla types (24%), Kwakina Polychrome (10%), and Pinnawa Glaze-on-white (3%). Two sherds each of Puerco Black-on-white (0.3%) and Reserve Black-on-white (0.3%) were also found. The assemblage is similar to the one found at Pescado West. The main difference is the much larger percentage of Pinnawa Glaze-on-white. The occupation probably began late in transitional complex DE and ceased near the end of complex F (from after A.D. 1300 to about 1375).

35. *Heshot uła* (Fig. 4.38)
(Heshotauthla, Hecota'utlIa)

Identification

Site Numbers: Spier 78, ZAP:NM:12:Y2:103, LA15605, NM G:14:7(ASM), YH206.

Bibliography: Fewkes (1891: 105–109, plan; 1909), Bandelier (1892a: 329, 333, Plate I Fig. 32), LeBlanc (1978), Spier (1917: 236–237), Hunter-Anderson (1978: 79–82, Fig. 8).

Discussion: Heshot uła was excavated by Cushing as part of the Hemenway Expedition. The fieldwork was under the supervision of Hodge (1888), who sent occasional reports back to Cushing at Zuni. Simpson appeared to be describing this ruin in his account of his 1849 trip, although McNitt's footnote to the account identifies it as another ruin on the opposite side of the river (Simpson 1964: 121–122, footnote 141). If my supposition is correct, Heshot uła has been identified as an ancestral Zuni site as far back as 1849 (Simpson 1964: 124).

Environmental Setting

Elevation: 2030 m (6660 feet).

Exposure: Open.

Landforms: Heshot uła is built next to the Pescado River. Sandstone outcrops appear on the mesa side about 150 m north of the site.

Plant Communities: The site is located in the plains grassland of the Pescado River Valley. A juniper-pinyon woodland is on the mesa to the north.

Archaeological Remains

Architecture: The pueblo is roughly oval with a central plaza and is built of tan sandstone. The Hemenway Expedition site map published by Fewkes (1891: 133) shows the

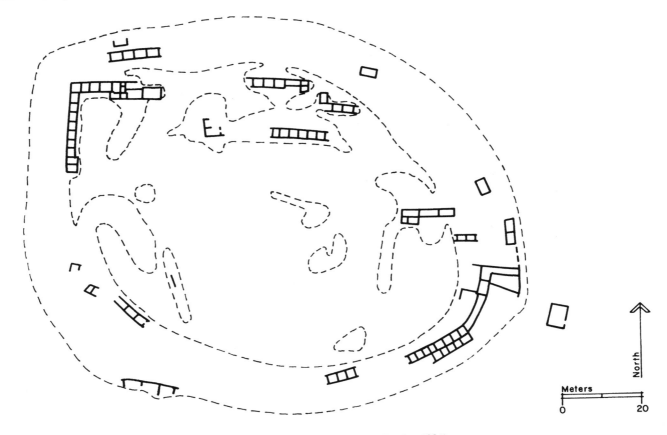

Figure 4.38.   Heshot uⱡa (after Fewkes 1891).

basic outline and contours of the site. In describing the excavations, Fewkes (1909: 45–62) indicates that the ruin may have had a free-standing outer wall forming a sort of "moat" around the room clusters. Excavations in the central part of the ruin revealed no walls. Outside the outer wall on the south, structures identified as communal ovens were found. Today additional features are difficult to see because the site is thickly covered with wolfberry and other shrubs. Southwest of the main ruin are walls washing into the Rio Pescado, which, judging from the pottery, are from an earlier component of the site.

Dimensions: 107 m by 128 m, oval.

Room Estimate: It is difficult to estimate the number of rooms from the plan published by Fewkes. The only other available map is the one published by Hunter-Anderson. Although in general this map is not satisfactory, it is probably more adequate for room estimation. This map shows about 530 ground floor rooms and a room area of about 5634 square meters. The rubble mound around the perimeter of the site ranges from 1 m to 4 m in height, suggesting a three-story structure. Fewkes (1909: 46) indicates that the mound was 15 to 20 feet (5 m to 6 m) high. Multiplying 530 rooms by 1.75 for a three-story pueblo, the total estimate is 875 rooms. In one place Fewkes (1891: 106) emphasizes that the rooms average 4 feet square (1.5 square meters) and elsewhere (1909: 47) says the average was 10 feet square (9.3 square meters), which seems much more likely.

Ceramic Samples: Quantitative by Spier, Kintigh; diagnostic by Spier, Kintigh (3).

Temporal Placement: I made a quantitative sample of 48 sherds in 1979. The major ceramics represented are Pinedale Black-on-white (10%), Heshotauthla types (13%), gray ware (44%), and buff corrugated (15%). Puerco Black-on-white, Tularosa Black-on-white, and Kwakina Polychrome were each represented by one sherd (2%). Spier's quantitative sample of 76 sherds shows, in addition, Reserve Black-on-white (1%), St. Johns types (2%), Pinnawa Glaze-on-white (1%), and Kechipawan Polychrome (1%). A variety of diagnostic samples also have Red Mesa Black-on-white (3 sherds), Springerville Polychrome (1), and Matsaki types (6). Pinnawa Glaze-on-white vessels are represented in the excavated Hemenway collection; however, no Matsaki vessels were found. There is an earlier structure west of the large pueblo that probably dates to transitional complex DE (about A.D. 1300). The ceramic evidence tends to indicate that the area was continually occupied through complex F (about A.D. 1375). There is not sufficient evidence to attribute the single Kechipawan Polychrome sherd or the Matsaki pottery to the major occupation, especially given the absence of black ware, the physical location of the site, and the pueblo's importance in Zuni tradition (which has probably resulted in historic visitation of the site). The major pueblo might have been constructed during complex E (about A.D. 1325), although there is insufficient evidence for adequate support of this supposition.

36. *Rainbow Spring Ruin* (Fig. 4.39)

Identification

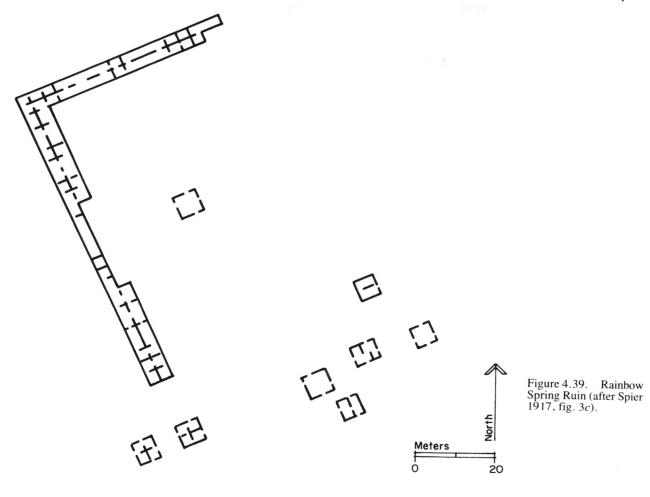

Figure 4.39. Rainbow Spring Ruin (after Spier 1917, fig. 3c).

Meters

North

0   20

Site Numbers: Spier 11, ZAP:NM:13:A:8.
Bibliography: Spier (1917: 221–222, Fig. 3c), Ferguson (1981a), Upham (1982).

Environmental Setting
Elevation: 1935 m (6350 feet).
Exposure: Northeast.
Landforms: The ruin is near the base of a hill on the southern edge of the broad bottomland of Ojo Caliente, which is now extensively used for irrigation agriculture. A major spring, Rainbow Spring, is located about 240 m to the northwest. A volcanic outcrop is on a hill only a few meters west of the main room block. The site of Kechiba:wa is visible on the top of the mesa about 2 km north of the site.
Plant Communities: The site is in an area transitional between the juniper-pinyon woodland of the hillslopes and plains grassland of the valley bottom.

Archaeological Remains
Architecture: The major architectural feature of the Rainbow Spring Ruin is an L-shaped room block that is two rooms wide in most places. A number of isolated rooms and room blocks of not more than four rooms each are scattered on the top of a knoll east of the main room block. The rubble mound is low and is composed mainly of basalt blocks.
Dimensions: 83 m by 55 m, L-shaped, two rooms wide.
Room Estimate: Spier's map indicates that there are 76 rooms in the main room block and about 32 rooms in the isolated room clusters. The low height of the mound indicates that there was probably only a single story. Consequently, the total count is estimated to be 108 rooms. The area covered by rooms is about 917 square meters, with room sizes ranging from 7.7 to 9.2 square meters.
Artifacts: The artifact scatter was light. I collected all sherds that could be found. Many of these were located in an arroyo that bisects the site.
Ceramic Samples: Quantitative by Spier, Kintigh (2).
Temporal Placement: Spier's collection of 127 sherds at the site is probably the most reliable. The sample includes mainly Heshotauthla types (6%), Kwakina Polychrome (8%), Salado polychromes (3%), Pinnawa Glaze-on-white (6%), gray ware (28%), and black ware (8%). A single St. Johns sherd was found (1%). My quantitative collection of 56 sherds produced, in addition, single sherds of Puerco Black-on-white, Tularosa Black-on-white, and Puerco Black-on-red. This assemblage suggests a short occupation during complex F (about A.D. 1350 to 1375), although the starting date might be somewhat earlier. The few earlier sherds probably derive from earlier sites in the area. The black ware and Salado polychrome sherds must be regarded as somewhat anomalous; none of these types were found in my recent collection. It seems possible that Spier's black ware was associated with later prehistoric or historic use of the spring.

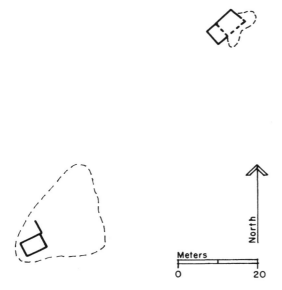

Figure 4.40.   Hambassa:wa
(after Mindeleff 1891, fig. 15).

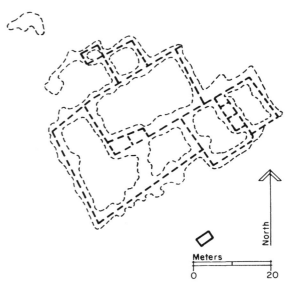

Figure 4.41.   Binna:wa (after
Mindeleff 1891, fig. 16).

37. *Hambassa:wa* (Fig. 4.40)

(Hampassawa, Hampassawan)

Identification

Site Numbers: Spier 32, ZAP:NM:12:L3:38.

Bibliography: Mindeleff (1891: 83–84, Fig. 15), Spier (1917: 225), Hodge (1937: 57), Ferguson (1981a), Upham (1982).

Environmental Setting

Elevation: 1892 m (6208 feet).

Exposure: Open.

Landforms: Hambassa:wa is located on a low knoll rising from the Zuni River Valley bottom. The river runs about 50 m north of the site. The nearest known sandstone outcrop is on the base of the mesa about 1.4 km to the south of the site.

Plant Communities: The site is in a large area of plains grassland. The riparian deciduous community along the river is just to the north of the site.

Archaeological Remains

Architecture: An exact determination of the nature of the architectural remains is not possible without some testing. This was apparently true also at the time of Mindeleff's visit, as his map is not especially helpful. The top and sides of the knoll, an area of about 20 m by 30 m, are covered with rubble, and occasional wall lines are visible. About 30 m to the northwest is a much smaller rubble mound.

Dimensions: 20 m by 30 m, 8 m in diameter.

Room Estimate: Using the 7.9 square meters of rubble area per room developed at Hawikku (see the room estimate section for Hawikku, site 39), I estimate that the main rubble mound area of 296 square meters includes 36 rooms. Surface remains suggest that no more than three rooms existed in the area of the smaller rubble mound. The total estimate for the site is 39 rooms. This estimate should not be regarded as reliable, but it is the most reasonable based on the available data.

Artifacts: The artifact scatter around the site is of moderate density. It indicates that there were as many as three tem-

porary components, including an historic one.

Ceramic Samples: Quantitative by Kintigh; diagnostic by Kintigh (3).

Temporal Placement: A quantitative sample of 99 sherds included a range of late ceramics: Heshotauthla types (6%), Kwakina types (7%), Pinnawa Glaze-on-white (6%), Kechipawan Polychrome (1%), unidentified buff ware (4%), gray ware (6%), black ware (27%), and historic Zuni ware (11%). A single sherd of Wingate pottery was also found. Other early types in the diagnostic samples were Kiatuthlanna Black-on-white (1 sherd), Red Mesa Black-on-white (1), and Puerco Black-on-white (1). Late types also appeared in the diagnostic samples: Matsaki types (3 sherds), Hopi buff ware (1), and Salado polychrome (1).

This ceramic evidence suggests an early component, with the major occupation in a second component through complex G into early complex H (about A.D. 1375 to 1425). Finally, there is a late (post–1692) historic Zuni component evidenced by the Zuni wares.

38. *Binna:wa* (Fig. 4.41)

(Pinnawa, Pinawa, Pinaua, Pinawan)

Identification

Site Numbers: Spier 33, ZAP:NM:12:K3:69, NM M:1:36(ASM).

Bibliography: Mindeleff (1891: 86, Fig. 16, Plate 56), Fewkes (1891: 112–113), Bandelier (1892a: 338), Kroeber (1916: 22), Spier (1917: 225–226), Hodge (1937: 57), Romancito (1980), Ferguson (1981a), Upham (1982).

Environmental Setting

Elevation: 1911 m (6270 feet).

Exposure: Open.

Landforms: Binna:wa occupies the top of a knoll surrounded by Zuni River Valley bottomland. The river runs about 100 m to the north. Sandstone outcrops occur on the north slope of the site.

Plant Communities: The ruin is in an area of plains grassland, although a deciduous riparian ribbon follows the river about 50 m to the north.

Archaeological Remains

Architecture: Mindeleff reports that a historic corral occupied the major area of the site at the time of his visit in the 1880s. Although a large number of walls are visible on top of the hill, it is impossible to determine the extent of the prehistoric site because of the historic structures. Although Bandelier believed it to be a compact pueblo, the high density of prehistoric artifactual material suggests a substantial ruin. Certainly the best architectural information available comes from Mindeleff. He reports that he was able to follow prehistoric walls and his map depicts a ruin of irregular shape that he compares to Kechiba:wa. The masonry is of red tabular sandstone.

Dimensions: Approximately 42 m by 58 m, irregular shape.

Room Estimate: The area covered by rubble, as measured from Mindeleff's map and ground observations, is about 1764 square meters. If Mindeleff is correct and the layout is similar to Kechiba:wa, then about half of the area would be open, as is the case there. Thus, a rubble area of 882 square meters of rooms, divided by the Hawikku estimate of 7.9 square meters of rubble per room, yields an estimate of 112 ground floor rooms. Assuming that one-half of these have two stories, the total estimate is 168 rooms.

Artifacts: The artifact scatter associated with Binna:wa is large and, in places, quite dense. Recent excavations northeast of the hill yielded a substantial amount of prehistoric trash (Romancito 1980).

Ceramic Samples: Quantitative by Kintigh (3); excavated by Spier (6); diagnostic by Kintigh (5).

Temporal Placement: Six of Spier's 13 levels of a trench excavated at Binna:wa were analyzed, in addition to several surface collections. The dominant ceramics in my three quantitative surface samples (197 sherds) were Kwakina Polychrome (3%), Matsaki types (8%, plus 7% unidentified buff ware), gray ware (5%), and black ware (45%). Heshotauthla types (2%), Salado polychromes (2%), Pinnawa Glaze-on-white (2%), Kechipawan Polychrome (1%), and buff corrugated (2%) are additional late ceramics. Puerco Black-on-white (1%) and St. Johns types (2%) also occur in small quantities, but may be safely disregarded considering the earlier sites close by (Schreiber 1979a). In four diagnostic surface collections (220 sherds) Reserve Black-on-white, Tularosa Black-on-white, Pinedale Black-on-white, Springerville Polychrome, Pinedale Polychrome, Hopi buff ware, and historic Zuni ware also appear.

Spier's deepest excavated level, M (117 sherds), appears to indicate a start of occupation in complex G. The major ceramics represented are Heshotauthla types (16%), gray ware (18%), and black ware (12%), with Pinnawa Glaze-on-white (1%) and Kechipawan Polychrome (2%) also present. The black ware to gray ware ratio is 0.64:1. As expected, the next two higher levels, K and L (328 sherds), date slightly later, perhaps early in complex H. The percentage of Hesotauthla types decreases (to 7%), while Kwakina Polychrome (4%), Pinnawa Glaze-on-white (4%), Pinnawa Red-on-white (1%), and Kechipawan Polychrome (2%) are present in significant amounts. Gray ware (14%) decreases, while black ware (35%) increases substantially; the black ware to gray ware ratio increases to 2.5:1. Two sherds (1%)

of Matsaki types were also found, suggesting an occupation early in complex H. Levels H and J, with 752 sherds, seem even later, with Heshotauthla types continuing to decrease (to 4%). Gray ware (13%) and black ware (30%) make up most of the identifiable portion of the collection, and the black ware to gray ware ratio of 2.3:1 remains about the same. Other ceramics amounting to 2 percent or more of the collection were Puerco Black-on-white (2%), Kwakina Polychrome (2%), Salado polychromes (3%), Kechipawan Polychrome (3%), and Matsaki types (2%). These levels seem to date early in complex H. The uppermost level analyzed, level D (175 sherds), also appears to be associated with complex H. Heshotauthla types (2%) decrease, while gray ware (7%), buff corrugated (12%), and black ware (47%) comprise most of the identifiable assemblage. The black ware to gray ware ratio is again 2.5:1. Ceramics totaling 2 percent or more are Pinnawa Glaze-on-white (3%) and Matsaki types (2%).

The ceramic evidence from Binna:wa indicates an occupation starting in complex G and lasting into complex H (from after A.D. 1375 to about 1500). The depth and density of refuse excavated suggest a relatively long and intense occupation. Substantial quantities of buff ware were not found in the levels analyzed; however, Spier's tabulations show a maximum of 11 percent buff ware in Level A. Recent quantitative surface collections with 197 sherds included Matsaki types (8%), unidentified buff ware (8%), gray ware (5%), and black ware (45%), indicating an occupation lasting well into complex H.

39. *Hawikku* (Figs. 4.42, 4.43)
(Hawikuh, Hawwikku, Hauicu)

Identification

Site Numbers: Spier 25, ZAP:NM:13:A:2, LA37, NM M:1:1(ASM).

Bibliography: Mindeleff (1891: 80–81, Plates 46–48), Bandelier (1892a: 338, Plate I Fig. 34), Spier (1917: 224), Hodge (1918a, 1918b, 1920b, 1921a, 1921b, 1922, 1923, 1924a, 1924b, 1924c, 1926, 1937, 1952), Hrdlička (1931), Smith and others (1966), Woodbury (1979: 467–468), Ferguson (1981a), Upham (1982).

Discussion: Extensive excavations were conducted at Hawikku by Hodge between 1917 and 1923 (Fig. 4.43). The results are discussed in a number of brief reports by Hodge, but were not comprehensively reported until published in 1966 by Smith, Woodbury, and Woodbury. Collections from these excavations are housed at the Museum of the American Indian, Heye Foundation. Hawikku was the pueblo at which Coronado first confronted the Zuni in 1540 and may have been the one at which Estevan, a member of Fray Marcos' expedition, was killed in 1539.

Hodge believed that there were two distinct temporal components at Hawikku, an "ancient" one and an historic one, occupied by different cultural groups and separated by a substantial interval of time (Smith and others 1966: 150–151). As Smith and the Woodburys (1966: 6, 40–42) discuss, understanding these earlier remains was not the primary goal of the expedition and they did not receive the attention paid the materials Hodge considered historic. It seems clear today that although there probably was an earlier component, evidenced by the site known as "Circular Kivas

Figure 4.42.   Hawikku (after Smith and others 1966, fig. 1; Mindeleff 1891, plate 46).

near Hawikuh'' (Hodge 1923), most of the prehistoric remains underlying the historic structures were part of a continuous occupation of the pueblo from Pueblo IV times (or perhaps earlier) until the late 1600s.

Environmental Setting
Elevation: 1899 m (6230 feet).
Exposure: Open, southern.
Landforms: Hawikku is located on top of a ridge, along the southern slope of the ridge, and on the bottomland at the base of the ridge. The ridge has a number of sandstone outcrops in the vicinity of the ruin. The site overlooks the junction of the Zuni River with Plumasano Wash, which drains the Ojo Caliente area. There are extensive open bottomlands to the west and south in the Zuni River Valley, and to the east and south toward Kechiba:wa and Ojo Caliente. To the north, the ridge joins a low mesa.
Plant Communities: The site is located primarily in an area of plains grassland. The top of the ridge is covered with an open juniper-pinyon woodland.

Archaeological Remains
Architecture: Hawikku is a large ruin of irregular shape built on the top and the southern and eastern slopes of the low point of a mesa. The construction of this multistory pueblo on

top of and down the slope of a hill doubtless made it look to the Spaniards as though it had six or more stories, as they reported. There are at least seven major room blocks constructed mainly of tan and red sandstone. While Hodge excavated extensively, there is apparently one room block he did not touch. This room block does not show on the map in Smith and others (1966, Fig. 1), but it can be seen on the map presented by Mindeleff and the one included here (Fig. 4.42). A number of inhumations were found in room fill but most of the cremations and inhumations, nearly a thousand in all, were found in clusters located to the north, west, and south of the pueblo (Smith and others 1966, Fig. 37). Walls were found beneath almost 5 m of refuse in one plaza excavation. The remains of an adobe church and monastery, established in 1629, lie melting at the base of the mesa point.
Dimensions: 120 m by 152 m, multiple room blocks.
Room Estimate: At Hawikku, 370 rooms were excavated and a high-quality map of most of the site is in Smith and others (1966: 2, Fig. 1). On this map, 327 rooms are visible in room blocks A through E (not including room block F or the church). However, shown on Mindeleff's map are substantial architectural remains to the east, only a small portion of which (room block F) was excavated by Hodge. The 327 rooms of room blocks A through E correspond to an area of

Figure 4.43. Collapsed kiva at Hawikku excavated by the Hendricks-Hodge Expedition, 1921. Note the depth of deposits above the kiva roof. (Photograph courtesy of the Museum of the American Indian, Heye Foundation, Negative No. 7437.)

2591 square meters of concentrated rubble on Mindeleff's map. Using this correspondence, a rubble area of 7.9 square meters per room is derived. This figure, when divided into the remaining rubble area mapped by Mindeleff (1018 square meters), indicates an additional 130 ground floor rooms. This estimate of 457 ground floor rooms corresponds fairly well with the 470 ground floor rooms estimated by Smith and the Woodburys. Using the 457-room figure, and assuming one-half of the rooms had second stories and that one-fourth of the rooms had third stories, the total estimate is 800 rooms. The rooms range in size from 8.4 to 9.2 square meters with an average of about 8.6 square meters.

Artifacts: The artifact scatter is relatively heavy on the site. In all probability, this quantity results from the extensive excavations that were not back-filled and from the early practice of not collecting all of the sherds. A much earlier ruin, Circular Kivas near Hawikuh (Hodge 1923), is a short distance west of the site and it probably contributed many of the early sherds to the Hawikku sample.

Ceramic Samples: Quantitative by Kintigh (2); diagnostic by Kintigh (3).

Temporal Placement: The combined quantitative surface assemblage from Hawikku (268 sherds) contains unidentified red ware (5%), Kwakina Polychrome (1%), Salado polychromes (1%), Pinnawa Glaze-on-white (1%), Pinnawa Red-on-white (1%), Kechipawan Polychrome (0.4%), Matsaki types (12%), unidentified buff ware (13%), gray ware (1%), buff corrugated (0.4%), black ware (55%), and Hawikuh types (1%). Based on the diagnostic surface collections, the unexcavated eastern portion appears to date relatively late in the occupation of the pueblo, although this observation may be due to the differential disturbance of the areas.

Hodge's stratigraphic trench, with 14,094 sherds analyzed, provides evidence that is somewhat difficult to interpret. The trench was 75 feet (22.9 m) long, 11 feet (3.4 m) wide, and 15 feet (4.6 m) deep, and was excavated in one foot (30.5 cm) levels. Smith and the Woodburys have presented Hodge's ceramic tabulations with their interpretation of the modern typological equivalents. Black ware and unidentifiable sherds were not counted by Hodge (Smith and others 1966: 151). Because of the inevitable mixing of stratigraphic deposits in a trench 75 feet long, because of terminological differences, and because of the absence of black ware and unidentifiable sherds, it is difficult to base solid conclusions

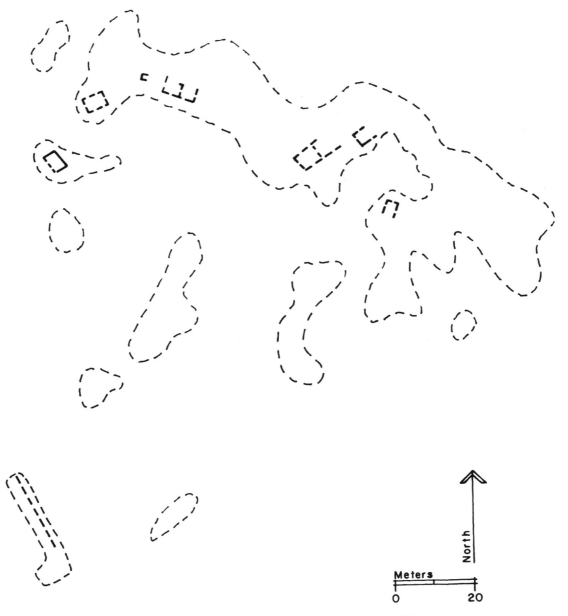

North

Meters

0   20

Figure 4.44.   Mats'a:kya (after Mindeleff 1891, plate 55).

on these data. In the following discussion, the percentages are based only on *identifiable* decorated wares.

In this trench, substantial quantities (5% or more) of Hawikuh types appear in the upper six levels. The fourth through second levels show an increase from 20 percent to 64 percent of Hawikuh types. This assemblage seems to be evidence of a substantial post–1620 occupation. No other sites seem to have this density of late material, and these percentages of Hawikuh glaze wares are difficult to understand, considering the low percentages now found on the surface.

Levels 7 through 11 are dominated by Matsaki types, with lesser percentages of Heshotauthla types, Kwakina Polychrome, Pinnawa Glaze-on-white, Salado polychromes, and Hopi ware, and small amounts of corrugated. The assemblage seems to correspond to Spier's levels A through C at the site of Mats'a:kya, implying a date during historic complexes H and I. Levels 12 through 14 are dominated by Heshotauthla types, Kechipawan Polychrome, and Matsaki types. Kwakina

Polychrome and Salado polychromes also make up significant portions of the assemblage, with small quantities of Pinnawa Glaze-on-white, corrugated, and Hopi ware. These levels date somewhat earlier in complex H.

The large quantities of Kechipawan Polychrome (up to 44%) and Salado polychromes (up to 16%) in Hodge's trench, especially when compared with his percentages of Pinnawa Glaze-on-white (maximum of 2%), seem most unlikely when no percentages even approaching these appear in other assemblages analyzed here. Along with the high percentages of Hawikuh types in the upper levels, these observations underscore the unresolvable problems of classification in Hodge's tabulations (intensified by the fact that the sherds have been discarded). However, the fractions of Heshotauthla types (28% in level 14) and Matsaki types (7% in level 14) compare well with the earliest level (I) at Mats'a:kya (site 40), when roughly comparable percentages based on slip colors (29% and 10% respectively) are compiled, suggesting a date early in complex H.

Figure 4.45.   Ruin of Mats'a:kya in 1899. Note the extensive rubble scatter on slope of ridge and the corn growing in the foreground. (Photograph by Adam Clark Vroman, courtesy of the Smithsonian Institution, National Anthropological Archives, Bureau of American Ethnology Collection, Negative No. 2347A.)

Therefore, I conclude that the occupation of Hawikku started at about the same time as the occupation of Mats'a:kya early in complex H (about A.D. 1400), and continued into historic times. However, because the deepest deposits at Hawikku probably have not been sampled, it is certainly possible that the site's occupation could have started much earlier. Historical information suggests that the pueblo continued to have a substantial population up until 1680 when it was finally abandoned.

40. *Mats'a:kya* (Figs. 4.44, 4.45)
(Matsaki, Matzaki, Maçaque, Maça)

Identification
Site Numbers: Spier 48, ZAP:NM:12:K3:62, NM M:1:33(ASM).
Bibliography: Mindeleff (1891: 86, Plate 55), Fewkes (1891: 110), Bandelier (1892a: 336–337), Kroeber (1916: 22), Spier (1917: 231–232), Hodge (1937), Ferguson (1981a), Upham (1982).
Discussion: Mats'a:kya was occupied at the time of the Spanish entrada and was said by many to be the largest of the Zuni towns.

Environmental Setting
Elevation: 1932 m (6340 feet).
Exposure: Open.
Landforms: Mats'a:kya is located on the top, sides, and base of a large knoll on the Zuni River floodplain, about 200 m south of the river. The mesa, Dowa Yalanne, is about 2 km to the southeast.
Plant Communities: The major plant community on and around the site is plains grassland. A riparian community occurs along the Zuni River and an adjacent tributary.

Archaeological Remains
Architecture: Like Kyaki:ma (site 41), extensive areas of Mats'a:kya are covered with rubble, but at Mats'a:kya, even rough outlines of major room blocks are difficult to discern. Bandelier, however, suggests that the pueblo could have been polygonal. The best projection of the site configuration is a major room block completely covering the knoll, with several additional room blocks southwest of the knoll.
Dimensions: The portion of the site with architecture is contained in an area of 140 m by 150 m.
Room Estimate: It seems likely, particularly in reviewing the historical accounts, that Mats'a:kya was a large site with multiple stories. Bandelier (who certainly was aware of the historical accounts) believed it to be large. It may be noted, however, that neither Mindeleff nor Fewkes thought that Mats'a:kya was very large. Nonetheless, supposing the ruin to be large and using Mindeleff's map as a base, I determined on the ground the major area believed to be covered with architecture. This area of 8144 square meters of rubble was assumed to be about one-half open area, similar to Kechiba:wa. The rubble area of 4072 square meters was divided by the Hawikku figure of 7.9 square meters of rubble area per room to get an estimate of 515 ground floor rooms. Using a figure of one-half two-story and one-fourth three-story rooms, the total estimate is 901 rooms. This estimate, however, must be regarded as highly tentative.
Artifacts: Sherds are not abundant on the surface. Most of the sherds visible in 1979 were adjacent to potholes and rodent holes.
Ceramic Samples: Quantitative by Kintigh (2); excavated by Spier (9); diagnostic by Kintigh (3).
Temporal Placement: Spier's nine-level Mats'a:kya trench provides the best stratigraphic evidence for the protohistoric period, although it is difficult to correlate with the trench at

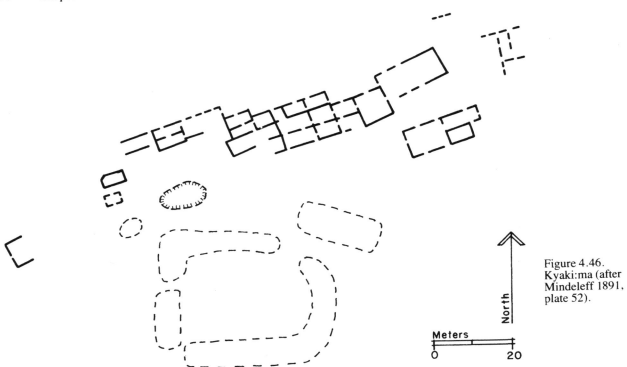

Figure 4.46.
Kyaki:ma (after
Mindeleff 1891,
plate 52).

North

Meters
0   20

Binna:wa. The deepest Mats'a:kya level (I), with 101 sherds, has Pinnawa Glaze-on-white (4%), Pinnawa Red-on-white (5%), Kechipawan Polychrome (3%), Matsaki types (1%), gray ware (44%), and black ware (36%). The ratio of black ware to gray ware (0.8:1) is almost identical to the value of this ratio in the deepest level (M) at Binna:wa (site 38; 0.6:1). The presence of Matsaki types and the slightly higher ratio of black ware at Mats'a:kya suggest a slightly later date for the Mats'a:kya level. Level M at Binna:wa has many more Heshotautha sherds and more unidentified red ware than does Mats'a:kya Level I (54% as compared with 6%), while Pinnawa Glaze-on-white, Pinnawa Red-on-white, and Kechipawan Polychrome are more frequent in Level I (in total 12%, as compared with 3%). Overall, Mats'a:kya Level I probably dates early in complex H.

The next two higher levels, G and H, with 217 sherds, show an increase in the black ware to gray ware ratio to 4.0:1 (55% black ware to 14% gray ware) and a large increase in Matsaki types to 6% (with another 6% unidentified buff ware). The glazed white ware types decrease in percentage: Pinnawa Glaze-on-white (4%), Pinnawa Red-on-white (2%), and Kechipawan Polychrome (1%). Kwakina Polychrome (2%), unidentified red ware (6%), and Salado polychromes (0.5%), are also present. These levels doubtless date later in complex H.

The next three levels (D, E, F), with 266 sherds, reveal another increase in the black ware to gray ware ratio to 25.4:1 (67% to 3%), with similar percentages of Matsaki types (7%), unidentified buff (4%), Heshotauthla (1%), unidentified red ware (7%), Kwakina Polychrome (2%), Pinnawa Glaze-on-white (2%), and Kechipawan Polychrome (1%). A single Salado sherd (0.4%) was found. These levels seem yet later in complex H.

The top three levels (A, B, C), with 105 sherds, clearly date to the historic period of complexes H and I, with a single sherd of Hawikuh Glaze-on-red found in Level C. Gray ware has completely disappeared, while black ware is dominant. Matsaki types (18%) and unidentified buff ware (10%) make up most of the rest of the assemblage. Other ceramics represented are Heshotauthla types (1%), Kwakina Polychrome (1%), Salado polychromes (1%), Pinnawa Glaze-on-white (2%), Pinnawa Red-on-white (1%), and Kechipawan Polychrome (1%).

This trench indicates a continuous occupation from early in complex H (about A.D. 1400) into historic complex I. The degree of overlap with the Binna:wa trench is debatable, but relying mainly on the black ware to gray ware ratio, I argue it to be substantial.

For future reference, the main constituents of the surface assemblage (84 sherds) are unidentified red ware (10%), Kwakina Polychrome (4%), Matsaki types (13%), unidentified buff ware (23%), gray ware (4%), and black ware (37%).

41. *Kyaki:ma* (Figs. 4.46, 4.47)
(Kyakkima, Kiakime, Kiakima)

Identification
Site Numbers: Spier 45, ZAP:NM:12:K3:10, NM G:13:2(ASM).
Bibliography: Mindeleff (1891: 85–86, Plates 52–54), Fewkes (1891: 109–110), Bandelier (1892a: 337), Kroeber (1916: 22), Hodge (1937), Ferguson and others (1977), Ferguson (1981a), Upham (1982).
Discussion: This famous pueblo was occupied at the time of the Spanish arrival in 1539. In his 1885 report Cushing (Green 1979: 172–175) indicates that according to Zuni tradition, Estevan was killed at Kyaki:ma (not Hawikku). Eggan and Pandey (1979) gave Cushing's translation for the name of the village as "house of eagles."

Figure 4.47. Ruins of Kyaki:ma at the base of Dowa Yalanne. Note the vertical stone slabs in the lower left of the photograph.

Environmental Setting
Elevation: 1969 m (6460 feet).
Exposure: South.
Landforms: Kyaki:ma is located on a steep hill in a protected cove at the base of the mesa known as Dowa Yalanne. Sheer sandstone cliffs bound the ruin on the north. The site overlooks the broad area of bottomland where Galestina Canyon and Mullen Canyon join the Zuni River Valley. A permanent spring lies about 200 m west of the site.
Plant Communities: The primary plant community at Kyaki:ma is plains grassland. A small riparian community exists around the spring and a small juniper-pinyon woodland occurs along the base of the mesa.

Archaeological Remains
Architecture: As indicated on Mindeleff's map, extensive portions of the site are covered with rubble. A major area at the top of a hill is shown by Mindeleff to have visible wall outlines. In addition, occasional walls can be seen on the higher areas that surround the depression, immediately south of the obvious room block. The best assessment seems to be that there was a single linear room block at the top of the ridge that extends from the edge of the mesa. Another square room block (or square composition of linear room blocks) surrounded a deep depression. As Mindeleff notes, several large

sandstone slabs are set vertically in the ground east of the upper room block.
Dimensions: The room blocks are in an area of 70 m by 140 m.
Room Estimate: An accurate room estimate cannot be made. Using Mindeleff's map as a base, I made on-the-ground decisions concerning the probable area of architecture. It is estimated that 1972 square meters of rubble area were covered with rooms. Using the estimate derived at Hawikku of 7.9 square meters of rubble per ground floor room, I estimate 250 ground floor rooms for Kyaki:ma. Without adequate surface evidence to determine the number of stories, I consider Kyaki:ma to have one story.
Ceramic Samples: Quantitative by Spier (2), Kintigh; excavated by Spier (1); diagnostic by Spier, Kintigh (3).
Temporal Placement: Spier's two quantitative samples, with a total of 161 sherds, have similar characteristics. Various ceramic types appear, most with low frequencies. The main ceramics are Pinnawa Glaze-on-white (3%), Matsaki types (9%), unidentified buff ware (6%), gray ware (4%), and black ware (45%). Several early types (14%) are indicative of the adjacent early site noted by both Spier and Kroeber. Heshotauthla types (2%), unidentified red ware (9%), Kwakina Polychrome (2%), Salado polychromes (1%), and Hopi buff ware (1%) probably relate to the main period of occupation. Historic Zuni sherds indicate later visitation at the site, where there is now an active shrine.

Quantitative samples collected by Spier (58 sherds) and me (44 sherds), and my diagnostic samples (62 sherds), add only Pinnawa Red-on-white, Kechipawan Polychrome, and buff corrugated to the list of late types. These collections date the occupation to complexes H and I, but give little hint as to the start of habitation. Spier's excavation at the site does not help significantly. The ceramics found in the excavated sample are St. Johns types (6%), Kwakina Polychrome (3%), Pinnawa Glaze-on-white (1%), Pinnawa Red-on-white (1%), Matsaki types (8%), gray ware (7%), and black ware (57%), an assemblage that probably puts the beginning of occupation sometime during complex H. Notable here is the relatively low percentage of Matsaki types in a pueblo we know was occupied in historic times. The surface sample has proportions almost identical to those from Binna:wa and very similar to those from Kwa'kin'a. An occupation through most of complexes H and I (starting about A.D. 1400), similar to that of Mats'a:ka (site 40), is suggested.

Interestingly, Hawikuh Glaze-on-red and Polychrome do not appear, suggesting that the occupation of the site ended by the time these types were introduced at the end of complex I (about A.D. 1630).

42. *Kwa'kin'a* (Fig. 4.48)
(Kwakina)

Identification
Site Numbers: ZAP:NM:12:L3:12, LA 1053.
Bibliography: Fewkes (1891: 99), Bandelier (1892a: 339), Spier (1917: 229), Hodge (1937), Ferguson (1981a), Upham (1982).
Discussion: Kwa'kin'a was mentioned by early visitors to Zuni, including Fewkes, Bandelier, and Spier, although apparently none of them visited the ruin. Spier, however, was told of its approximate location. Eggan and Pandey

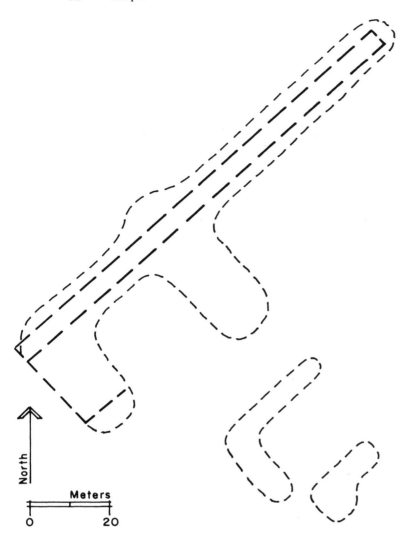

Figure 4.48.   Kwa'kin'a.

(1979: 481) give a translation of "town of the entrance place," citing Cushing by way of Hodge.

Environmental Setting
Elevation: 1887 m (6190 feet).
Exposure: Open.
Landforms: Kwa'kin'a is located on a ridge overlooking the Zuni River Valley. The river runs about 1.3 km southeast of the ruin. No sandstone outcrops are apparent in the immediate vicinity of the site, although outcrops are visible on the mesa slopes southeast of the river, about 1.8 km to the south.
Plant Communities: The site is in a transitional area between the juniper-pinyon woodland of the high country to the north, and the plains grassland of the slopes and river valley. A deciduous riparian community extends in a narrow strip along the river.

Archaeological Remains
Architecture: The actual configuration of the site is difficult to determine. It is well buried and has not been subject to any significant disturbance, either natural or cultural. One large F-shaped mound and two smaller L-shaped mounds are

evident. These mounds are located on the tops of natural features. The three mounds do not appear to be architecturally connected, but it is not possible to say this with certainty. Room outlines on the largest room block are clearly visible. The major building material is tan sandstone.
Dimensions: 126 m by 45 m, F-shaped; 35 m by 25 m and 20 m by 12 m, both L-shaped.
Room Estimate: The large F-shaped room block had a large number of visible room outlines, indicating that the rooms were about 2.7 m by 3 m (8.1 square meters). This room block appeared to be only two rooms wide. Not enough walls could be observed in the other two mounds to enable accurate estimates of their size. Using the large mound as a model, I made the room estimate from a map by fitting 2.7 by 3 m rooms, two rooms wide, into the observed mounded areas. The resulting figures were 141 rooms in the F-shaped room block, 30 rooms in one of the L-shaped mounds and 15 rooms in the other, for a total of 186. The large mound did not seem especially high, while the smaller ones appeared higher. However, lacking better data, I assume that all room blocks had only a single story.
Artifacts: Sherds are sparsely scattered around the site, with concentrations occurring near rodent holes and small erosional areas.
Ceramic Samples: Quantitative by Kintigh (3); diagnostic by Kintigh (3).
Temporal Placement: The 151 sherds in the three quantitative samples have Puerco Black-on-white (1%), Tularosa Black-on-white (1%), Heshotauthla types (9%), unidentified red ware (1%), Kwakina Polychrome (1%), Pinnawa Glaze-on-white (1%), Matsaki types (11%), unidentified buff ware (8%), gray ware (8%), buff corrugated (1%), black ware (42%), and Hawikuh types (1%). The diagnostic samples add Reserve Black-on-white, Pinedale Black-on-white, a Wingate type, St. Johns types, Pinnawa Red-on-white, Kechipawan Polychrome, Hopi buff ware, and historic Zuni ware.
    The quantitative sample has type proportions similar to the quantitative surface samples from Kyaki:ma and Mats'a:kya. While dating the start of occupation cannot be done accurately using surface evidence for a site with a long occupation such as Kwa'kin'a, it seems safest to assume that the habitation period is similar to that of Mats'a:kya, that is, during most of complexes H and I (starting about A.D. 1400).

43. Chalo:wa (Fig. 4.49)
(Tca'lowa, Chalowe)

Identification
Site Numbers: Spier 8, ZAP:AZ:15:H:17.
Bibliography: Fewkes (1891: 100–101), Mindeleff (1891: 83), Spier (1917: 221), Ferguson (1981a), Upham (1982).
Discussion: Mindeleff describes the site of Chalo:wa as a series of small ruins across the valley east of the large ruin Spier located. This confusion is discussed by Spier (1917: 225). Mindeleff's sites with this name probably include Achiya:Deyała, a ruin that is described above (site 31). Mindeleff indicates he was told that the ruins of Chalo:wa had been occupied at the time of Spanish contact. This statement probably refers to the large ruin discussed here, not the ruins identified by Mindeleff.

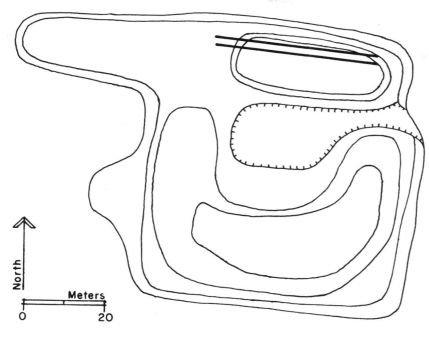

Figure 4.49. Chalo:wa. Mounded areas are indicated by arbitrary contours. Parallel heavy lines indicate walls.

Environmental Setting
Elevation: 1868 m (6130 feet).
Exposure: Open.
Landforms: Chalo:wa is located on a low knoll that drops off sharply to the east, south, and north, and more gradually to the west. It is on the floodplain of the Zuni River, which runs about 100 m to the east. To the west lies a row of hills. No nearby outcrops were noted.
Plant Communities: The ruin is in a desert scrub plant community, while the hills to the west are covered with a juniper-pinyon woodland.

Archaeological Remains
Architecture: The pueblo appears to be roughly rectangular (60 m by 64 m), somewhat rounded on the southwest and southeast corners, with two linear appendages on the western side, the larger of which has visible architecture. In contrast, Spier records the ruin as a circular mound, about 64 m in diameter, with a 37 m diameter depression in the center that I interpret as a plaza. The rubble mound is well buried so that it is difficult to determine the exact shape of the ruin. The rubble mound stands from 2 m to 4 m above the valley floor, and although it is evident that the pueblo lies on a natural hill, it is not clear how much of the elevation of the mound is due to the underlying landform and how much is a result of cultural activity. Architectural remains apparently are substantial and quite deep, although they are visible mainly in a few potholes on the site. Spier also found an earlier ruin a short distance away on the southwest part of the hill. A sherd scatter confirms this fact, but no architectural remains of this earlier ruin are visible.
Dimensions: 60 m by 64 m, rectangular.
Room Estimate: No accurate estimate of the number of rooms can be made because of the buried condition of the ruin. From my plan, it appears that about 2610 square meters of the main ruin are filled with rooms. Dividing by the 9 square meters per room seen at Hawikku (site 39), I estimate

a ground floor total of 290 rooms. Assuming a two-story pueblo, 435 rooms are estimated for the main ruin, to which 20 one-story rooms in the northern extension may be added for a total of 455 rooms.
Artifacts: Ceramics cover the mound. The western slope has a high percentage of earlier types while the remainder has predominately late types.
Ceramic Samples: Quantitative by Spier, Kintigh; excavated by Spier (2); diagnostic by Kintigh.
Temporal Placement: The two quantitative surface samples from the site show ceramic evidence of two temporal components. Spier's sample has 188 sherds and mine has 106 sherds; they are combined for the present analysis. The early component, located on the western slope of the mound, is dated by Puerco Black-on-white (1%), Reserve Black-on-white (0.3%), Tularosa Black-on-white (1%), Puerco Black-on-red (1%), Wingate types (1%), St. Johns types (1%), and gray ware (7%) to the time of transitional complex AB.

The remainder of the surface assemblage has Heshotauthla types (2%), unidentified red ware (4%), Salado polychromes (1%), Kwakina Polychrome (1%), Pinnawa Glaze-on-white (1%), Kechipawan Polychrome (1%), Matsaki types (6%), unidentified buff ware (5%), gray ware (as mentioned above, 7%), buff corrugated (0.3%), and black ware (61%). The ratio of black ware to gray ware (and buff corrugated) is 8.5:1. The diagnostic sample adds only two Hopi sherds and a single Hawikuh type sherd. This assemblage seems to indicate a relatively late occupation in complex H, slightly later than Mats'a:kya (site 40) Levels G and H.

Spier excavated two trenches in the site from which he selected random collections from specific depths. The larger of the two samples is from the trench on the southeast slope of the site, where 48 sherds were selected from depths between 28 inches (71 cm) and 52 inches (132 cm) beneath the surface. Along with 15 percent composed of earlier ceramics, the following were found: unidentified red ware (19%),

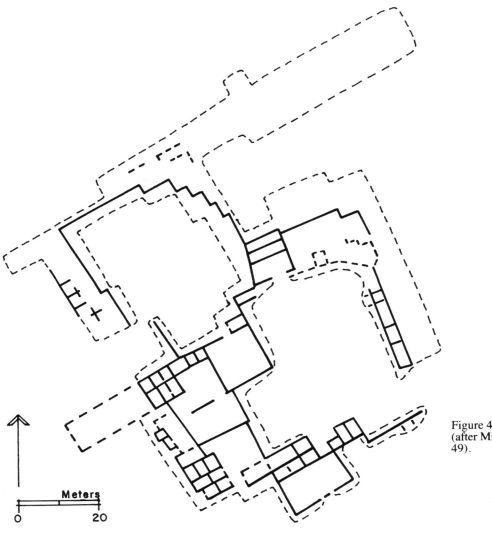

Figure 4.50.   Kechiba:wa (after Mindeleff 1891, plate 49).

Kwakina Polychrome (15%), Kechipawan Polychrome (2%), Matsaki types (4%), unidentified buff ware (2%), gray ware (10%), and black ware (29%). The black ware to gray ware ratio is 2.8:1 in this sample. (This figure is probably too low for the late occupation; it is lowered by the gray ware from the earlier component.) Although the sample is small, a complex H date, approximately contemporary with Mats'a:kya Levels G and H (about A.D. 1425), is suggested for the beginning of the later component.

Occupation of Chalo:wa ended some time near A.D. 1540. The available evidence is not sufficient to establish whether or not this site was occupied at the time of the Spanish entrada because we lack absolute dates for the ceramic changes involved. However, there is some historical evidence that this pueblo might be the "missing" seventh city. In Bandelier's mysterious references to Chyan-a-hue (1890a: 133, note 2; 1892a: 338–339), he seems to be talking about Kechiba:wa, although he mentions Kechiba:wa by name as a separate place in one of them. There is also the Zuni informant's report noted by Mindeleff that the pueblo was occupied at the time of Spanish contact.

If there was a seventh city, in addition to the six that are firmly established by Hodge (1937), the most likely candidate

seems to be Chalo:wa. The only other possibility is the site of Binna:wa. It was apparently abandoned before Chalo:wa, because it has substantially smaller proportions of buff ware in the excavated samples, and a lower black ware to gray ware ratio as well.

44. *Kechiba:wa* (Fig. 4.50)
(Kechipaun, Kechipauan, Kechipawan, Kettcippawa, Ketchipauan, K'ianawa, Kianawe)

Identification
Site Numbers: Spier 13, ZAP:NM:13:A:3, NM M:1:34(ASM).

Bibliography: Mindeleff (1891: 81–83, Plates 49–51), Fewkes (1891), Bandelier (1892a: 338–339), Spier (1917: 222), Hodge (1920a; 1937), Bushnell (1955), Kaemlein (1967), Ferguson (1981a), Upham (1982).

Discussion: The Hendricks-Hodge Expedition conducted excavations at Kechiba:wa from 1919 to 1923. A total of 90 rooms, including one kiva, and 100 inhumations and 66 cremations were excavated. The artifacts recovered were divided between the Museum of the American Indian, Heye Foundation, and the Cambridge University Museum of Archaeology and Ethnology (Kaemlein 1967). The field notes are also at Cambridge (Bushnell 1955: 568). Nusbaum apparently dug some trenches at an earlier date (Bushnell 1955: 568). Bandelier (1892a: 338) visited this ruin and refers to it as Chyan-a-hue. There is some confusion because in the same passage he discusses the site of Ketchip-a-uan, which he also describes as being near Hawikku. Kechiba:wa means, in Zuni, "gypsum place" (Eggan and Pandey 1979: 481) from the whiteish rock on which the pueblo was built.

Environmental Setting

Elevation: 1966 m (6450 feet).

Exposure: Open.

Landforms: Kechiba:wa is located on a knoll at the top of a mesa. The mesa drops off steeply about 75 m south of the ruin. To the west the mesa slopes down gradually, while to the northeast it slopes gradually uphill. The site of Hawikku, about 3 km to the west, is visible from Kechiba:wa. To the south, the site overlooks the irrigated agricultural lands in the area of the modern town of Ojo Caliente. There is a spring located at the bottom of the mesa about 750 m south of the ruin.

Plant Communities: The site is located in an area of plains grassland but is surrounded by a juniper-pinyon woodland.

Archaeological Remains

Architecture: Kechiba:wa has a rather complex shape that results from the composition of a number of room blocks that form two or three plazas. The rubble mounds are often quite high and distinct. The pueblo is built mainly of tan sandstone. Standing walls of a Spanish *visita*, established between 1629 and 1663, are located on the site. Mindeleff discusses a reservoir 110 feet (34 m) in diameter and 4 feet (1.2 m) deep. The reservoir was formed by a wall across a drainage near where it discharges over the edge of the mesa. Hodge reports trash deposits 7 feet (2 m) deep to the south of the ruin. Burials were found in the trash.

Dimensions: 100 m by 116 m, multiple room blocks.

Room Estimate: A precise room estimate for this site cannot be made. From Mindeleff's map, however, it appears that the area covered with rubble was about 3720 square meters. Using the figure of 7.9 square meters of rubble area per room developed for Hawikku (site 39), the estimate is 471 ground floor rooms. (Hawikku is contemporary to Kechiba:wa and also has a similar layout.) Assuming that one-half of the rooms were two story and that one-fourth were three story, the total estimate is 824 rooms.

Artifacts: The artifact scatter in the area of the rubble mounds is light. Two trash mounds (or possibly backdirt piles), one to the south and one to the northwest near major areas of architecture, had dense surface scatters.

Ceramic Samples: Quantitative by Spier, Kintigh (2); excavated by Spier (1); diagnostic by Kintigh (3).

Temporal Placement: Three quantitative samples and a single excavated sample from a depth of 42 inches (107 cm) to 54 inches (137 cm) below the surface are available. Spier's excavated sample has only 25 sherds and includes only Matsaki types (6 sherds) and black ware (11) in substantial numbers.

My surface samples were taken from trash heaps (or possibly backdirt piles from the excavations). The sample to the north showed a later assemblage with more buff ware and less gray ware. Combined, the two samples have 376 sherds

distributed mainly among the following: unidentified red ware (9%), Kwakina Polychrome (1%), Pinnawa Glaze-on-white (1%), Matsaki types (15%), unidentified buff ware (17%), gray ware (4%), and black ware (43%). The black ware to gray ware ratio is 11.5:1. Puerco Black-on-white (1%), St. Johns types (1%), a Heshotauthla type (0.3%), Hawikuh types (1%), and a historic Zuni ware (0.3%) also appear. This assemblage is notable for a high percentage of buff ware.

Spier's quantitative sample had 249 sherds distributed as follows: unidentified red ware (9%), Matsaki types (12%), unidentified buff ware (7%), gray ware (1%), black ware (48%), and Hawikuh types (5%). Also appearing are early white ware and red ware sherds (3%), Heshotauthla types (1%), Pinnawa Glaze-on-white (0.4%), Pinnawa Red-on-white (0.4%), Hopi buff ware (1%), and a Zuni ware (0.4%). The lower proportion of gray ware and higher proportion of Hawikuh types suggest a slightly later assemblage.

On the basis of surface evidence, the start of occupation cannot be placed precisely within the span of complex H. The surface assemblages appear to be similar to the quantitative collections from Hawikku, but somewhat later than those from Mats'a:kya, Kyaki:ma, and Kwa'kin'a (indicating a start about A.D. 1425). However, this may well have more to do with the intensity of occupation in the historic period than with the start of occupation.

45. *Halona:wa North*

Identification

Site Numbers: ZAP:NM:12:K3:1.

Bibliography: Mindeleff (1891: 97–99, Plate 76), Spier (1917: 228–229), Kroeber (1916: 12–13; 1917), Caywood (1972), Ferguson (1981a), Ferguson and Mills (1982), Upham (1982).

Discussion: The site referred to as Halona:wa North (see the discussion under Halona:wa South, site 26) is the prehistoric ruin underlying the modern pueblo of Zuni. No major archaeological work has been done at Zuni Pueblo, although Spier dug several stratigraphic trenches within the pueblo. In addition, Louis Caywood did extensive archaeological work in the immediate vicinity of the Catholic mission at Zuni, adjacent to the old pueblo. Modern construction and excavation of water and sewer line trenches have yielded additional archaeological materials. Excellent maps of the late 19th and 20th century pueblo are given by Mindeleff, Kroeber (1917, Map 6), and most recently by Ferguson and Mills. It may be noted that the scale for Mindeleff's large map was computed by Kroeber (1917: 190) as 43 feet to the inch (1:516).

Environmental Setting

Elevation: 1920 m (6300 feet).

Exposure: Open.

Landforms: Halona:wa North is on a knoll just north of the Zuni River and is essentially surrounded by the floodplain.

Plant Communities: The site is located in an area of plains grassland. Until recently, substantial agriculture was carried out in the immediate vicinity of the site.

Archaeological Remains

Architecture: The prehistoric pueblo of Zuni is completely buried by the modern village. Some of the walls of the prehistoric ruin may have been used in the modern pueblo (as illustrated by Mindeleff). However, it is difficult to determine from available archaeological evidence what the size of the prehistoric village was.

Dimensions: Not available.

Room Estimate: The size of Halona:wa North cannot be estimated from available archaeological data. Historic data, discussed in Chapter 5, indicate a size of about 200 rooms.

Artifacts: Because of the intensive modern occupation of the area, prehistoric sherds generally are not present on the surface.

Ceramic Samples: Excavated by Spier (14).

Temporal Placement: Caywood (1972) reports 24 tree-ring dates from Halona:wa North, mostly from his work on the restoration of the mission. The dates form four broad clusters from A.D. 1478 to 1549, 1591 to 1700, 1841 to 1856, and 1883 to 1900. The first mission at Halona:wa appears to have started in 1630 (Caywood 1972: 7) and the history of the present mission started around 1700 (Caywood 1972: 14). Therefore, all the wood from the early cluster and much from the next cluster is probably reused wood from the pueblo, suggesting occupation in the immediate area started at least by the late 1400s.

Spier recovered 422 sherds from his 14–level trench M in a plaza of modern Zuni pueblo. The top six levels are almost entirely composed of historic Zuni types and black ware and date to complex J. In the next two levels the glazed Hawikuh types appear, indicating a complex I assemblage. Thus, the top eight levels seem to date to the post–1630 occupation. In these levels (274 sherds), the major ceramics are black ware (60%) and Zuni types (20%). The only other types with more than two sherds are Matsaki (1%, 3 sherds) and Hawikuh (1%, 3 sherds).

The next four levels down (I through L), with 87 sherds, appear to be fairly similar to one another in terms of chronological indicators. They contain Kwakina Polychrome (6%), Pinnawa Glaze-on-white (6%), Matsaki types (10%), gray ware (13%), and black ware (32%). Several other types, notably Kechipawan Polychrome (1%), appear in quantities of three sherds or less. Others are Red Mesa Black-on-white (1%), Puerco Black-on-white (1%), Tularosa Black-on-white (2%), Wingate types (3%), St. Johns types (2%), Pinnawa Red-on-white (1%), and an historic Zuni type (1%). Notable is the absence of Heshotauthla types. These four levels seem to be indicative of an occupation fairly early in complex H, considering the percentages of gray ware and Matsaki types.

The two deepest levels (M and N, with 61 sherds) have only Heshotauthla types (15%), gray ware (48%), and an anomalous presence of black ware (8%). These levels date the occupation to the time of complex E, indicating a substantial temporal gap with the levels just above.

The chronological sequence revealed in this trench shows two discontinuities. First, it is not possible to connect the early complex H deposits with the complex I deposits, probably a hundred years or more later. However, another of Spier's trenches that was analyzed by Barbara Mills does seem to fill this gap. She has generously provided me with these data. The top five levels of that trench (72 sherds) apparently date to the post–1680 complex J; the dominant

ceramics represented are historic Zuni ware (50%, plus 22% plain red that is probably also historic Zuni), along with black ware (18%) and gray ware (6%). The next three levels (38 sherds) seem to show a chronological break with a dramatic increase in black ware (53%) and decrease in Zuni ware (3%, 1 sherd). Heshotauthla types (5%), Matsaki types (8%), and gray ware (8%) are also found. These levels are difficult to place, but appear to date sometime in complex H.

The deepest four levels in the trench Mills analyzed, with 221 sherds, clearly date to mid-complex H, as indicated by the percentages of the Matsaki types and black ware. Matsaki types (24%) are the dominant decorated types, with only small quantities of Heshotauthla types (2%), Kwakina Polychrome (2%), Salado polychromes (1%), Pinnawa Glaze-on-white (3%), and Kechipawan Polychrome (2%). Black ware makes up most of the remainder of the assemblage (53%), along with historic Zuni ware (2%). These levels seem to fill the later gap in the sequence between early complex H and complex I that appeared in the trench I analyzed.

The tabulation of the decorated pottery from levels 2 through 9 of a test pit made by Caywood (1972, Fig. 3) provides information regarding the earlier discontinuity in Spier's trench, between complexes E and H. We are missing the assemblages expected for complexes F and G, in which we would expect Heshotauthla types with glazed white ware but without Matsaki buff ware types. In his tabulation of Level 10, Caywood lists Pinnawa Polychrome, Kwakina Polychrome, Heshotauthla Polychrome, Gila Polychrome, and culinary corrugated. Taken at face value, this suggests a complex E assemblage. However, since Pinnawa Polychrome is an obsolete pottery type name for a rare variant of Kwakina, it may be that Pinnawa Glaze-on-white was intended, because this type was not included in the figure. If this is the case, Level 10 would date to complex F. Levels 7 and 9 (Level 8 has no sherds indicated) appear to date to complex G, because in addition to the types in Level 10, Kechipawan Polychrome appears in substantial quantities. Levels 5 and 6 indicate a complex H date, since Matsaki types are added to the aforementioned inventory. Levels 2 through 4 have such small quantities of sherds that they are not useful chronological indicators.

Thus, while the evidence is not conclusive, it appears that the area may well have been occupied continuously from the time of the complex D occupation of Halona:wa South (before A.D. 1300) up to the historic period. Indeed, with the exception of a brief period after the Pueblo revolt of 1680, it has been occupied up to the present day. However, it is also possible that the area was repeatedly occupied during this period, resulting in the characteristically discontinuous stratigraphic sections analyzed. Relying on Spier's data from the pueblo itself, I will assume the major occupation started somewhat later (about A.D. 1425) than at Mats'a:kya. (In terms of proportions of Matsaki types and gray ware, Levels C and H at Mats'a:kya are similar to Levels I through L in Spier's Trench M at Halona:wa North.) The archaeological evidence seems fairly strong for a continuous occupation from complex H up to the historic period. Historical evidence indicates that Halona:wa was occupied from 1540 to 1680 and then reoccupied from about 1693 to the present. Thus, the archaeological evidence clearly places contact-period Halona:wa on the north side of the Zuni River.

5. EVALUATION OF SITE DATING AND SITE SIZE ESTIMATES

In discussing the 45 sites under consideration (Chapter 4), I paid particular attention to estimates of site size and to approximations of the occupation span based on the ceramic complexes developed in Chapter 3. Before these data are summarized to yield a demographic picture of the Zuni area for the period A.D. 1250 to 1540, some of the chronological assignments made are compared with interpretations by other archaeologists and some refinements are suggested. Site size estimates for the historic pueblos are compared with historical accounts and certain discrepancies are discussed.

COMPARISON OF EL MORRO VALLEY CHRONOLOGIES

Seriation by William Marquardt

Excavation units from six of the sites in the El Morro Valley were also seriated by Marquardt (1974). In his analysis, Marquardt used factor analysis to order excavated collection units chronologically, based on their values on several temporally sensitive ceramic indices such as the red ware to white ware ratio and the mean exterior white line width. Marquardt's (1974: 166–171) conclusions about the relative sequence of sites do not differ drastically from those developed by the techniques used here. However, because his conclusions are based on more data and on a more refined analysis, it seems worthwhile to revise the relative dating of these sites based on his seriation. The sites considered by Marquardt are: Scribe S, Mirabal, Tinaja, Cienega, Pueblo de los Muertos, and Atsinna.

The results of the chronological analysis presented in Chapter 4 for these El Morro Valley sites are graphically presented in Table 5.1. The revisions to this analysis suggested by Marquardt's work are presented in Table 5.2. Marquardt's results concur in several respects with the conclusions reached in Chapter 4. In both analyses, the Scribe S Site dates early in the sequence and overlaps with the occupation of the Mirabal Ruin. In both analyses, Tinaja Ruin overlaps with the Cienega Site and Pueblo de los Muertos. In both cases, Pueblo de los Muertos and the Cienega Site are basically contemporaneous, and the site of Atsinna overlaps these two sites in time but also continues to be occupied later.

The major revisions suggested by Marquardt's analysis involve the Tinaja and Mirabal ruins. Marquardt's analysis indicates that the Mirabal Ruin started its occupation later and ended later. The Tinaja Ruin appears to have started and ended earlier in Marquardt's scheme. Although Marquardt's results indicate that the occupation of Atsinna began later than the occupation of Pueblo de los Muertos and Cienega,

his sample from Atsinna was limited, and a contemporaneous starting date is maintained for the purposes of this study.

Considering the fact that Marquardt was dealing with a much shorter time period, with much better understood ceramic changes, and with a fairly large number of excavated collections, the extent of the agreement between his and my analyses is encouraging support of the more inductive technique used here. Marquardt's analysis, like the one I have presented, does not allow the determination of absolute dates for most of these sites.

Absolute Dating of the El Morro Sequence

Absolute dates corresponding to this sequence are not well established. Only the Scribe S Site has been well dated with tree-rings: the main construction occurred in the years from A.D. 1250 to 1275 (Watson and others 1980: 205). Based on a lack of tree-ring dates postdating 1288, Watson and others (who accept Marquardt's sequence) believe that the occupation of the El Morro Valley ended in the early 1300s. However, there are only a few cutting dates from the five later sites analyzed. Fourteen are shown by Watson and others; they recognize the difficulty of reconciling the amount of deposition at the later sites with the tree-ring data (Watson and others 1980: 212–213), and indicate that the absolute time span may be left an open question.

The interpretation suggested here uses essentially the same relative sequence, but extends the absolute time range to late in the 1300s. Part of the difference in these two interpretations rests on my identification of Pinnawa Glaze-on-white from Pueblo de los Muertos, the Cienega Site, and Atsinna, and my acceptance of Woodbury's report of Pinnawa Glaze-on-white and Kechipawan Polychrome from Atsinna. Watson and others (1980: 213–214) indicate that no Pinnawa Glaze-on-white or Kechipawan was found in their work at these sites. However, my analysis of their material (as well as Spier's collections) from these sites did reveal significant (but small) quantities of Pinnawa Glaze-on-white in excavated and surface contexts. It seems likely that the small quantities of these sherds were interpreted as odd pieces of Tularosa or Pinedale Black-on-white pottery.

Although no Kechipawan Polychrome turned up in my analysis of Atsinna ceramics, I see no reason to doubt Woodbury's identification. Considering that Pinnawa Glaze-on-white was found in floor contexts at Atsinna (for example, in Woodbury's Room 12), and that the overwhelming majority of the material that Woodbury worked with was from excavated contexts, the suggestion of Watson and others that the presence of this type is due to postabandonment deposition

TABLE 5.1
**Occupation Spans of El Morro Valley Pueblos
Based on Ceramic Chronology**

No.	Site	Approximate Year A.D.					
		1200	1300	1400	1500	1600	1700
10.	Scribe S		— — —				
21.	Mirabal Ruin		— — —				
19.	Tinaja		— — ǀ —				
27.	Cienega		· ǀ — — — — —				
29.	Pueblo de los Muertos		· · ǀ — — — — — —				
30.	Atsinna		· · ǀ — — — — — — —				

Ceramic Complex: A | AB | B | C | D | E | DE | F | G | H | H | H | I | J

Note: — — = major occupation, · · = minor occupation.

TABLE 5.2
**Occupation Spans of El Morro Valley Pueblos
Revision Based on Marquardt (1974)**

No.	Site	Approximate Year A.D.					
		1200	1300	1400	1500	1600	1700
10.	Scribe S		— — —				
21.	Mirabal Ruin		— — ǀ — —				
19.	Tinaja		— — — —				
27.	Cienega		· · ǀ — — — — —				
29.	Pueblo de los Muertos		· · ǀ — — — — —				
30.	Atsinna		· ǀ — — — — — —				

Ceramic Complex: A | AB | B | C | D | E | DE | F | G | H | H | H | I | J

Note: — — = major occupation, · · = minor occupation.

must be rejected. It must be recalled that both Pinnawa Glaze-on-white and Kechipawan Polychrome were types that *never* made up large fractions of an assemblage, even in the period when they undoubtedly were manufactured.

Finally, in this connection, Watson and others note Spier's identification of buff ware at these sites. This identification is a result of an error in his Table I (Spier 1917: 261–262). For sites 140, 146, 149, and 161 all of the columns of percentages except corrugated should be transposed one column to the right. In addition, in his Table I the sample labeled as being from site 152 is actually from 149, Atsinna. These corrections correspond to the discussion in Spier's text and to the same data retabulated elsewhere in the monograph. With these corrections, the anomalous presence of buff ware and black ware is eliminated and the mysterious apparent absence of red ware is explained. Once these corrections are made, only a single buff ware sherd is reported by Spier, from the highest level of the trench at the Lookout Site. (My reanalysis identified buff ware in the diagnostic collections made by both Spier and CARP at this site.) Watson and others were aware of this mistake in Spier's report with reference to the problem of black ware (discussed in their footnote 23), but they apparently failed to recognize its significance with respect to buff ware.

The results of tree-ring dating of 15 additional samples from Atsinna, obtained after the ceramic analysis had been completed, lend strong support to the conclusion that the El Morro Valley was occupied well into the 14th century. Most of these samples date between A.D. 1260 and 1320, and six of them date *after* 1288, which is the latest date obtained in the more than 200 dated samples excavated by CARP in the El Morro Valley (Watson and others 1980: 207). Most importantly, one sample dates to 1349, demonstrating that the occupation of Atsinna lasted at least until 1350, and supporting the more general argument for a later occupation of the Valley.

SUMMARY AND EVALUATION OF THE CHRONOLOGY OF SITES

The relative sequence of the El Morro Valley sites developed here agrees reasonably well with the results of Marquardt's more detailed analysis. Based on Marquardt's study, the relative sequence of the El Morro Valley sites has been revised with respect to the dating of the Tinaja and Mirabal ruins. In contrast to the argument presented by Watson and others that the occupation of the El Morro Valley ends very early in the 1300s, I argue that the occupation lasts

TABLE 5.3
Occupation Spans of Late Prehistoric Zuni Pueblos

No.	Site	Rooms	Approximate Year A.D. 1200	1300	1400	1500	1600	1700
1.	Spier 81	43						
2.	Miller Ranch Ruin	60.						
3.	Spier 61	122						
4.	Upper Deracho Ruin	30						
5.	Vogt Ranch Ruin	39						
6.	Kay Chee Ruin	255						
7.	Pettit Site	125						
8.	Pescado Canyon Ruin	723						
9.	Lower Deracho Ruin	609						
10.	Scribe S Site	410						
11.	Heshoda Yala:wa	150						
12.	Box S Ruin	473						
13.	Shoemaker Ranch Ruin	17						
14.	Day Ranch Ruin	574						
15.	Lookout Site	300						
16.	Jack's Lake Ruin	245						
17.	Archeotekopa II	1412						
18.	Fort Site	216						
19.	Tinaja Ruin	163						
20.	Kluckhohn Ruin	1142						
21.	Mirabal Ruin	743						
22.	Yellowhouse	425						
23.	Ramah School House Ruin	186						
24.	North Atsinna Ruin	180						
25.	Upper Nutria Village	180						
26.	Halona:wa South	375						
27.	Cienega Site	500						
28.	Upper Pescado Ruin	405						
29.	Pueblo de los Muertos	880						
30.	Atsinna	875						
31.	Achiya:Deyala	5						
32.	Lower Pescado Village	420						
33.	Pescado West Ruin	445						
34.	Lower Pescado Ruin	180						
35.	Heshot ula	875						
36.	Rainbow Spring Ruin	108						
37.	Hambassa:wa	39						
38.	Binna:wa	168						
39.	Hawikku	800						
40.	Mats'a:kya	901						
41.	Kyaki:ma	250						
42.	Kwa'kin'a	186						
43.	Chalo:wa	455						
44.	Kechiba:wa	824						
45.	Halona:wa North	200						

Ceramic Complex: A | AB | B | C | D | DE | E | F | G | H | H | H | I | J

Note: — = major occupation, · · = minor occupation.

until the middle or late 1300s. This conclusion is based on different identifications of the ceramic types present and on additional tree-ring dates from Atsinna.

The sequence of site occupations for the Zuni area derived in Chapter 4 and revised slightly in this chapter is summarized in Table 5.3. In this table, the number of rooms in each site is listed, and the occupation span is plotted with respect to the ceramic complexes developed in Chapter 3. From this figure the period of occupation of each site may be compared with the occupation spans of the other sites and demographic trends over time may be inferred.

Some caution must be exercised in evaluating this figure. The absolute dates are tentative because few data exist to date accurately most of the ceramic transitions of interest here. Beyond that, Table 5.3 suggests a degree of definiteness and a precision that are not completely warranted by the data and their analysis. In most cases, site ending dates (with respect to the ceramic complexes) are more reliable than the starting

TABLE 5.4
Estimates of the Sizes of Historic Zuni Villages

No.	Village	Archaeological Data		Historical Data (A.D. 1581)		
		No. of rooms	No. of houses[1]	No. of houses[2]	No. of stories[2]	No. of rooms[3]
41.	Kyaki:ma	250	59	75	2 and 3	600
40.	Mats'a:kya	901	212	100	4 and 5	800
45.	Halona:wa North			44	3 and 4	352
42.	Kwa'kin'a	186	44	60	3 and 4	480
43.	Chalo:wa (?)	455	107			
39.	Hawikku	800	188	118	3 and 4	944
44.	Kechiba:wa	824	194	40	3 and 4	320

1. Obtained by dividing the number of rooms by 4.25 (see the text for the derivation of this estimate).
2. Derived from Hodge's (1937: 61) presentation of Martín de Pedrosa's account of the Rodriguez–Chamuscado expedition, 1581.
3. Obtained by multiplying the number of houses by 8; Gallegos states (Hodge 1937: 61) that there were at least 8 rooms per house.

dates. Most ending dates rely on the absence of later types, whereas the starting dates usually rely on a judgement of the significance of an assortment of earlier types present. In addition, as most dating determinations are made on the basis of surface collections, the earlier material is generally less visible and more difficult to evaluate.

HISTORICAL ACCOUNTS OF VILLAGE SIZES

In Chapter 4, the number of rooms in the historic towns is estimated on the basis of meager archaeological evidence. The archaeological site size estimates derived are given in Table 5.4. Because of the overburden and the deteriorated condition of most of these sites, it may be useful to compare the archaeologically estimated sizes with the contact-period historical accounts. These accounts are discussed in more detail by Hodge (1937: 60–61), Bandelier (1892b: 36–43), and Winship (1896).

Based on ethnographic and archaeological evidence, the historical accounts of the number of stories in these villages do not appear to be accurate. The villages reportedly had two to seven stories, an appearance that probably was due partly to the natural contours underlying the pueblos and partly to the fact that the number of different roof terraces was not the same as the number of stories. While there may easily be seven observably distinct roof levels in modern Zuni, there are probably no more than three stories in any one place (see Ferguson and Mills 1982).

The earliest report on village sizes comes from Mendoza, writing in 1540. His is not a firsthand observation, but rather is a report based on information Diaz obtained from Indian informants who had been to Zuni. The report states that there were seven places, a short day's march from one another. Three of the towns were very large and four not so big (Hodge 1937: 47–48). If we assume that Halona:wa North was not one of the large pueblos, then the estimates presented here conform with Mendoza's report (three have 800 or more rooms and three have 455 or fewer rooms).

Coronado, writing a firsthand report in 1540, says that Hawikku had about 200 houses with a total of about 500 families (Hodge 1937: 49–50). A nearby town is larger, another is about the same size, and the other four are smaller.

In this case the nearby town is almost certainly Kechiba:wa. Again this account conforms with our data.

More definite information comes from the *Relación Postrera de Sivola,* derived from the 1540 expedition. Three of the villages, including Hawikku, are said to have about 200 houses, the remainder "somewhere between sixty and fifty and thirty houses" (Hodge 1937: 51–52). If we take the archaeological room counts of the three largest sites (which average 842 rooms) as indicative of 200 historic houses, it may be inferred that the number of rooms per house is about 4.25. Applying this figure to the other three sites for which we have room estimates, we can obtain comparable house estimates. As may be seen in Table 5.4, these estimates correspond reasonably well with the size range of thirty to sixty houses. However, if Chalo:wa is one of the seven towns, it was perhaps substantially smaller in 1540 than our estimate of 455 rooms. From this analysis, Halona:wa North may be inferred to have between 128 and 255 rooms, because it was reported to have between 30 and 60 houses.

On the other hand, the *Relación del Suceso,* also describing the 1540 expedition, reports (Hodge 1937: 52–53) that:

> The villages have from one hundred and fifty to two hundred and three hundred houses; some have the houses of the village all together, although in some villages they are divided into two or three sections [room blocks], but for the most part they are all together, and their courtyards [plazas] are within, and in these are their hot rooms [kivas], and they have their summer ones outside the villages.

Castañeda, writing many years later about Coronado's expedition, reports that Mats'a:kya was the largest village (Hodge 1937: 53–55), an observation that corresponds well with the archaeological estimates given in Chapter 4 and Table 5.4. Through reports of the 1540 expedition, three large villages have been identified by name or had their identity strongly implied in the historical accounts: Hawikku, Kechiba:wa, and Mats'a:kya.

Gallegos' relación of the 1581 Rodriguez-Chamuscado Expedition, written in 1582, names five of the six then-occupied towns. An appendix to this relación by Martín de Pedrosa gives six village names and village sizes. Gallegos

TABLE 5.5
Size, Room Area, and Estimated Population of Zuni Pueblos

No.	Site	Rooms	Total Room Area[1] in square meters	Average Room Area in square meters	Estimated Population[2]
1.	Spier 81	43	293	7.5	56
2.	Miller Ranch Ruin	60	540	9.0	78
3.	Spier 61	122	1366	11.2	159
4.	Upper Deracho Ruin	30	261	8.7	39
5.	Vogt Ranch Ruin	39	341	8.8	51
6.	Kay Chee Ruin	255	1415	8.3	332
7.	Pettit Site	125		7.2	163
8.	Pescado Canyon Ruin	723	3304	8.0	940
9.	Lower Deracho Ruin	609	2504	7.2	792
10.	Scribe S Site	410			533
11.	Heshoda Yala:wa	150	1365	9.1	195
12.	Box S Ruin	473	3804	14.1	615
13.	Shoemaker Ranch Ruin	17			22
14.	Day Ranch Ruin	574	3284		746
15.	Lookout Site	300	1615	8.0	390
16.	Jack's Lake Ruin	245	1400	10.0	319
17.	Archeotekopa II	1412	8072		1836
18.	Fort Site	216	1673	13.6	281
19.	Tinaja Ruin	163	1537	9.4	212
20.	Kluckhohn Ruin	1142	7614		1485
21.	Mirabal Ruin	743	4354	8.8	966
22.	Yellowhouse	425	2522	10.4	553
23.	Ramah School House Ruin	186	1143	9.0	242
24.	North Atsinna Ruin	180			234
25.	Upper Nutria Village	180			234
26.	Halona:wa South	375			488
27.	Cienega Site	500			650
28.	Upper Pescado Ruin	405	2700		527
29.	Pueblo de los Muertos	880	3266	6.4	1144
30.	Atsinna	875		9.3	1138
31.	Achiya:Deyała	5			7
32.	Lower Pescado Village	420			546
33.	Pescado West Ruin	445	2540		579
34.	Lower Pescado Ruin	180	1200		234
35.	Heshot uła	875	5634	10.6	1138
36.	Rainbow Spring Ruin	108	917	8.5	140
37.	Hambassa:wa	39	296		51
38.	Binna:wa	168	1764		218
39.	Hawikku	800	3609*	8.6	1040
40.	Mats'a:kya	901	4072*		1171
41.	Kyaki:ma	250	1972*		325
42.	Kwa'kin'a	186	1507	8.1	242
43.	Chalo:wa	455	4095		592
44.	Kechiba:wa	824	3720*		1071
45.	Halona:wa North	200			260

1. Rubble area rather than room area indicated by *.
2. Assumes 65 percent of rooms occupied and two persons per room (see Chapter 4).

notes that: "There is not a house of two or three stories that does not have eight rooms or more" (Hodge 1937: 61). Using the modern equivalent names determined by Hodge, this list is presented in the third column of Table 5.4 (Hodge 1937: 58–61), along with an estimate of the historic village size in rooms obtained by multiplying the number of houses by eight.

The information provided by Gallegos and Martín de Pedrosa does not correspond well to either the archaeological evidence or to the earlier historical evidence. Hawikku and Mats'a:kya are still considered the largest sites, but not by nearly as large a margin as in the 1540 accounts, and Kechiba:wa is reported as small, with 40 houses. Of these six sites, Kechiba:wa and Kwa'kin'a, with 60 houses, are the only ruins (other than Hawikku) where the character of the archaeological remains can be determined with reasonable accuracy. There is no question that Kechiba:wa is several times the size of Kwa'kin'a. We must conclude that the relación is reporting erroneous information; that Kechiba:wa was largely abandoned by 1582, having been much larger in 1540; or that the early accounts were wrong and that Kechiba:wa grew much larger after 1581. The first two suggestions seem to be the most likely in this case.

Summary of Site Size Comparison

From all these accounts, the conclusion drawn is that the archaeological data seem to compare well with the early historical accounts. The data do not strongly suggest modifying any of the site size estimates. All accounts seem to agree that Halona:wa was a reasonably small village. Because no reliable archaeological data are available, an estimate of 200 rooms (between the 128 and 255 rooms suggested by the 1540 accounts) will be used for Halona:wa North in the demographic reconstruction presented below.

Site size information is compiled and presented in Table 5.5. Sites are presented in chronological order from early to late occupation periods. The table lists the number of rooms and, where available, the total area covered with rooms and an average room area. Average or typical room areas are derived from reports of room size, or from measurements on the ground or from maps. Usually the sample on which this estimate is based is not adequate to derive additional descriptive statistics or to calculate a meaningful standard deviation. At sites where a room size based on other data has been assumed (for example, Day Ranch), no room size figure is listed. Populations for each of the sites are estimated by assuming (as described in Chapter 3) that 65 percent of the rooms were occupied at any one time, and that each of the occupied rooms had two inhabitants. Although some of the room size data in this table are of dubious accuracy, it appears that the sizes of rooms ranged from 6.4 to 13.6 square meters, but that there were no clearcut trends in changing room size over time.

6. DESCRIPTIVE SUMMARY OF SETTLEMENT PATTERNS

The purpose of this review is to present synchronic and diachronic descriptive summaries of the corpus of data contained in the previous two chapters. First, the data for the period represented by each ceramic complex are summarized. For each period, the sites occupied are discussed with respect to their general location, topographic situation, architectural layout, and size, as indicated by the number of rooms. Second, the obvious changes in these settlement pattern variables through time are discussed with reference to tabular and graphical displays of the settlement information.

SYNCHRONIC SUMMARY OF SETTLEMENT PATTERNS

Through the analyses of Chapters 4 and 5, a refined chronology of late prehistoric Zuni area sites has been developed. The three centuries considered here were divided into a series of periods, each of which is identified by a ceramic assemblage indicative of a ceramic complex. Each ceramic complex, in turn, is divided into two or more temporal intervals that represent the smallest increments of time that are resolved in this study. For the purposes of summarizing the data, the periods indicated by each ceramic complex are discussed separately, but the settlement changes that occur within a complex are not discussed in detail. However, in order to avoid the problem of overestimated maps (Ammerman 1981: 77) in which an artificially high site density is implied, all maps in this chapter show a set of sites that were occupied at the *same* time (that is, during a single minimal time increment), not all the sites that were occupied at *some* time during that ceramic complex. (Figure 4.1 provides a map of all site locations.)

Ceramic Complexes AB and B
(A.D. 1175–1250)

The sample of sites chosen for this study was designed to include all the large, planned pueblos and all sites with Springerville Polychrome or later types (complex C or later). Several smaller and earlier sites (dating to complexes AB and B) were included in order to provide comparative data for the early end of the period under consideration. Of the many small pueblos in the area that are known to date to complex AB, only two are included in this study: Spier 81 and Miller Ranch Ruin. For complex B, five small pueblos were added: Upper Deracho Ruin, Vogt Ranch Ruin, the Pettit Site, the Scribe S Site (which was a series of small pueblos), and Shoemaker Ranch Ruin. Six large, presumably planned villages apparently began their occupation during complex B: Spier 61, Kay Chee Ruin, Pescado Canyon Ruin, Lower Deracho Ruin, Heshoda Yala:wa, and the Box S Ruin. Figure 6.1 shows the locations of these pueblos (all of which were occupied at the end of complex B).

Considering the conclusions of other investigators, it was somewhat surprising to see that the large, plaza-oriented pueblos made their first appearance during complex B, rather than in complex C (containing Springerville Polychrome and Pinedale Black-on-white) or, more likely, complex D (Kwakina Polychrome). Of these six large pueblos, the occupations of the last four mentioned extended into the next period (that is, they have Springerville Polychrome or Pinedale Black-on-white), and could conceivably have started in complex C rather than in complex B. However, the occupation periods of the first two pueblos appear to have been restricted to complex B. Even if the absence of Springerville Polychrome at Spier 61 and at the Kay Chee Ruin were discounted and the starting date of all the large pueblos was in complex C, the appearance of these large pueblos is still earlier than archaeologists had thought previously.

The smaller sites in this group are typical of the larger Pueblo III ruins in the area, with linear, C- or L-shaped, or irregular arrangements of rooms, usually with less than fifty rooms in a room block. These seven pueblos were in the eastern half of the study area, and three (Scribe S, Upper Deracho, and the Pettit Site) were in the immediate vicinity of later large sites. Vogt Ranch Ruin and Spier 81 were on the valley floor at the base of a mesa; Scribe S and Miller Ranch Ruin were on ridges that extend onto valley floors; Upper Deracho was on a mesa slope; Shoemaker Ranch was on a mesa top; and the Pettit Site was both on the top and at the base of a butte.

Four of the larger pueblos were more or less rectangular (Spier 61, Kay Chee, Box S, and Heshoda Yala:wa), one was oval (Lower Deracho), and one had an irregular plan (Pescado Canyon Ruin). However, it is possible that in some of these pueblos the earliest occupation was not associated with the architecture that is now visible. Although these large sites are concentrated in the eastern half of the study area, a diversity of topographic settings was utilized. The Pescado Canyon Ruin was built on top of a mesa, and Heshoda Yala:wa was placed on a bluff overlooking the Zuni River, while the other pueblos were located on or near good-sized expanses of bottomland.

Ceramic Complex C
(A.D. 1250–1275)

The distribution of the 15 pueblos occupied at the end of complex C is shown in Figure 6.2 (all pueblos that were occupied at any time in complex C were still occupied at the

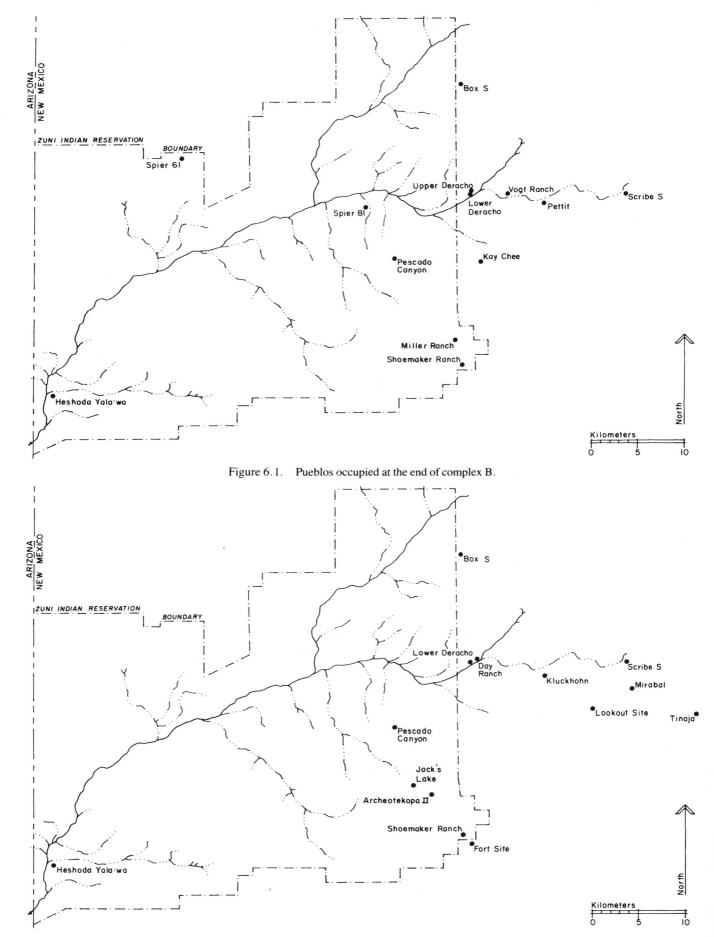

Figure 6.1. Pueblos occupied at the end of complex B.

Figure 6.2. Pueblos occupied at the end of complex C.

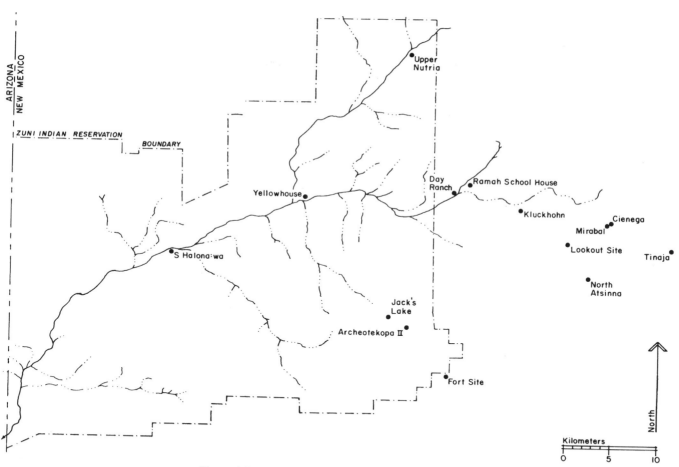

Figure 6.3. Pueblos occupied at the end of complex D.

end of the complex). Dating to complex C are three small sites (the Pettit Site, Scribe S, and Shoemaker Ranch) and twelve large sites (Pescado Canyon, Lower Deracho, Heshoda Yala:wa, Box S, Day Ranch, Lookout, Jack's Lake, Archeotekopa II, Fort Site, Tinaja, Kluckhohn, and Mirabal). Few other known sites in the study area date to this time interval, and it is likely that by its end virtually the entire population of the area lived in large pueblos.

Of the dozen large pueblos, four were round or oval (Lower Deracho, Day Ranch, Mirabal, and Jack's Lake), four were roughly rectangular (Box S, Heshoda Yala:wa, the Fort Site, and the Lookout Site), two were composite square and round (Kluckhohn and Archeotekopa II), and two had irregular plans (Pescado Canyon and Tinaja). It is clear from this that the rectangular and oval architectural forms were contemporaneous, and that the occupation of the only two composite square and round pueblos began at about the same time.

These 14 pueblos were spread out over the eastern half of the study area, much like the preceding period. Only one site, Heshoda Yala:wa, was in the southwest corner of this region, and the entire northwest section of the study area was unoccupied from this period until the refuge period in historic times. Four of these pueblos were built on the tops of mesas (Pescado Canyon, the Fort Site, Shoemaker Ranch, and the Lookout Site) and appear to be in defensible positions with a commanding view of at least some directions. Jack's Lake and Archeotekopa II were in the high valleys, but were not in particularly defensible locations. Heshoda Yala:wa was on a

butte overlooking the Zuni River, and Tinaja occupied both bottomland and the top of a small butte. The Scribe S Site was on a ridge extending into the El Morro Valley, and Lower Deracho, Box S, Day Ranch, Kluckhohn, and Mirabal were all on bottomland, either at the base of a mesa or out on a valley floor.

Ceramic Complex D
(A.D. 1275–1300)

The 17 villages occupied during complex D include only one small site, Shoemaker Ranch. The distribution of pueblos at the end of complex D is shown in Figure 6.3. During this period, as with the previous one, the population was concentrated in the eastern portion of the study area. In addition, during complex D there was an expansion to the west, down the Zuni River Valley to Yellowhouse and Halona:wa South. Heshoda Yala:wa, Shoemaker Ranch, and Box S were apparently abandoned some time during complex D (and therefore are not shown on the map), and there was no new occupation of the extreme southwest corner of the study area during this time interval. However, Upper Nutria Village replaced Box S in the north-central portion of the area.

As with the previous complexes, both mesa top and bottomland locations were used. The only small pueblo (Shoemaker Ranch) and three of the large ones were on mesa tops (North Atsinna, Fort Site, and the Lookout Site). Two pueblos were in high valleys (Jack's Lake and Archeotekopa II), one (Tinaja) was both on bottomland and on top of a small butte, one was on a bluff overlooking the Zuni River

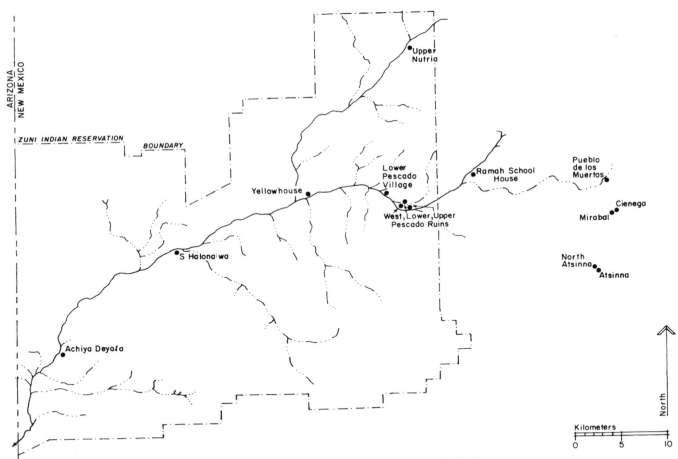

Figure 6.4.   Pueblos occupied at the end of complex DE.

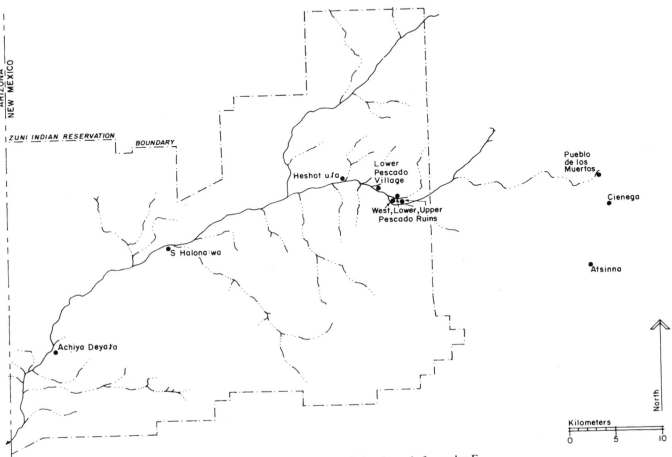

Figure 6.5.   Pueblos occupied at the end of complex E.

(Heshoda Yala:wa), and the remainder were on bottomland (Box S, Day Ranch, Kluckhohn, Mirabal, Yellowhouse, Ramah School House, Upper Nutria Village, Halona:wa South, and Cienega).

Four pueblos had round or oval outlines (Day Ranch, Cienega, Mirabal, and Jack's Lake); eight had approximately rectangular outlines (Box S, Heshoda Yala:wa, Fort Site, Lookout Site, Ramah School House, North Atsinna, Yellowhouse, and Halona:wa South); two were composite round and square pueblos (Kluckhohn Ruin and Archeotekopa II); one was of irregular form (Tinaja); and one appears to have been C-shaped (Upper Nutria Village).

Ceramic Complex DE
(A.D. 1300–1325)

In transitional complex DE, the south-central part of the reservation was abandoned and the population was almost completely concentrated in the El Morro Valley and the Rio Pescado and Zuni River bottomlands. The only exception was Upper Nutria Village, which was abandoned during this period. The focus of occupation moved farther west, and became much more concentrated in a single east-west corridor along the main drainage. Figure 6.4 shows the distribution of pueblos at the end of complex DE. The map shows all pueblos occupied during complex DE except the Kluckhohn Ruin, which was abandoned during this time.

By the end of complex D, the Fort Site in the south-central portion of the study area had been abandoned, as had the two pueblos in Knife Hill Canyon, Jack's Lake and Archeotekopa II. In addition, three pueblos in the Ramah–El Morro area had been abandoned (the Lookout Site, Tinaja, and Day Ranch), while two new pueblos were established in the same general area (Pueblo de los Muertos and Atsinna). Kluckhohn, North Atsinna, Cienega, Mirabal, and the Ramah School House Ruin continued their occupation of the Ramah–El Morro area. Four new pueblos were established in the Pescado Springs area (Lower Pescado Village, Pescado West, Lower Pescado, and Upper Pescado). Farther downstream, occupation of Yellowhouse and Halona:wa South continued, while the small pueblo of Achiya:Deyaʎa was built even farther downstream. In the north-central part of the region, Upper Nutria Village was still inhabited. With the exception of Atsinna and North Atsinna on El Morro, all the pueblos were located on bottomland.

Architectural plans of the 15 pueblos occupied during complex DE are varied. Six pueblos were square or rectangular (Ramah School House, North Atsinna, Atsinna, Pueblo de los Muertos, Halona:wa South, and Yellowhouse), while five were oval (Cienega, Mirabal, Lower Pescado Village, Pescado West, and Lower Pescado). One of the composite square and round pueblos was abandoned immediately before this period (Archeotekopa II), and the other (the Kluckhohn Ruin) was abandoned during this time. The remainder had a variety of forms: C-shaped (Upper Nutria Village), irregular (Upper Pescado), small and linear (Achiya:Deyaʎa).

Ceramic Complex E
(A.D. 1325–1350)

By the end of ceramic complex E, all 10 pueblos still occupied were concentrated in a band along the Zuni River and the Rio Pescado, and in the El Morro Valley, as shown in

Figure 6.5. (The only other pueblo occupied during this time period was Upper Nutria Village, which seemingly was abandoned before the end of the complex.) This settlement pattern represents the continuation of a trend observed during the previous two complexes. Again, the focus of the population moved farther west and the pueblos became associated more strongly with the major drainages. With the exception of Atsinna (on a mesa top), all the pueblos were located on bottomland.

By the end of complex DE, four pueblos in the Ramah–El Morro area had been abandoned (Ramah School House, Kluckhohn, North Atsinna, and Mirabal), and only three large pueblos continued (Pueblo de los Muertos, Cienega, and Atsinna). Farther downstream, Yellowhouse was abandoned, but the larger pueblo of Heshot uʎa was built nearby. The four Pescado pueblos continued to be occupied, as did Halona:wa South and Achiya:Deyaʎa.

The mix of architectural plans is similar to that reported for the last complex. Of the 10 pueblos occupied throughout this interval, three were square or rectangular (Pueblo de los Muertos, Atsinna, and Halona:wa South), five were circular or oval (Cienega, Lower Pescado Village, Pescado West, Lower Pescado, and Heshot uʎa), Upper Pescado was irregular in shape, and Achiya:Deyaʎa was a small linear room block.

Ceramic Complexes F and G
(A.D. 1350–1400)

All the pueblos that were occupied at the end of complex E were also inhabited during the initial part of complex F. Rainbow Spring, a pueblo on bottomland near Ojo Caliente was added during this period. This pueblo had an L-shaped room block and a scatter of isolated rooms or small room clusters. The settlements occupied at the end of Complex F are shown in Figure 6.6.

In complex G, the only pueblos occupied were the rectangular, mesa-top pueblo of Atsinna (which may have been abandoned before the end of this period), and Hampassa:wa and Binna:wa, which were added to the settlement distribution during complex G. These two new pueblos were both on natural hills adjacent to the Zuni River. Binna:wa apparently had a rectangular layout, but the shape of the small site of Hambassa:wa is unknown.

Ceramic Complex H
(A.D. 1400–1625)

Binna:wa and Hambassa:wa, plus four of the six historic towns (Hawikku, Mats'a:kya, Kyaki:ma, and Kwa'kin'a), were occupied at the beginning of complex H. Soon thereafter they were joined by Chalo:wa, Kechiba:wa, and Halona:wa North. The small pueblo of Hambassa:wa was abandoned, followed by the eventual demise of Binna:wa and then Chalo:wa. The six known historic towns then continued their occupation into the 17th century. The distribution of pueblos occupied in the middle of complex H is shown in Figure 6.7.

These pueblos were all located in the western third of the study area. All except Kyaki:ma and Kechiba:wa were located close to the Zuni River. Hawikku and Kechiba:wa were situated close to Plumasano Wash, which drains the springs of Ojo Caliente, and Kyaki:ma was on a major tributary of the Zuni River. Hawikku, Chalo:wa, Hambassa:wa,

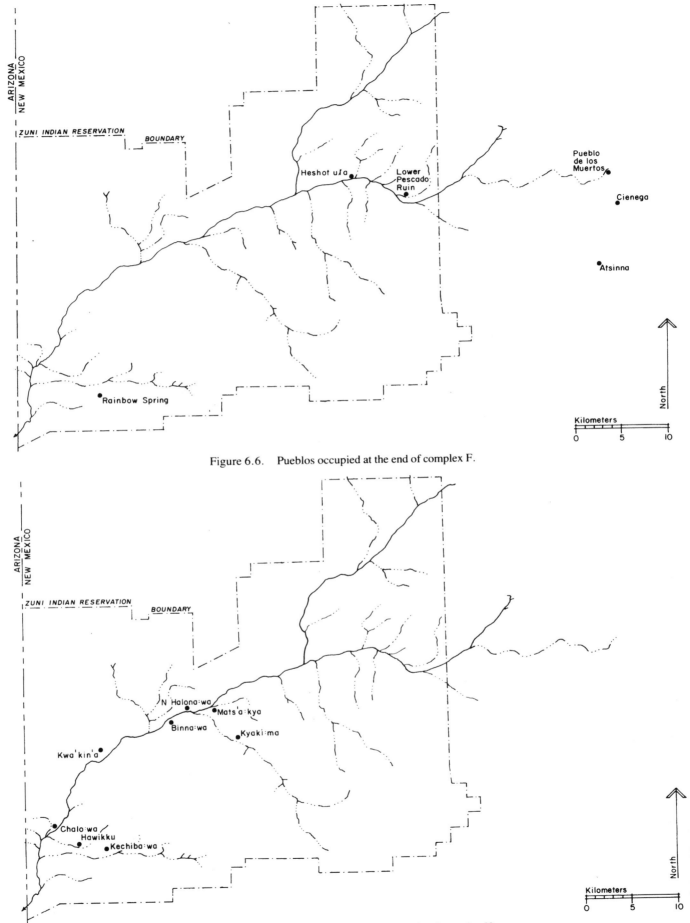

Figure 6.6.   Pueblos occupied at the end of complex F.

Figure 6.7.   Pueblos occupied in the middle of complex H.

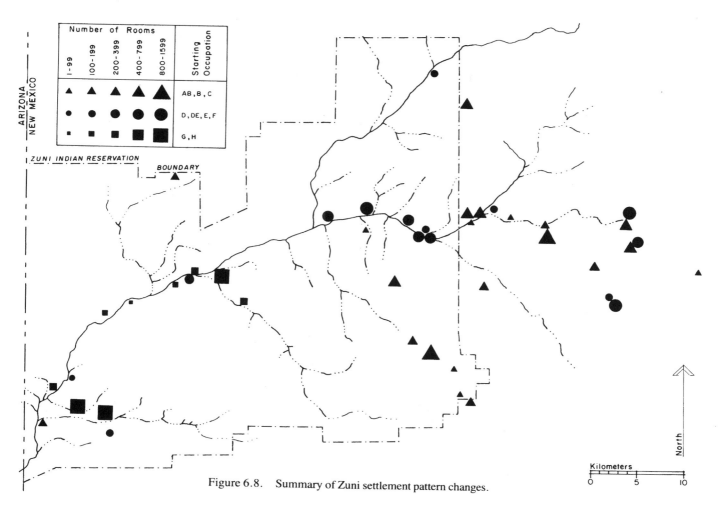

				Number of Rooms					Starting Occupation
	1-99	100-199	200-399	400-799	800-1599				
▲	▲	▲	▲	▲					AB, B, C
●	●	●	●	●					D, DE, E, F
■	■	■	■	■					G, H

ZUNI INDIAN RESERVATION

BOUNDARY

Figure 6.8.   Summary of Zuni settlement pattern changes.

Binna:wa, Halona:wa North, and Mats'a:kya were located on low natural hills, while Kyaki:ma and Kwa'kin'a were on somewhat more elevated land, and Kechiba:wa was on the top of a mesa.

Architectural plans for this complex are less certain than for any other period. The shapes of four of the villages are unknown (Hambassa:wa, Mats'a:kya, Kyaki'ma, and Halona:wa North); Kechiba:wa, Chalo:wa, and Binna:wa were rectangular; and Kwa'kin'a and Hawikku had multiple rectilinear room blocks. Some of the pueblos may have started with more regular layouts that were obscured by the growth of the pueblos over time.

DIACHRONIC SUMMARY OF SETTLEMENT PATTERNS

Site Location

The distribution of differently sized sites over time is graphically summarized in Figure 6.8. The sites are divided into three gross temporal periods (early, middle, and late) and five size classes, and are plotted on the base map for the area. Site size, shape, elevation, and topographic setting are tabulated in Table 6.1. From this information and previous discussions in this chapter, some trends in the settlement pattern changes emerge.

During the early period (complexes AB, B, and C), the initial aggregation in the 13th century occurred in the high country in the eastern part of the Zuni reservation and in the El Morro Valley. It is clear that, at this time, pueblos were distributed over a much larger portion of the eastern half of the study area than they were during the middle period. Small dispersed pueblos were much more common in the early period than in either the middle or late periods.

From the early to the middle period (complexes D through F), pueblos became much more closely associated with the main east-west drainage formed by the Rio Pescado and the Zuni River. The settlements gradually moved downstream (to the west) from the Ramah area, to the Pescado Springs area, and to Yellowhouse, Heshot uła, and Halona:wa South.

A dramatic difference between the middle and the late period (complexes G and H) is evident. After the ceramic discontinuity about A.D. 1400 (between complexes G and H), there was an abrupt settlement shift to the western third of the study area. The late period (protohistoric) pueblos were all on elevated ground with extensive areas of river bottomland in the vicinity, and all were closely associated with major drainages.

Topographic Setting and Elevation

The general trend toward locations at lower elevations in the western part of the study area is evident from the site elevation data aggregated in Table 6.2. There was a rise in mean elevation (weighted by the number of rooms) between complexes B and C, which is probably a reflection of the increased use of mesa top locations in complex C. Following complex C, the mean elevation decreased gradually through complexes D, DE, and E. However, between complexes F and H the mean elevation dropped dramatically (by 238 m).

TABLE 6.1
Archaeological and Environmental Variables for Zuni Sites

No.	Site	Rooms	Shape	Planned	Elevation (meters)	Topographic Location
1.	Spier 81	43	U	−	2060	Base of mesa
2.	Miller Ranch Ruin	60	Linear	−	2219	Ridge top
3.	Spier 61	122	Rectangular	+	2039	Base of mesa
4.	Upper Deracho Ruin	30	Linear	−	2103	Mesa terrace
5.	Vogt Ranch Ruin	39	U	−	2115	Base of mesa
6.	Kay Chee Ruin	255	Rectangular	+	2167	Ridge top
7.	Pettit Site	125	Multiple	−	2134	Mesa top, base
8.	Pescado Canyon Ruin	723	Complex	−	2252	Mesa top
9.	Lower Deracho Ruin	609	Oval	+	2088	Base of mesa
10.	Scribe S Site	410	Multiple	−	2231	Ridge top
11.	Heshoda Yala:wa	150	Rectangular	+	1875	Bluff top
12.	Box S Ruin	473	Rectangular	+	2106	Valley floor
13.	Shoemaker Ranch Ruin	17	Multiple	−	2274	Mesa top
14.	Day Ranch Ruin	574	Oval	+	2091	Valley floor
15.	Lookout Site	300	Rectangular	?	2271	Mesa top
16.	Jack's Lake Ruin	245	Oval	+	2225	Base of mesa
17.	Archeotekopa II	1412	Round-Rect.	+	2256	Base of mesa
18.	Fort Site	216	Rectangular	+	2289	Mesa top
19.	Tinaja Ruin	163	Multiple	−	2240	Butte top, base
20.	Kluckhohn Ruin	1142	Round-Rect.	+	2137	Base of mesa
21.	Mirabal Ruin	743	Oval	+	2198	Valley floor
22.	Yellowhouse	425	Rectangular	+	2012	Valley floor
23.	Ramah School House Ruin	186	Rectangular	+	2099	Valley floor
24.	North Atsinna Ruin	180	Rectangular	+	2268	Mesa top
25.	Upper Nutria Village	180	C	+	2079	Valley floor
26.	Halona:wa South	375	Rectangular	?	2050	Valley floor
27.	Cienega Site	500	Oval	+	2201	Valley floor
28.	Upper Pescado Ruin	405	Complex	?	2067	Valley floor
29.	Pueblo de los Muertos	880	Square	+	2219	Base of mountain
30.	Atsinna	875	Rectangular	+	2265	Mesa top
31.	Achiya:Deyaʌa	5	Linear	−	1878	Ridge top
32.	Lower Pescado Village	420	Oval	+	2048	Valley floor
33.	Pescado West Ruin	445	Oval	+	2060	Valley floor
34.	Lower Pescado Ruin	180	Oval	+	2060	Valley floor
35.	Heshot uʌa	85	Oval	+	2030	Valley floor
36.	Rainbow Spring Ruin	108	L	+	1935	Base of mesa
37.	Hambassa:wa	39	Unknown	?	1892	Hill top
38.	Binna:wa	168	Rectangular	?	1911	Ridge top
39.	Hawikku	800	Multiple	?	1899	Ridge top, slope
40.	Mats'a:kya	901	Unknown	?	1932	Hill top, slope
41.	Kyaki:ma	250	Unknown	?	1969	Base of mesa
42.	Kwa'kin'a	186	Complex	−	1887	Ridge top
43.	Chalo:wa	455	Rectangular	+	1868	Ridge top
44.	Kechiba:wa	824	Rectangular	+	1966	Mesa top
45.	Halona:wa North	200	Unknown	?	1920	Valley floor

TABLE 6.2.
Elevation Changes of Zuni Site Locations by Ceramic Complex

Ceramic Complex	Approx. Date A.D.	No. of Sites	Elevation (m)			Standard Deviation	Weighted Mean	Elevation Change (m)
			Min.	Max.	Mean			
End B	1250	13	1875	2274	2128	103	2149	
End C	1275	14	1875	2289	2181	109	2184	+35
End D	1300	14	1913	2289	2163	108	2167	−17
End DE	1325	14	1878	2268	2097	116	2140	−27
End E	1350	10	1878	2265	2074	119	2121	−19
End F	1375	6	1935	2265	2118	118	2163	+42
Mid H	1450	8	1868	1969	1919	33	1925	−238

TABLE 6.3
Topographic Settings of Zuni Sites by Ceramic Complex

Topographic Setting	Ceramic Complex (A.D.)						
	End B 1250	End C 1275	End D 1300	End DE 1325	End E 1350	End F 1375	Mid H 1450
Mesa Top	3	5	3	2	1	1	1
Ridge	5	2	0	1	1	0	4
Mesa Base	5	4	3	1	1	2	1
Valley Floor	0	3	8	10	1	2	1
Total	13	14	14	14	10	6	8

The topographic settings of the sites are examined for that time in each ceramic complex for which distribution maps are provided above. Table 6.3 indicates that mesa tops were inhabited throughout the entire time period studied, but their frequency of occupation decreased after complex C. Living on ridges extending into the valley floors was common in both of the earliest two complexes and in the latest complex (H). Although the distinction between a site at the base of a mesa and one out on the valley floor is not always clear, it seems that following complex C valley floor locations became the most common by far, up until complex H when there was a movement back to the ridge tops and slopes.

This summary of the changes in site elevation and topographic setting highlights the dramatic break in settlement patterns between complexes F and H. The mix of topographic settings used changed from a pattern in which valley floor locations were preferred to one in which ridge tops and slopes extending into the valleys were the most common topographic situation.

Demographic Data

When the proposed site sequence (Table 5.3) is translated into numbers of rooms in pueblos occupied during each arbitrary time interval within each ceramic complex, the demographic curve of Figure 6.9 is derived. In this context, it must be emphasized that the site sequence presented in Figure 6.9 and in Chapters 4 and 5 is determined solely by ceramic evidence. The dates have not been rearranged in order to yield a more coherent demographic picture.

Ceramic Complexes AB, B, C, and D

Only a small fraction of the pueblos occupied during complexes AB and B are included in this study. For this reason, the dramatic increase in the number of occupied rooms through complexes AB and B that is shown in Figure 6.9 is not necessarily reflective of an actual population increase for the study area during this time; rather it is an indication of the replacement of small pueblos (such as Spier 81) by large planned pueblos.

Figure 6.9 indicates that during complex C the number of rooms reached a maximum. However, because the number of rooms in small sites during complex B remains unknown, it is not possible to say whether the number of rooms occupied during complex C is greater or less than the number of rooms occupied during complex B.

Although it is not possible to estimate the number of rooms in sites that are not included in this study for complexes AB and B, it would take about 350 pueblos with 20 rooms each to

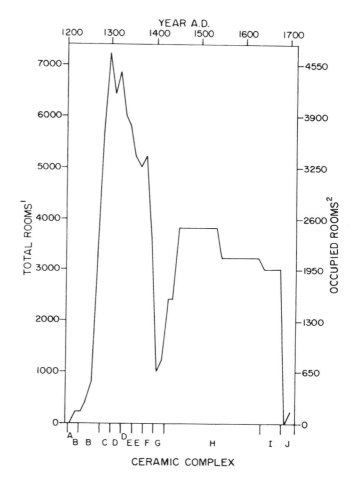

Figure 6.9. Number of rooms and occupied rooms by ceramic complex. 1, the number of rooms in occupied pueblos; the sum of the size estimates for all pueblos occupied in each time interval. 2, estimated number of occupied rooms; the number of rooms in occupied pueblos less 35 percent for rooms unoccupied at any time.

total the large-pueblo room count of over 7000 indicated for complex C. (In a survey of Miller Canyon covering about 4.25 square kilometers, a total of 170 rooms were found that dated to complex B; Kintigh 1980.)

The situation in complex D is similar to that of complex C. A large number of rooms continued to be occupied, probably about the same number as in complex C. During complex D the number of simultaneously occupied large pueblos reached a maximum of 14.

Ceramic Complexes DE, E, F, and G

The number of occupied rooms apparently declined slightly in complex DE, and remained about the same during complex E even though the number of occupied pueblos decreased somewhat. The plot of occupied rooms against time (Figure 6.9) shows a precipitous drop in the number of occupied rooms after the initial interval of complex F, from about 5000 rooms in occupied pueblos down to only 900 at the beginning of complex G. This dramatic drop is discussed further in Chapter 8.

Ceramic Complex H

The number of rooms occupied seems to have increased sharply at the beginning of complex H, and rose again when occupation began in three of the large pueblos. Thereafter, the number of rooms in occupied pueblos leveled off at about 3000. The reason for the first increase in rooms occupied is discussed in more detail in Chapter 8. The second rise likely is a more straightforward consequence of the lack of data, and the inability of the analytical procedures used to detect changing pueblo sizes over time or to date ceramic assemblages accurately within the long period included in complex H. The actual number of occupied rooms might well have remained approximately constant.

Of the ceramic samples analyzed, only those from one trench at Binna:wa, one at Halona:wa North, and one at Mats'a:kya yielded apparently stratified prehistoric material dating to this period. At sites as large as these, the limited excavations easily could have missed the earliest materials. The great diversity of the ceramics in the Halona:wa North trench (Spier 1917) is testimony to this problem.

The six historic towns all had long occupations that unfortunately make surface collections less useful than they have been elsewhere. No significant data from excavations are available for Kechiba:wa, Kwa'kin'a, or Kyaki:ma, and Hodge's information from Hawikku is not comparable to the other data analyzed here. The start of occupation at these complex H pueblos is dated only by the similarity of the surface collections (or in the case of Kyaki:ma, the unstratified refuse deposit) to the surface collection at Mats'a:kya. What is perhaps as unfortunate as the poor control over site dating is the lack of evidence for the actual sizes of the villages over their long periods of habitation; we have only the present surface remains.

Thus, the archaeological data are not sufficient to indicate the true nature of the room occupation curve through complex H, nor are they strong enough to enable choice between a model of gradual decline up to 1540 or of an approximately constant number of rooms occupied through the same period. However, the surface data do seem to argue against a substantial decline in the number of occupied rooms from the beginning of complex H to the historic period.

Summary of Demographic Data

Large planned pueblos appeared in the Zuni area in the mid–1200s, earlier than previously thought (see Watson and others 1980), and probably prior to the introduction of Springerville Polychrome. The replacement of the earlier form of small pueblos by large pueblos with regular outlines was apparently accomplished within a very short time in the mid–13th century (during ceramic complexes B and C), and

it was essentially complete by the time Kwakina Polychrome was introduced about 1275 (complex D). This transition period also appears to be shorter than scholars had thought (see Woodbury 1956: 558).

There was an apparent peak in the number of rooms occupied in the late 1200s (during complexes C and D), followed by a gradual decline through the time that Pinnawa Glaze-on-white (complex F) was introduced, sometime in the mid–1300s (Fig. 6.9). Using a figure of 65 percent room occupancy and two people per room (see Chapter 4), the estimated population peak is 9300 people, followed by a fairly stable population of about 6500 people.

Shortly after the introduction of Pinnawa Glaze-on-white and prior to the introduction of Kechipawan Polychrome (complex G) and Matsaki buff ware (complex H), the room occupation curve (Fig. 6.9) shows a decline down to about 900 people, followed by a population increase about the time that buff ware was introduced. This apparent discontinuity may be due to a massive abandonment, although that seems unlikely intuitively; it may be due to a substantial change in ceramic manufacture that seriously violates the assumptions of the dating methods used; or it may be due to the fact that the major protohistoric pueblos started their occupations earlier than the present evidence indicates. This question is discussed in more detail in Chapter 8.

From the start of the Matsaki buff wares until late in the 16th century, there apparently was a relatively constant room count at a level perhaps one-third less than during the 1300s. The quality of the data for this particular period does not strongly support the gradual decline in rooms during complex H that is indicated in Figure 6.9.

Using the figures of 65 percent room occupancy and two people per room, the population estimate is 4100 for the middle to late 1500s. This population corresponds fairly closely to Obregon's indirect estimate of 4500 people (Hodge 1937: 72). For comparison, Bandelier (1892b: 43) estimates 2000 to 3000 and Hodge (1937: 72) conservatively estimates 3000 to 3500. Considering the sources of the data and the assumptions involved in making the archaeological estimates presented here, the close correspondence is striking. A drastically different picture is presented by Upham (1982: 46, 199–200), who proposes a 1583 Zuni population of 13,280, including a group he identifies as the Querechos who probably did not live in the major villages. However, that number of people could not have lived in the known villages, and to my knowledge, there are absolutely no archaeological data that lend any support to Upham's claim that there were people living outside these villages.

Site Size

The changing distribution of site sizes through time can be examined through histograms of site sizes for each ceramic complex. Figure 6.10a is a histogram of site sizes for sites from all time periods combined. In this histogram, one can see five possible size modes. Sites with fewer than 100 rooms are mainly the small pueblos indicative of earlier periods. Next, a sizable mode from 100 to 250 rooms can be observed, followed by smaller modes around 400 and 850 rooms. Finally, there are the two pueblos with more than 1000 rooms.

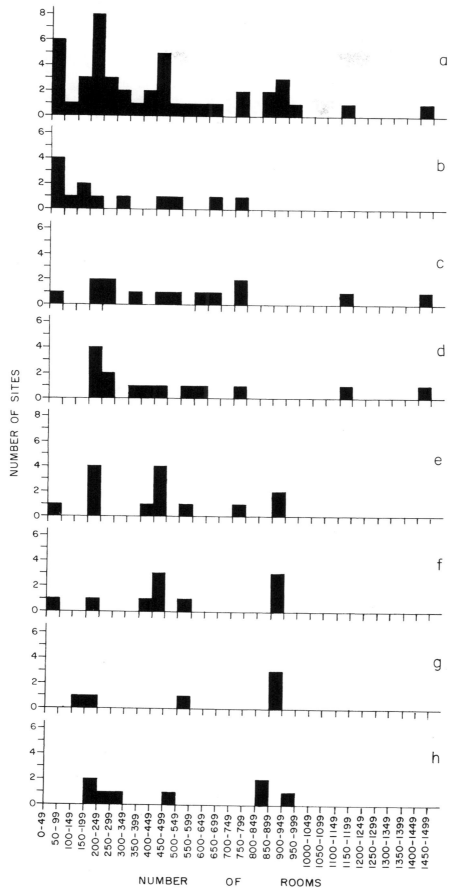

Figure 6.10.   Histograms of Zuni site size through time. *a*, all complexes combined; *b*, end of complex B; *c*, end of complex C; *d*, end of complex D; *e*, end of complex DE;*f*, end of complex E; *g*, end of complex F; *h*, middle of complex H.

TABLE 6.4
Size and Shape Distribution of Zuni Sites by Ceramic Complex

End B 1250		**End C 1275**		**End D 1300**		**End DE 1325**		**End E 1350**		**End F 1375**		**Mid H 1450**	
Size[1]	Shape[2]	Size	Shape	Size	Shape	Size	Shape	Size	Shape	Size	Shape	Size	Shape
17	M	17	M	163	M	5	I	5	I	108	L	168	R
30	I	150	R	180	C	180	O	180	O	180	O	186	M
39	U	163	M	180	R	180	C	375	R	500	O	200	?
43	U	216	R	186	R	180	R	405	X	875	O	250	?
60	I	245	O	216	R	186	R	420	O	875	R	455	R
125	M	300	R	245	O	375	R	445	O	880	R	800	M
122	R	410	M	300	R	405	X	500	O			824	R
150	R	473	R	375	R	420	O	875	O			901	?
255	R	574	O	425	R	425	R	875	R				
410	M	609	O	500	O	445	O	880	R				
473	R	723	X	574	O	500	O						
609	O	743	O	743	O	743	O						
723	X	1142	CR	1142	CR	875	R						
		1412	CR	1412	CR	880	R						

1. Size = number of rooms.
2. Shape categories: C, C-shaped; CR, Circular-Rectangular (composite); I, Linear; L, L-shaped; M, Multiple room blocks; O, Oval; R, Rectangular; X, Complex; ?, Unknown.

TABLE 6.5
Descriptive Statistics for Zuni Site Size By Ceramic Complex

Ceramic Complex	All Sites				Large Sites			
	No. of Sites	Mean	Std. Dev.	Total	No. of Sites	Mean	Std. Dev.	Total
End B	13	223	232	3031	6	389	229	2332
End C	14	513	381	7177	12	563	381	6750
End D	14	474	371	6641	14	474	371	6641
End DE	14	414	258	5799	13	446	240	5794
End E	10	496	284	4960	9	551	245	4955
End F	6	570	330	3418	6	570	330	3418
Mid H	8	461	301	3689	8	461	301	3689

When histograms are compiled for each point in time for which a map was presented in the first part of this chapter, it is clear that the complete size range of sites appears early, but that a pattern of modal site sizes developed over time (Fig. 6.10b–h). The data from which these histograms were drawn are presented in Table 6.4.

In complex B (Fig. 6.10b) there were, of course, a number of small pueblos. The earliest large pueblos, in complex B, ranged in size from 122 to 723 rooms, with no clear modalities in size. By complex C (Fig. 6.10c) the small pueblos had essentially disappeared. During complexes C and D (Figs. 6.10c, 6.10d) the two largest pueblos of any time period (the Kluckhohn Ruin and Archeotekopa II) were both occupied; the remaining pueblos had a range of 150 to 743 rooms.

In complex DE (Fig. 6.10e), clear size modalities are visible. The mode centered around 180 rooms is apparent during complex D but becomes more pronounced in complex DE. Other modes appear around 425 and 875 rooms. Occupation of the two largest pueblos ceased before complex DE. In complex E (Fig. 6.10f), the 180-room size mode disappears almost completely, but the modes around 425 and 875 seem to continue. The small number of pueblos dating to complex F (Fig. 6.10g) prevents drawing any strong conclusions, although the modes around 425 and 875 may continue.

A range of sizes from 168 to 901 rooms occurs in the middle of complex H (Fig. 6.10h). These sites might be divided into two groups: four pueblos between 168 and 455 rooms, and three between 800 and 901 rooms. Additional patterns in size for these pueblos may have been obscured by their long periods of occupation.

Aggregate data on site size over time are presented in Table 6.5. During the time that the site size modalities appear to be clearest (DE and E), the standard deviation of the site size drops somewhat. However, the mean of the large sites (excluding pueblos with fewer than 100 rooms and those made up of many room blocks) is high in complex C, decreases through complex DE, and then increases through complexes E and F (as the small site size mode drops out of the distribution).

Architectural Plan

Changes in pueblo layout show some correspondence with changes in other settlement characteristics discussed above. Table 6.6 shows the distribution of architectural plans over

TABLE 6.6
Architectural Plans of Zuni Sites by Ceramic Complex

Architectural Plan	Ceramic Complex (A.D.)						
	End B 1250	End C 1275	End D 1300	End DE 1325	End E 1350	End F 1375	Mid H 1450
Round–Oval	1	4	4	6	5	3	
Rectangular	4	4	6	6	3	2	3
Composite		2	2				
Linear, L, U, C	4		1	1	1	1	
Multiple	3	3	1				2
Complex	1	1		1	1		
Unknown							3
Total	13	14	14	14	10	6	8

time (see also Table 6.4). In the earliest period, complex B, the typical Pueblo III layouts of linear, L-shaped, U-shaped, and C-shaped room blocks, and multiple room blocks of these shapes were common among the small pueblos, while the large pueblos were mainly rectangular. However, one of the large pueblos was oval and one had a complex shape.

During complexes C and D, oval, rectangular, and composite square and round pueblos were the primary forms. Two earlier small pueblos with multiple room blocks remained occupied and a single large pueblo with multiple room blocks began its occupation during this period. The two composite round and square pueblos were the largest in the area for any time period, and they had almost identical occupation spans.

It is now clear, as Spier (1917: 325) suggested, that the round and oval-shaped pueblos were contemporaneous with the square or rectangular ones. This viewpoint is contrary to Fewkes' (1891: 123) proposition that the oval pueblos were earlier than the rectangular ones and the composite round-square pueblos were a transitional form.

The diversity of architectural plans utilized was at a minimum during complex DE, in which the frequency of oval and rectangular pueblos was approximately equal. Complex DE was also the period during which site size modalities first appeared clearly. Through complexes E and F, rectangular and oval shapes dominated.

The transition from complex F to complex H is characterized by a dramatic change in pueblo layouts, corresponding with dramatic changes in other settlement characteristics during this interval. Although original layouts may be obscured by long occupation, it appears that the oval plan completely disappeared, and that large, plaza-oriented pueblos were largely replaced by unplanned villages containing multiple room blocks and, perhaps, multiple plazas.

SETTLEMENT CHANGES

This descriptive synthesis of the late prehistoric settlement data for the Zuni area discussed site size, shape, topographic situation, elevation, and the distribution of site locations over the study area. In many ways, there seems to be a correspondence among changes in these variables over time.

There was a tendency toward an increasing uniformity in the settlement patterns leading up to complex DE. The diversity of topographic situations used in complex DE was much less than in complex D. The site size distribution shows strong modalities starting in complex DE, and the diversity of pueblo layouts used in complex DE was much less than in complex D.

The most obvious changes occurred between complexes F and H, between the prehistoric and protohistoric pueblos. There was a marked change in settlement location to the west along the Zuni River, reflected by a drop in average elevation of over 230 m between complexes F and H. Also, at this time there were changes in the topographic settings that were utilized, in the site size distribution, and in the distribution of architectural layouts. In addition, there was an apparent discontinuity in the population curve through this time.

Using the synchronic and diachronic descriptions of the settlement patterns and information on the natural environment and agricultural technology presented next, the settlement data are further analyzed and interpreted in Chapter 8.

7. ZUNI AREA ENVIRONMENT AND AGRICULTURAL TECHNOLOGY

The Zuni area, as defined by this study, includes 3400 square kilometers of the southeastern portion of the Colorado Plateau drained by the New Mexico portion of the Zuni River (see Fig. 1.1). Most of the area is a relatively high plateau sloping down from east to west, extensively dissected by streams and washes. The resulting topography is characterized by large mesas cut by both narrow canyons and broad flat plains, spotted with isolated buttes and hills (Ferguson 1980: 9; Schreiber 1979b: 1).

THE NATURAL ENVIRONMENT

Topography and Geology

The area is bounded on the northeast and east by the Zuni Mountains, which reach a height of over 2740 m (9000 feet). The malpais, on the southeastern edge of the study area, is at an elevation of about 2286 m (7500 feet), while the southwestern corner of the area on the Zuni River plain is at an elevation of only about 1830 m (6000 feet). The northern edge, the divide between the drainages of the Zuni River and Whitewater Arroyo, is at an elevation near 2134 m (7000 feet).

The entire area is drained by the Zuni River, which, with its major tributaries, the Rio Pescado and the Rio Nutria, forms a northeast-southwest oriented Y through the area. These three drainages have fertile floodplains that are, in places, several kilometers wide. In addition to these rivers, the mesas are also cut by many smaller drainages. Elevations on the major drainage range from 2200 m (7200 feet) in the El Morro Valley and 2075 m (6800 feet) at Nutria, down to 1845 m (6050 feet) on the Zuni River at the Arizona border. Mesa top elevations range from about 2285 m (7500 feet) in the east and south, to above 1950 m (6400 feet) in the southwest.

The geologic basement of the Zuni area is formed by Precambrian granitic crystalline rock that generally is overlain by 750 m or more of sedimentary deposits. The Precambrian rocks are unconformably overlain by geologic units of Permian age, the uppermost of which are Glorietta Sandstone and San Andres Limestone. Over the Permian rocks are the Triassic Chinle Formation and Wingate Sandstone. In some places within the Chinle Formation, erosion has exposed beds of petrified wood, which was used in prehistoric stone tool manufacture. The Triassic formations are overlain by Jurassic Zuni Sandstone, which may be covered by Cretaceous Dakota Sandstone and Gallup Sandstone, intertongued with Mancos Shale. The Tertiary Bidahochi Formation is overlain by Quaternary alluvium, which may be more than 60 m deep, and by basalt flows (Orr 1982; Schreiber 1979b; Ferguson

1980). Southeast of the study area is a barren malpais with a number of cinder cones.

The soils in the area and their agricultural potential are discussed in more detail below. In general, the mesa tops and slopes are covered with shallow, rocky soils. These poor soils also cover a substantial part of the floor of the El Morro Valley. However, most of the bottomlands in the area have a cover of deep, permeable soils suitable for agriculture.

Water Resources

Before the turn of the century, Mindeleff (1891: 80) observed that the Zuni River was a perennial stream that generally disappeared a few miles below Zuni (Fig. 7.1) but that flowed to the Little Colorado River during the rainy season. Although it now is dry much of the summer, in the mid–19th century it was investigated as a possible part of a navigable route from the Continental Divide to the Pacific Ocean (Crampton 1977: 102–103). Early in this century, Leslie Spier (1917: 216–217) described other water resources in the area:

> Beginning at the east, there are springs near Tinaja and a permanent waterhole in the ruin of Cienega (percolating from under the lava sheet). The basin here presents an inhospitable appearance, but water is not far from any of the ruins even at this season [early summer]. A fair-sized stream has its source in the foot of the Zuni Range and runs westward past Pueblo de los Muertos to Ramah which is situated at the junction of several drainages capable of cultivation. Further north, Nutria Creek also rises in the mountains as a permanent stream. It is of considerable size and in the neighborhood of Nutria village irrigates an area fully two miles long. At Pescado village six miles west of Ramah are two groups of large copious springs which, gushing from under the lava fault at this point, constitute the perennial source of the Zuni River. Water is now diverted from the springs into irrigation ditches, as it undoubtedly was in prehistoric times. Many ruins are clustered in the vicinity, duplicating the situation at Ramah. . . . The large wash leading towards Zuni from the north, and others near the foot of Towwayallanna [Dowa Yalanne] to the south may be pointed out as typical areas cultivated by dry farming. Even sand bars in the bed of the river are utilized. Other washes occurring at intervals further down the basin are now cultivated. The Zuni River ceases to be a source of water supply in the lower basin; for it sinks into the ground a few miles below Zuni and only a few pools stand in the lower reaches of its bed. At Ojo Caliente the so-called hot springs burst forth under the edge of the lava sheet in great quantity and permit the irrigation of a large area. . . . Portions of the washes in the valley above the springs also sustain cultivation.

Figure 7.1. Zuni River and the Pueblo of Zuni in 1911. (Photograph by Jesse Nusbaum, courtesy of the Smithsonian Institution, National Anthropological Archives, Bureau of American Ethnology Collection, Negative No. 2303–C–1.)

In prehistoric times, the major potential sources of water (other than direct rainfall) were the Zuni River and its major tributaries, shallow wells, and springs. The current availability of water resources has been compiled by Orr (1982) and is summarized below. Records from 1911 to 1930 indicate that the Zuni River, measured at Black Rock Reservoir, had a mean annual runoff of 23,664,000 cubic meters per year (19,192 acre-feet per year), although there is a great deal of both seasonal and annual variation. (Records from 1969 to 1979 show a greatly lowered stream flow, although much of the difference can be accounted for by evaporation from the many reservoirs that have since been constructed upstream of Black Rock Reservoir.) Operating wells dug in alluvium along the Zuni River are from 2 m to 12 m deep with an average depth of less than 6 m. These wells are commonly hand dug and generally yield less than 0.63 liters per second (10 gallons per minute).

Major springs exist at Ojo Caliente, Nutria, and Pescado, and there are other substantial springs within the area. Rainbow Spring and Sacred Spring at Ojo Caliente together discharge about 888,000 cubic meters of water per year (720 acre-feet per year), and an additional 107,000 to 134,000 cubic meters per year (87 to 109 acre-feet per year) seep into Plumasano Wash from the same source. Nutria Spring produces about 100,000 cubic meters per year (81 acre-feet per year). Both the Nutria and Ojo Caliente Springs are fed by an aquifer within the Glorietta Sandstone and San Andres Limestone that is recharged mainly at exposed outcrops in the Zuni Mountains. A spring comparable in size to Nutria Spring is located at the base of Dowa Yalanne near Kyaki:ma. This Dowa Yalanne spring is fed by an aquifer in the Chinle Formation that is primarily recharged along the hogback (the Nutria Monocline). Upper and Lower Pescado Springs are fed by alluvial groundwater in buried channel deposits (associated with basalt flows) and have a combined output of about 986,000 cubic meters per year (800 acre-feet per year). The same source of water is tapped by Black Rock Spring. Although there is seasonal variation in the output of these springs, they are perennial sources of water. It must be noted that modern pumping from wells drilled into these aquifers

has probably reduced spring flow substantially from the prehistoric levels.

Flora and Fauna

The life zones of the study area have been identified by Lowe (1964). The Transition life zone in the Zuni area occurs on mesa and mountain slopes and tops mostly at elevations over 2225 m (7300 feet) (Schreiber 1979b: 19). This zone is dominated by a ponderosa pine (*Pinus ponderosa*) forest. Lower elevations in the area are part of the Upper Sonoran life zone, which is divided into four floral associations. Plains grassland and Great Basin desert scrub dominate the flat lands between 1830 m and 2225 m (6000 to 7300 feet). Plains grassland, which is dominated by grasses such as grama (*Bouteloua* spp.), has been replaced in many areas by Great Basin desert scrub vegetation, dominated by shrubs such as sagebrush (*Artemesia* sp.) and rabbit brush (*Chrysothamnus nauseosus*). Juniper-pinyon woodlands are common along tops and slopes of the mesas. Stands of juniper-pinyon woodlands are common along tops and slopes of the mesas. Stands of juniper-pinyon woodland along the bases of the mesas often grade into the desert scrub or grasslands. At lower elevations juniper (*Juniperus* spp.) is most common, and as the elevation increases, juniper is replaced by pinyon (*Pinus edulis*). Riparian woodlands occur along streams and around springs. Riparian woodlands are composed largely of cottonwood (*Populus* spp.) and willow (*Salix* spp.).

Marquardt (1974: 4), Schreiber (1979b: 24–25), and Ferguson (1980: 22) list the animals that are found (or were aboriginally) in the different life zones of the study area. Among others, elk (*Cervus canadensis*), mule deer (*Odocoileus hemionus*), and mountain sheep (*Ovis canadensis*) are found in the Transition zone. Some of the animals found in the Upper Sonoran life zone are: antelope (*Antilocapra americana*), white-tailed deer (*Odocoileus virginianus*), coyote (*Canis latrans estor*), jackrabbit (*Lepus californicus*), and cottontail (*Sylvilagus* sp.), along with a variety of small rodents.

TABLE 7.1
Rainfall in the Zuni Area

Station	Elevation		Mean Rainfall (mm)					Years of Record
	m	feet	Annual	May-Oct	Nov-Apr	June-Sept	Oct-May	
Zuni	1963	6440	301	183	119	144	159	62–66
Ramah	2194	7200	357	207	149	169	195	13–16
El Morro Monument	2200	7218	338	200	133	158	159	37–41
El Morro Airport	2170	7120	278	210	68	174	104	5

Station	Elevation		Standard Deviation of Annual Rainfall			Years of Record
	m	feet	Annual	May-Oct	June-Sept	
Zuni	1963	6440	85	66	58	62–66
Ramah	2194	7200	95	79	73	13–16
El Morro Monument	2200	7218	79	· 63	53	37–41
El Morro Airport	2170	7120	92	92	77	5

Station	Mean Monthly Rainfall (mm)													Years of Record
	Jan	Feb	Mar	Apr	May	June	July	Aug	Sept	Oct	Nov	Dec	Total	
Zuni	21	20	23	15	13	10	52	48	32	26	17	23	301	62
Ramah	22	32	23	29	19	12	52	58	44	24	19	18	357	13
El Morro Monument	25	21	28	18	13	13	48	65	33	27	17	24	333	37
El Morro Airport	11	11	15	7	9	17	48	80	29	27	9	18	278	5

Station	Standard Deviation of Monthly Rainfall													Years of Record
	Jan	Feb	Mar	Apr	May	June	July	Aug	Sept	Oct	Nov	Dec	Total	
Zuni	17	14	19	12	14	11	33	29	26	28	15	15	85	62
Ramah	19	25	25	29	18	17	35	44	40	23	22	16	95	13
El Morro Monument	21	14	19	14	14	11	23	37	26	26	14	16	79	37
El Morro Airport	9	11	9	10	9	17	23	71	17	14	8	8	92	5

Modern Climate

The modern climate has been systematically recorded at four locations in the study area (see Fig. 1.1): the Zuni Airport at Black Rock, Ramah, El Morro National Monument, and El Morro Airport (National Weather Service 1908–1981). The Zuni station (it is called both Black Rock and Zuni in the National Weather Service Reports) has by far the longest record (71 years were available to me). El Morro Monument also has a relatively long record (44 years). Records from the other two stations are too short and too incomplete to be considered reliable indicators of climate. (Records were available from Ramah for only 17 years and from El Morro Airport for only 6 years.)

Rainfall

The Zuni area has a semiarid climate with seasonal rains subject to considerable variation. Table 7.1 indicates that the average annual rainfall at Zuni is 301 mm (11.9 inches), with a standard deviation of 85 mm (3.3 inches). Reviewing the monthly rainfall data for each station for each year of record showed that the maximum rainfall recorded at Zuni (in 1941) was 496 mm (19.5 inches), and the minimum (in 1950) was 112 mm (4.4 inches; Kintigh 1982b).

A typical year has light winter rains from November until March, scant rainfall in April, May, and June, and heavy summer rains from July through October. The average June rain at Zuni is only 10 mm (0.40 inch), and in 15 of the 68 years recorded less than 0.5 mm (0.02 inch) of rain fell. On

the other hand, the average July rain is 52 mm (2.05 inches) at the same station, and the maximum July rain recorded was 159 mm (6.25 inches).

Although it is widely believed that the amount of rainfall is well correlated with elevation in a given area (Watson and others 1980: 214; Ferguson 1980: 16), these data indicate that the difference attributable to elevation is relatively small. The highest and lowest stations (El Morro National Monument and Zuni) differ in elevation by 237 m (778 feet), but they differ in average annual precipitation by only 8 percent or 23 mm (less than an inch) over each station's entire period of record.

The difference is somewhat larger if the annual totals are averaged for the 34 years with recordings at both stations; El Morro National Monument has an average of 41 mm (1.6 inches) more rainfall than Zuni. It is difficult to rely on data from the other stations; however, for the 13 years that the Ramah Station recorded total rainfall, it averaged only 20 mm (0.8 inch) more than Zuni (337 mm in those same years), which is more than 230 m lower in elevation. For the four years that the three stations have common records, Ramah had 26 mm more rainfall than Zuni (1.0 inch), and El Morro Monument had 24 mm (0.9 inch) more than Ramah.

Rainfall data from El Morro Airport are somewhat puzzling. It is 30 m lower in elevation and less than 5 km distant from El Morro National Monument, yet in the two years that both stations recorded rainfall, the Monument recorded an average of 75 mm (3 inches) more rainfall. And, for the three

TABLE 7.2
Length of the Growing Season in the Zuni Area

Station	Elevation		Last 0° C		First 0° C		No. of Days		Years of
	m	feet	Mean	Std. Dev.	Mean	Std. Dev.	Mean	Std. Dev.	Record
Zuni	1963	6440	May 16	15	Oct 12	12	150	21	65
Ramah	2194	7200	June 3	21	Sept 22	15	97	35	2
El Morro Monument	2200	7218	June 6	11	Sept 27	11	113	17	43
El Morro Airport	2170	7120	June 25	4	Sept 19	11	86	9	4

years that have recorded totals for Zuni and El Morro Airport, Zuni had 6 mm (0.2 inch) *more* rainfall than the much higher El Morro Airport.

It may be that there is some local orographic effect on the rainfall patterns that causes the airport to get less, or the Monument to get more, rainfall than the surrounding area. However, because most summer rainfall comes from thunderstorms that characteristically produce a patchy distribution of rain, and because the period of years at El Morro Airport is so small (5 years), it seems likely that much of the difference in precipitation between El Morro National Monument and El Morro Airport is due to sampling error. With a longer record, it seems likely that the differences would be much smaller. These data do serve to point out that within any given year, there may be localized but dramatic differences in rainfall patterns.

While it appears that higher elevations may get somewhat more rainfall, the maximum difference in rainfall between major parts of the study area that were intensively inhabited almost certainly averages somewhere between 20 and 40 mm (0.8 and 1.6 inches), or between 7 percent and 13 percent of the average rainfall at Zuni (much less than the standard deviation at that station). Furthermore, within this general trend, there is substantial, highly localized, but essentially random variation in total rainfall. Finally, although there are no available data, it is likely that the orographic effect on rainfall on the Zuni Mountains, and perhaps on other large, high landforms, produces systematic differences in rainfall, with more rain falling on these topographic features.

Growing Season

Much more dramatic than the effect elevation has on rainfall is the difference in the average length of the growing season at the stations of different elevations (Table 7.2). (In the more recent records, the growing season is defined as the number of days between the last spring day with a temperature of 0° C [32° F] or below, and the first fall day with a temperature of 0° C or below; in the earlier records, it is the number of days between frosts.) For El Morro Monument the average growing season is 113 days, while at Zuni Airport it is 150 days—37 days longer. If the averages are computed for the same set of 38 years, the difference is 33 days (the growing seasons are 111 and 144 days, respectively). For Zuni, the average date of the last spring frost is May 16, while at El Morro Monument it is June 3. On the average, the first fall frost comes on October 12 at Zuni and on September 22 at El Morro.

Like rainfall, the growing season is subject to considerable annual variation. At Zuni the standard deviation in the length of the season is 21 days and at El Morro National Monument it is 17 days. Based on the annual records listed in Table 7.3,

the minimum growing season recorded at Zuni is 107 days, and the minimum at El Morro National Monument is 72 days. At El Morro, 10 of the 43 years recorded have seasons less than 100 days long.

In addition to this annual variation, it appears that the growing season also may be subject to substantial local variation. In the four years (1945–1948) that records were kept at both El Morro stations, El Morro Airport had a growing season that was an average of 40 days shorter, with a range of 11 to 69 days difference. Although this average difference may not be reliable, there are some reasons to believe that there is a systematic difference in temperature between these two stations. The station at El Morro Monument is near the base of the east side of a 70 m (230-foot) high mesa, but the airport is on the valley floor approximately two kilometers from any major mesa or hill. Two factors would tend to keep temperatures at the Monument higher, and thus the growing season longer. First, night-time drainage of cool air off the mesa top would tend to produce air movement and mixing of warm and cool air near the base of the mesa, whereas because of the nighttime inversion, cool air would settle on the valley floor. Second, enough heat probably is radiated off the mesa at night to warm the air in the vicinity of the Monument station.

The average annual temperatures at El Morro National Monument and Zuni differ by an average of 1.6° C (2.9° F). On a monthly basis (Table 7.4), the difference is relatively constant, between 1° C and 2° C.

There apparently is a general trend toward lower temperatures and shorter growing seasons at higher elevations. The particular location of the El Morro National Monument weather station probably causes it to have substantially higher nighttime temperatures than would be observed on nearby valley floors that are farther from mountains or large mesas. Thus, the growing season differences due to elevation in fact may be greater than are suggested by a comparison of the Zuni data with the El Morro National Monument data. However, the Zuni station at Black Rock is on a hill and is close to Black Rock Reservoir, which may cause it to show a longer growing season than is characteristic of valley floor locations in its area. In general, nighttime temperatures in areas on or near the lower slopes of large mountains or mesas will be moderated by the effects of cold air drainage, and for that reason, those locations would be advantageous for fields in areas where the length of the growing season presents a problem.

Paleoclimatic Data

Information concerning the prehistoric environment may be reconstructed from variation in tree-ring widths. The University of Arizona Laboratory for Tree-ring Research has

TABLE 7.3
Annual Growing Season Records for Zuni Area Weather Stations

Year	Zuni			Ramah			El Morro National Monument			El Morro Airport		
	Last 0° C	First 0° C	No. of Days	Last 0° C	First 0° C	No. of Days	Last 0° C	First 0° C	No. of Days	Last 0° C	First 0° C	No. of Days
1981	147	289	142				166	277	111			
1980	147	289	142				157	278	121			
1979							171	279	108			
1978	138	288	150				173	263	90			
1977	147	298	151				150	274	124			
1976	164						178	279	101			
1975	144						177	266	89			
1974							161	271	110			
1973							157	267	110			
1972	143	303	160				147	270	123			
1971	155	262	107				156	248	92			
1970	128	280	152				167	258	91			
1969	127	278	151				160	278	118			
1968	136	290	154				163	261	98			
1967	135	280	145				149	257	108			
1966	111	287	176				134	281	147			
1965	130	264	134				153	264	111			
1964	130	286	156				151	281	130			
1963	132	305	173				160	287	127			
1962	142	301	159				168	274	106			
1961	133	283	150				154	247	93			
1960	141	292	151				153	267	114			
1959	147	268	121				153	261	108			
1958	123	294	171				164	268	104			
1957	141	281	140				145	258	113			
1956	136	293	157				148	287	139			
1955	136	280	144				155	264	109			
1954	158	288	130				158	285	127			
1953	151	287	136				155	269	114			
1952	119	257	138				144	257	113			
1951	153	279	126				161	256	95			
1950	129	302	173				160	255	95			
1949	127	282	155				153	282	129			
1948	133	281	148				144	279	135	171	256	85
1947	133	288	155				137	289	152	173	256	83
1946	151	280	129				152	280	128	179	278	99

compiled tree-ring data for the Cibola Station. Almost all of those data were collected from within the study area and, for the time period of interest, mainly from sites under consideration here. These data, presented in Table 7.5 and Figure 7.2, are taken from Dean and Robinson (1977). The decade departure index is a standardized climatic index where the units are standard deviations from the average for the entire tree-ring sequence for the area. A negative index is interpreted as a decade with lower than normal precipitation and higher than normal temperatures; a positive index indicates a decade of higher rainfall and lower temperatures.

Perhaps most notable in these data is the large amount of variation. Among the 40 decades shown in Figure 7.1, 12 decades (30 percent) are one standard deviation or more above normal, 13 (33 percent) are more than one standard deviation below normal, and only 15 (38 percent) of the decades are within one standard deviation of the normal value.

The period from A.D. 1270 to 1370 deserves some additional comment. There were three hot, dry decades from 1270 to 1300 (the Great Drought), immediately followed by a four-decade cool, wet period from 1300 to 1340. The climate in the following three decades alternated between very hot and dry and very cool and wet. The period from 1370 to 1540 was characterized by substantial variation, although not as severe as in the century between 1270 and 1370.

The height of the water table and degree of arroyo-cutting through time are important for evaluating the viability of different agricultural technologies. Although specific data are not available for the Zuni area, Euler and others (1979: 1096–1097) argue that the three available hydrologic sequences (Black Mesa, Navajo Reservoir, and Chaco Canyon) agree fairly well with each other and with the regional dendroclimatic record. They conclude that: "hydrologic and climatic changes in the eastern and western parts of the Colorado Plateaus were essentially synchronous." These data are particularly valuable because the portion of the hydrologic sequence that is relevant to this research has been well dated using tree-rings.

TABLE 7.3
(continued)

Year	Zuni Last 0°C	Zuni First 0°C	Zuni No. of Days	Ramah Last 0°C	Ramah First 0°C	Ramah No. of Days	El Morro National Monument Last 0°C	El Morro National Monument First 0°C	El Morro National Monument No. of Days	El Morro Airport Last 0°C	El Morro Airport First 0°C	El Morro Airport No. of Days
1945	152	272	120				169	257	88	180	257	77
1944	156	275	119				170	276	106			
1943	139	287	148				166	278	112			
1942	137	266	129				152	262	110			
1941	160	277	117	179	251	72	180	252	72			
1940	128	303	175				151	288	137			
1939	169	277	108				145	275	130			
1938	148	282	134									
1937	131	292	161									
1936	153	282	129									
1935	124	293	169		285							
1934	99	293	194									
1933	143	306	163	142								
1932	128	293	165		254							
1931	140	300	160	142	263	121						
1930	131	285	154									
1929	122	297	175		283							
1928	117	289	172		255							
1927	129	275	146									
1926	90	296	206									
1925	115	298	183									
1924	129	271	142									
1923	121	291	170									
1922	132	289	157									
1921	139	299	160									
1920	137	285	148									
1919	154	281	127									
1918	151	276	125									
1917	127	270	143									
1916	123	290	167									
1915	123	257	134									
1914	121	316	195									
1913	131											
1909	135	281	146									
1908	155	271	116									

TABLE 7.4
Mean Monthly Temperature in the Zuni Area

Station		Mean Monthly Temperature Jan	Feb	Mar	Apr	May	June	July	Aug	Sept	Oct	Nov	Dec	Annual	Years of Record
Zuni	°F	30	35	40	48	57	65	71	69	63	53	40	32	50	64
	°C	−1	1	4	9	14	19	22	21	17	11	5	0	10	64
El Morro Monument	°F	28	32	37	45	54	63	69	66	60	50	37	30	47	33
	°C	−2	0	3	7	12	17	20	19	16	10	3	−1	9	33

Euler and his colleagues (1979, footnote 83) also state that their data support the argument that arroyo-cutting occurs during periods of decreased moisture. They indicate that a climatically induced drop in the water table below plant roots affects the surface vegetation, and results in the onset of arroyo-cutting. Once begun, arroyos are cut down to the water-saturated strata.

If we accept the Black Mesa hydrologic sequence (Euler and others 1979: 1093) as representative, then the 1200s were hydrologically relatively stable with a high water table and shallow arroyos. A period of arroyo-cutting started about 1300 and lasted until nearly 1400. The century from 1400 to 1500 is characterized by deep arroyos and a low water table. Another arroyo-filling period started just before 1500 and lasted for about 90 years.

Although the hydrologic sequence, according to these authors, is dependent on climatically induced subsidence of the water table, there is no obvious correspondence between

TABLE 7.5
Cibola Station Tree-ring Decade Departure Values
(from Dean and Robinson 1977)

Decade	Departure	Decade	Departure
1200–1209	0.60	1400–1409	−0.70
1210–1219	−2.10	1410–1419	−1.90
1220–1229	0.20	1420–1429	2.00
1230–1239	1.00	1430–1439	2.10
1240–1249	1.00	1440–1449	−1.70
1250–1259	−1.20	1450–1459	−1.90
1260–1269	2.30	1460–1469	0.30
1270–1279	−0.20	1470–1479	−1.70
1280–1289	−3.70	1480–1489	1.50
1290–1299	−1.20	1490–1499	1.10
1300–1309	1.00	1500–1509	0.40
1310–1319	2.50	1510–1519	0.40
1320–1329	0.80	1520–1529	−0.70
1330–1339	2.20	1530–1539	0.50
1340–1349	−1.90	1540–1549	−0.60
1350–1359	1.80	1550–1559	0.40
1360–1369	−1.80	1560–1569	−0.80
1370–1379	0.40	1570–1579	−2.20
1380–1389	1.00	1580–1589	−4.10
1390–1399	−0.30	1590–1599	−1.70

the tree-ring decade departure index and the hydrologic sequence; that is, the wet and dry periods indicated by tree rings do not appear to be reflected by corresponding periods of arroyo-filling and cutting. Jeff Dean has informed me that this is a typical situation and that no such correspondence has been found either on a regional basis or in other tree-ring sequences. At present, it is not clear in what ways or over what time period the water table responds to the annual moisture indicated by tree rings.

Nonetheless, present information suggests that both the hydrologic and tree-ring data may be used with confidence in reconstructing characteristics of the prehistoric environment. The tree-ring data reflect (among other things) annual precipitation and temperature, while the hydrologic sequence reflects the longer-term processes of arroyo-cutting and filling and changes in the height of the water table.

ZUNI AGRICULTURAL TECHNOLOGY

Historic Zuni Subsistence and Land Use

Zuni land use has been given comprehensive treatment recently in the preparation of the Zuni land claims case (Ferguson 1980, 1981b; Hart 1980, 1981), as well as in other anthropological literature (Cushing 1920; Stevenson 1904, 1915; Bohrer 1960). However, several points relevant to the discussion that follows should be noted here.

At the time of the first Spanish contact, the Zuni were mainly sedentary agriculturalists, with maize the primary cultigen. Cushing (1920: 358) quotes Coronado writing to Viceroy Mendoza:

The victuals which the people of this countrey have, is Maiz, whereof they have great store, and also smalle white Pease [peas; beans?]: and Venison, which by all likelihood they feede upon, (though they say no) for wee found many skinnes of Deere, of Hares, and Conies [rabbits].

Wittfogel and Goldfrank (1943: 21–22) make a strong case for aboriginal canal irrigation (see also Hart 1980: 25). Zuni use of irrigation is suggested in chronicles deriving from Coronado's expedition, and definite references to irrigation are made in 1583, particularly at Quequina (Kwa'kin'a) and Hawikku (Ferguson 1981b: 343).

At the time of the earliest anthropological visits, starting in 1879, there was only one major pueblo, Halona:wa, and three major, seasonally occupied, farming villages at Nutria, Pescado, and Ojo Caliente. In all three farming villages, there was extensive use of spring-fed irrigation (Hart 1980: 32). Stevenson (1904: 351) describes the irrigation at Ojo Caliente as two large ditches, one of which watered an area 3.5 by 2.5 miles (5.6 km by 4.0 km; 22 square kilometers), and the other, a smaller area. Cushing (1920: 355–367) describes irrigation on a similar scale at Nutria where there was a ditch, fed by springs, that was 2 miles (3.2 km) long and included viaducts made of enormous hollow logs. The cultivated area was 1.5 miles (2.4 km) long, and nearly as wide, and supplied wheat for forty families (about 12 hectares per family). Fifteen or twenty plots of about 10 by 12 feet (3.0 m by 3.7 m) made up the patch of a poor man. A straight ditch ran through the middle of each enclosed plot.

Stevenson (1904: 353) indicates that no water measure was used and that disputes over water rarely arose. When they did, they were settled by the Governor. In contrast, in his description of the farming village of Nutria, Cushing (1920: 366–367) says that:

So limited is the supply of water during the dry months, that every householder keeps an account-stick hanging somewhere near the sky-hole. Every time he waters a set of his "earth-bins," he has to cut a notch in this account-stick; and as the latter is liable to inspection by the sub-chiefs any morning, he dares not, or rather does not, use more than his proper allowance of the water.

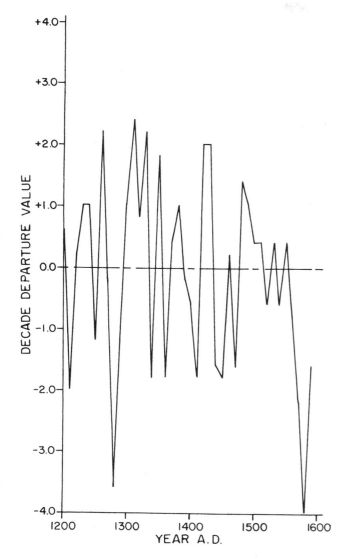

Figure 7.2. Cibola Station tree-ring decade departure values.

Stevenson (1904: 351) reports that: "Much of the corn and all of the wheat is raised in the farming districts of Nutria, Pescado, and Ojo Caliente. The cornfields also spread over the land near Zuni and elsewhere." Much of the corn not grown under irrigation was probably cultivated using flood-water farming of some sort.

Cushing (1920: 157–166, Plate 2) describes one type of floodwater farming for corn. Fields were formed, sometimes at a great distance from the pueblo, by constructing a dam across an arroyo and secondary embankments to spread the water over the field. The field was formed by the deposition of a layer of loam carried by the water and by accumulation of wind-laden sand and soil that was stopped by windbreaks constructed for this purpose and redistributed by the water.

The effect of the network of barriers is what the Indian prayed for, . . . namely, that with every shower, although the stream go dry three hours afterward, water has been carried to every portion of the field, has deposited a fine loam over it all, and moistened from one end to the other,

the substratum. Not only this, but also, all rainfall on the actual space is retained and absorbed within the system of minor embankments (Cushing 1920: 164–165).

Corn planting began in May, at the decision of the sun priest. Corn was planted in clusters, to the east of the stalks left from the previous year's planting. Twelve to twenty kernels were planted in a digging stick hole four to seven inches deep (Cushing 1920: 174–182). In the autumn, green corn that showed no promise of ripening was picked and baked (Cushing 1920: 204–208). Cushing (1920: 211) further implies that the main harvest came with the frost.

Bohrer (1960: 182; see also Stevenson 1904: 353) describes the waffle gardens (Fig. 7.3) extensively used at Zuni pueblo to grow herbs and vegetables:

> . . . a tidy series of planting beds built up about four inches above the ground and enclosed by an earthen wall about four inches higher. Each "waffle" measured one and a half to two feet on a side. These beds are placed in a single row with paths on each side, or they are contiguous over a larger area. Women water the squares by hand from metal pails that had been dipped from a nearby walk-in-well excavated into the river bed.

Waffle gardens on the south bank of the Zuni River are illustrated by Cushing (1920, Plate 1).

Late 19th and early 20th century accounts indicate that the Zuni tried to keep a one- or two-year supply of corn on hand in case of crop failure. In spite of this: "Starvation has sometimes compelled them to seek relief from other pueblos. Neighboring tribes have also sought aid from the Zunis for the same reason" (Stevenson 1904: 353; see also Adams 1981: 326–327).

In addition to agriculture, the Zuni collected a large number of wild plants (Stevenson 1915). The historic Zuni hunted a variety of animals including antelope, deer, and rabbit, over a wide area (see Hart 1980: 10–16; Ferguson 1981b: 19–20). The historic and prehistoric Zuni also raised domesticated turkeys (Ferguson 1981a: 343). Although gathering and hunting certainly played important roles in historic Zuni subsistence, agriculture was at the very core of the Zuni subsistence system.

The historic (and probably prehistoric) Zuni participated in a large trade network (Hart 1981, Riley 1975). However, there are indications that the Zuni did not typically trade for subsistence items on a large scale. Rather, it appears that most trade involved more exotic items such as salt (obtained from Zuni Salt Lake), turquoise, buffalo robes, cotton, and peridot (a form of olivine).

Environmental Requirements for Agriculture in the Zuni Area

Agricultural success or failure is determined by many factors: genetically determined requirements of the plants; the time between germination and the first killing frost; the absolute amount and timing of the water delivered to the plants (which is, in turn, dependent on several environmental variables discussed below); the properties of the soil; the agricultural methods used; and damage from wind, insects, and disease. Ford (1977: 147) states that of the crops grown under irrigation at Picuris (corn, wheat, beans, and squash),

Figure 7.3.   Waffle gardens at Zuni Pueblo, 1910–1911. (Photograph by Jesse Nusbaum, courtesy of the Museum of New Mexico, Negative No. 43170.)

the largest portion of the land is devoted to corn, and it requires more water than any of the other crops. Because of its water requirements and the primacy of corn in Zuni subsistence, this discussion focuses on corn cultivation. Unfortunately, the water requirements and growing seasons of the different varieties of aboriginal Zuni corn are not known, and I must rely mainly on data concerning modern corn and data for other varieties of Indian corn.

Growing Season

Hack (1942: 20) indicates that a growing season of 130 days is required for corn planted in the Hopi area, and that there may be some annual variation because dryness causes the crops to mature more slowly. Bradfield (1971: 6) indicates that 115 to 130 days is required for corn to mature at Hopi, depending on the season and the location. Because the season is apt to be shorter than the necessary period, crops are often lost to frost damage. The depth at which the corn is planted (10 to 15 inches, 25 cm to 38 cm) allows the seeds to reach subsurface moisture during the dry months of May and June (for germination and early growth), and also protects the seeds from late spring frosts. Cushing (1920:181) indicates that at Zuni corn is planted at a depth of 4 to 7 inches (10 cm to 18 cm).

The main planting by the Hopi is in mid-May (Hack 1942: 20), which is about the time of the last killing frost (Bradfield 1971: 6). The harvest starts about September 25, by which time frost has often already occurred (Hack 1942: 20). According to Bradfield (1971: 6), Hopi corn sprouts 10 days

to 2 weeks after planting, and any frost after sprouting results in death of the plant or severe retardation of its growth. He further indicates that a late spring frost is considered worse than an early fall frost.

Planting at Zuni was reported by Cushing (1920: 174) to be in May. Table 7.3 reveals that at Zuni if the planting were May 23 (day 143, one week after the average date of the last spring frost), then late spring frosts would come after the planting in 18 (28 percent) of the 65 recorded years, but in only two years (3 percent) would frosts come more than two weeks after the planting (that is, after the corn had sprouted). If the growing season for corn was 130 days, the first frost would have come before September 30 (130 days later, day 273) in only 10 (15 percent) of the 65 recorded years and in only two (3 percent) of the years would the first fall frost come more than two weeks before the maturation date. All together, only 13 years (20 percent) of the 65 recorded had a frost-free period less than 130 days.

The situation at El Morro is quite different. Only 7 of the 43 years of record have growing seasons *as long as* 130 days (that is, 84 percent do not). With a planting date of June 6 (day 157, the average date of the last spring frost), late spring frosts would come after the planting in 19 (44 percent) of the 43 years, and in four years (9 percent) they would come more than two weeks after the planting. However, if the corn required 130 days to mature, then the first fall frost would come before October 14 (day 287) in 39 years (91 percent) and more than two weeks before this date in 23 years (53 percent). With the intensive habitation of this area, it seems likely that corn was grown successfully on a regular basis, although the risk of crop failure due to frost must have been greater than at lower elevations.

Water Requirements for Agriculture

Although the water requirements of the varieties of prehistoric corn used in the area are not known, several studies have been conducted to determine the consumptive use of water by modern crops, including corn. (Consumptive use is defined as the amount of water used in building plant tissue and in transpiration, and in water evaporated from adjacent soil.) Factors that affect consumptive use are: crop-specific requirements, temperature, humidity, wind, and the amount of solar radiation (which is a function of the time of year, latitude, elevation, and cloud cover). Blaney and Criddle (1962) and Bordne and McGuinness (1973) discuss these studies and provide methods of estimating consumptive use of water based on climatic information and on the growth characteristics of the crops.

Bordne and McGuinness compare various estimation techniques and conclude that all methods surveyed provide satisfactory estimates. The simplest method they discuss, and the only one for which long-term records of the necessary climatic variables are available in the Zuni area, is the one presented by Blaney and Criddle (1962; also Blaney and Harris 1951). In this method, monthly consumptive use is the simple product of a crop-specific constant, the average monthly temperature, and the monthly percentage of daytime hours. The monthly values, summed over the growing season, determine the consumptive use of water by a crop. This formula is intended to produce an estimate of the minimum water requirements of the plants, and assumes that the water is delivered to the plants at the time it is needed. It does not include loss of water during its delivery to the field (which would be substantial), or loss due to surface runoff or percolation of water below the levels at which it is usable by the plants.

Using a growing season of June through September, the formula indicates that at Zuni the consumptive use of water by modern corn under irrigation would be 560 mm (22 inches), and at El Morro it would be 534 mm (21 inches, or 5 percent less than at Zuni); the difference is due to the lower temperature at El Morro. Under irrigation conditions, corn in the Zuni area would require about 14 cm (5.5 inches) per month, spaced out over the month, again neglecting water losses in irrigation (evaporation and ditch seepage), runoff, and deep percolation. Both Zuni and El Morro are at approximately 35 degrees north latitude. The percentage of daylight hours for each month at this latitude was derived from a table presented by Blaney and Harris (1951: 49). Average monthly temperatures for the two weather stations are given in Table 7.3, above. Because of the aridity of the area, the crop-specific constant used for corn (0.85) is at the high end of the range given by Blaney and Criddle (1962: 19).

Prehistoric southwestern varieties of corn probably required substantially less water than the modern varieties and were more resistant to periods of drought. Although the modern consumptive use figures may not be transferred directly to the prehistoric case, they do point out some significant considerations.

Perhaps most important, it seems unlikely in the absence of some method of water control that corn could get enough water to grow on rainfall alone. The total annual rainfall at Zuni (Table 7.1) is only a little more than half (54 percent) of the consumptive use requirement of modern corn. Although the water requirements of the plants in June might be supplied by groundwater remaining from the winter rains, the average July through September rainfall is only 132 mm (31 percent) of the July through September requirements of 422 mm. Also, in the absence of water control, a substantial fraction of the rainfall must be lost to runoff and deep percolation. Blaney and Harris (1951: 21) note that in each irrigation the first 13 mm to 25 mm (0.5 to 1.0 inch) of water are used in wetting the surface mulch and are lost to the plants, so brief showers in the summer (which may contribute substantially to the total rainfall) will have little value. Furthermore, for runoff agriculture Hack (1942: 20) indicates that 5 mm to 8 mm (0.2 to 0.3 inch) of rain are required to start arroyos running; rains less than this amount are effectively useless.

Second, considering the large discrepancy between the water requirements of corn and the amount of rainfall available (290 mm less than required for modern corn in June through September), it seems doubtful that the difference in seasonal or annual rainfall between Zuni and El Morro (14 mm difference in June through September rainfall; 37 mm annual difference) would be a major factor contributing to agricultural success or failure. Even if a much lower requirement for prehistoric corn is assumed, and the slightly lower water requirement at El Morro (26 mm less water is required at El Morro for modern corn) is taken into account, it is unlikely that the difference in rainfall would have been significant. It seems clear that additional sources of water would have been required at either Zuni or El Morro and, by extension, at any location in the study area.

Agricultural Properties of Zuni Area Soils

The only soil surveys of the Zuni area that have been comprehensive enough to include the entire study area were the county-by-county soil surveys conducted by the New Mexico State University Agricultural Experiment Station (Maker, Bullock, and Anderson 1974; Maker, Hacker, and Anderson 1974). These studies evaluated the agricultural potential of soils under irrigation. In these surveys, individual soils were classified and the associations of these soils were mapped. Based on their agricultural properties, the soils were classified into one of five categories with respect to their agricultural potential under irrigation. These classes were numbered 1 through 4, and 6 (there is no class 5).

The factors that affected the placement of land in the various irrigation land classes were: soil texture, including gravel and stone content; effective soil depth; available water-holding capacity; salinity; alkali; permeability; erosion; surface smoothness; slope; internal soil drainage; and surface drainage.

The classification system establishes four classes of irrigable land and one class of non-irrigable land. The limitations for use under irrigation increase from class 1 through 4. For example, class 1 has few or no limitations for use as cropland under irrigation. It is productive and well adapted to irrigation. High yields of most climatically adapted crops can be obtained on this land with good

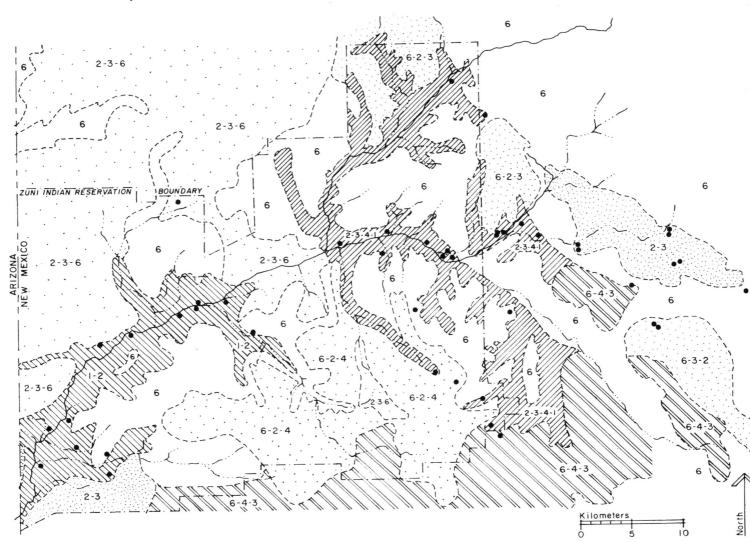

Figure 7.4.　Irrigation potential of the Zuni area (see text for key).

management. Class 2 land, although well suited to irrigation has slight, to moderate limitations for sustained use under irrigation. This is moderately productive land, or land that requires more than average management to produce high yields of climatically adapted crops. Class 3 land, which has moderate to severe limitations for sustained use under irrigation, is generally not as suitable for the production of as wide a range of the climatically adapted crops as land in classes 1 and 2. This land also has a more limited productivity for many of the climatically adapted crops, or requires a very high level of management for moderate to high yields. Class 4 land has a very severe limitation for sustained use under irrigation. The land included in this class is usually suited only to a relatively few of the climatically adapted crops. Some of this land may be adapted or used for the production of specialized crops under a very high level of management. Class 6 land is not suitable for irrigation (Maker, Bullock, and Anderson 1974: 4).

Soil associations, which are the combinations of soils that actually occur, are characterized by the proportion of soils of each irrigation class that are present in the association. Zones of these soil associations are shown in Figure 7.4 and are labeled by a sequence of numbers that use the irrigation potentials of each type of land included, in order of decreasing percentage of land in that irrigation class. The percentages of different land classes in each zone of different irrigation potential are given in Table 7.6. (A few minor adjustments were made in the figure and in the table to make data from the two counties compatible.)

The best agricultural soils are in the lower portions of the Zuni River Valley. The next most preferable soils are in relatively flat areas in the northwest portion of the study area and along the other major drainages. Portions of the El Morro Valley have productive soil, but other parts have poor soil. The upper mesa slopes and tops have, almost exclusively, poor agricultural soils.

This provides a relative evaluation of the agricultural potential of different areas, assuming the presence of adequate water for crops. While this evaluation may not be identical to an optimal evaluation of prehistoric agricultural potential for

TABLE 7.6
Classification of Zones by Irrigation Potential

Zone Label	Percent of Zonal Soil in Each Irrigation Class					Composite* Value
	Class 1	Class 2	Class 3	Class 4	Class 6	
1–2	52	28	8	2	10	0.78
2–3	4	47	32	4	13	0.56
2–3–4–1	15	29	25	18	13	0.54
2–3–6	9	45	20	11	15	0.56
6–2–3		16	15	4	65	0.21
6–2–4		39	5	15	41	0.36
6–3–2		18	22	5	55	0.26
6–4–3		13	16	20	51	0.23
6		4	3	8	85	0.07

*Composite productivity value, described in Chapter 8.

some specific crop, the basic factors considered in this evaluation probably were as important prehistorically as they are under modern irrigation.

Prehistoric and Historic Southwestern Water Control

If it is accepted that more water than is supplied by direct rainfall on a field is required to achieve agricultural success, there is a limited number of ways that additional water could be procured using prehistoric technology. The most obvious technique is to control surface runoff from slopes or on floodplains in order to divert some of it to fields. Perhaps the simplest method is to tap adequate sources of groundwater directly, either through seepage or a high water table; however, use of this strategy is limited to locations with the proper hydrology. Finally, fields may be irrigated from permanent springs or streams.

Historic Zuni agricultural technology was discussed above. Water-control techniques used by the historic Hopi, and archaeological evidence for water control in plateau and mountain areas of the Southwest, suggest additional mechanisms of water control that may have been utilized in the Zuni area and that should be considered in reconstructing the prehistoric settlement patterns of the area.

Hack (1942: 19–38) provides a typology of Hopi fields based on the way in which they were watered, and he describes in some detail four major categories of water-use strategies. His first category, fields watered by surface runoff (floodwater farming) includes: akchin fields (in which fields are formed at the fan of an arroyo); fields on the floodplains of large streams (in which spreaders and ditches are used to divert floodwater from a stream); fields on the flood terraces of large arroyos; fields in the bottoms of small arroyos; *trinchera* fields on artificial terraces in drainages; and fields watered by hillside wash. Cushing, in a passage cited above regarding historic Zuni practices, describes a related type of floodwater farming in which an arroyo is dammed to form a field at the base of a slope, a type combining characteristics of Hack's trinchera plots and akchin fields.

Hack's second category includes fields watered by rainfall: fields on sand dunes, and fields on alluvial and other soils at higher elevations. The third category is fields watered by underground seepage: either on sand dunes, on colluvial soils, or in dune hollows. His fourth category is made up of fields irrigated from either permanent streams or springs.

Woodbury (1961b: 8–16) provides a classification of agricultural field-related archaeological features at Point of Pines, Arizona. These included: terraced plots on slopes (which Hack calls trinchera fields), linear borders (rows of stones following elevation contours that served to slow runoff and erosion), grid borders (which are similar to linear borders, but form a grid rather than parallel lines), boundary markers, field houses, wells, and reservoirs.

This list was expanded by Vivian (1974: 95–97) in his summary of Anasazi water-control systems. Vivian's list includes: bordered gardens (Woodbury's grid borders), gravel-mulched bordered gardens (in which the gravel serves to retain moisture), check dams (similar to Hack's trinchera plots or Woodbury's terraces), contour terraces (linear borders), ditches, canals, headgates, diversion dams, and reservoirs. Using the information supplied by Fred Plog and Richard Woodbury, Vivian (1974: 102) indicates that several of these features occurred in the Zuni-Little Colorado area: check dams, contour terraces, ditches, and possibly bordered gardens. From our survey of Zuni sites (Chapter 4), reservoirs may be added to this list (at Atsinna and Kechiba:wa).

The potential applicability of these water-control methods for the Zuni area may now be evaluated. In the Hopi area, 73 percent of all cultivated lands were watered by surface runoff (Hack 1942: 26). Of these, akchin fields were the most common; they are placed at the mouths of arroyos that begin on the steep-sided Hopi mesas and drain into a broad, flat valley. At Zuni, though, the valleys are much narrower, and many of the mesas have slopes that are more gradual, especially in the eastern part of the Zuni area. The topographic possibilities for akchin fields are probably more limited in the Zuni area.

The possibilities for check dams and contour terraces (including the floodwater field type described by Cushing), however, are quite common in the Zuni area, in part because of the more gradual slopes at the bases of many of the mesas and the numerous large canyons with ample catchments.

As in the Hopi area, arroyo beds and terraces, and floodplains of streams could have been cultivated. However, also as at Hopi, these fields have a high probability of being washed out. There are some sand dunes in the Zuni area, but their potential for use in the types of agriculture described by Hack is unknown. Woodbury (1970: 4) suspects that there is less potential for sand dune agriculture at Zuni than at Hopi. Reservoirs are known prehistorically at Zuni, but their place in the agricultural system is not known (they may have only been sources of domestic water).

As mentioned above, there are large springs in the Zuni area that were used historically (and, I believe, prehistorically) as sources of irrigation water. There are other springs, such as the one mentioned by Spier near Tinaja, that potentially could have been used for irrigation.

In prehistoric times, the Zuni River was perennial and probably could have been used for irrigation. The Rio Nutria, the Rio Pescado, and the unnamed stream fed by Muerto Spring also may have been permanent sources of water usable for irrigation. However, in order for prehistoric irrigation to have been successful, it was necessary to have not only water in the streams through the summer, but also the appropriate topography in which to situate a headgate and run canals from the river to the fields. The topographic suitability of an area would have been determined partly by the depth the river channel was cut below the ground surface (which may have varied over time), and by the river gradient.

Agricultural Technology and Agricultural Potential

From this consideration of the modern and prehistoric environments and conceivable agricultural technologies, some general observations about the study area may be made. Although the data are insufficient to allow an evaluation of the absolute risk of agricultural failure at a particular location in prehistoric times, *relative* evaluations of the productivity and risk of crop failure under a given set of conditions can be made with some validity. In the next chapter these observations are used to aid in the inference of agricultural technology in the synchronic analyses of the settlement patterns for each period, and in examining the economic basis of settlement pattern changes in the diachronic analysis.

First, unless there was a great deal more rainfall prehistorically, it appears that sufficient water for corn agriculture could not have been obtained from direct rainfall on fields, and that one or more techniques of water control must have been utilized extensively. In fact, the tree-ring decade departure indices available for the modern period with climatic records, from 1910 to 1959, average +1.4, while for the period 1250 to 1540 they average −0.05, suggesting more rainfall during the modern period than characterized the late prehistoric period (data obtained from Dean and Robinson 1977).

Second, it appears that the rainfall differential within the study area was not enough to make a dramatic difference in the probability of agricultural success or failure in one place compared with another. However, orographic effects may have favored windward areas on or near the bases of major landforms such as the Zuni Mountains or large mesas.

Third, the difference in the length of the growing season over the study area is substantial and, particularly at the higher elevations, the short growing season appears marginal for corn agriculture, even during average years. Locations near the bases of mesas have more moderate nighttime temperatures, and hence slightly longer growing seasons than adjacent, more open areas.

Fourth, with the exception of a part of the El Morro Valley, soils on or near the valley bottoms have better soils than other landforms in the area. The best soils are in the lower Zuni River Valley, and the worst soils are on the upper mesa slopes and mesa tops.

Fifth, assuming that extensive water-control techniques were required, several methods conceivably could have been used prehistorically in the Zuni area: contour terraces, check dams, spring and river irrigation, and floodwater farming of arroyo bottoms and stream floodplains.

Sixth, if a large population had to be supported mainly from fields formed by check dams and contour terraces, the fields had to be located in areas with gradual slopes near the bases of mesas and mountains. Topographically, the eastern part of the study area, with its many relatively narrow canyons and valleys, was more suitable for locating a high density of these fields than was the western part. Other forms of floodwater farming could have been practiced in many parts of the region. Spring-fed irrigation was possible around major springs such as Nutria, Pescado, and Ojo Caliente. Because of the larger size of the river, the breadth of the floodplain, and the lower river gradient, riverine irrigation was a technique better suited to the southwestern part of the study area.

From the data presented in Chapter 6, I estimate that a peak population of approximately 9000 might have inhabited the valley at any one time. For the Rio Grande pueblo of Picuris in 1890, Ford (1977: 148) cites Walpole to the effect that scarcely more than 100 acres were irrigated for a population of 108. Based on this information, if we assume that approximately one acre (0.4 ha) of fields was planted per person (more may have been required for the more risky and probably less productive floodwater farming), then a population of 9000 would require in excess of 36 square kilometers of fields. Even for a conservative population estimate of 4500, 18 square kilometers would have been necessary. Bradfield (1971: 20–21) uses Stephen's (1936) data on agriculture using floodwater farming at Hopi (recorded in 1892) to argue that about 2.5 acres (1.0 hectare) per person were planted, mostly in corn. For a Zuni area population of 9000, this figure suggests a cultivated area of 90 square kilometers, and for a conservatively estimated population of 4500, 45 square kilometers. Thus, it appears that a substantial area must have been cultivated prehistorically in the Zuni area.

8. ZUNI SETTLEMENT PATTERNS AND SOCIAL ORGANIZATION

In this chapter, the synchronic views of the settlement patterns developed in Chapter 6 are used in conjunction with the information presented in the last chapter to infer aspects of the agricultural technology employed at different times, and to determine the extent to which settlement locations reflect the availability of natural resources. Further, an analysis of the lack of fit between resource availability and site location enhances our understanding of the social dimensions of these settlement patterns. In a diachronic synthesis, arguments relating changes in the settlement patterns to climatic variation and to technological evolution are presented and evaluated, and the settlement pattern changes are discussed with respect to their implications for the social organization of the inhabitants of these prehistoric pueblos.

SYNCHRONIC SYNTHESIS

Agricultural Technology

As discussed in Chapter 7, an agriculturally based subsistence system cannot succeed in the Zuni area using only rain falling directly on the fields. Either sources of groundwater must be tapped directly, runoff from slopes or streams (floodwater) must be captured and diverted to fields, or permanent springs or streams must be used to irrigate fields. In the Zuni region, the potential exists to use a variety of agricultural methods, although specific areas differ in their suitability for particular techniques. Many parts of the eastern, central, and northwestern portions of the region are well-suited to floodwater farming, and there is archaeological evidence that floodwater farming was practiced prehistorically in some of these areas. The narrow canyons provide a large number of arroyos that drain the higher elevations and cut across the gradual slopes at the bases of the mesas before emptying into the main canyon drainage. Irrigation from springs has been practiced throughout much of the historic period at the permanent springs at Nutria, Pescado, and Ojo Caliente. The topography and soils of the Zuni River floodplain appear to be suitable for river irrigation; in prehistoric and early historic times the Zuni River, and probably its major tributaries, flowed all year. It is difficult to evaluate the extent to which crops might have been able to tap sufficient groundwater directly, either in sand dunes or in areas with a high water table.

Ceramic Complexes AB and B
(A.D. 1175–1250)

The archaeological data are consistent with an interpretation that floodwater farming, particularly on slopes at the bases of mesas, was practiced near most of the pueblos occupied during complexes AB and B (Figs. 6.1 and 7.4). With a few exceptions, pueblos occupied during this period were situated in areas with extensive possibilities for fields created by check dams, like those described by Cushing (1920). Floodwater farming on floodplains, arroyo terraces, and arroyo bottoms may also have been practiced, but, as Hack (1942: 29–30) points out, such fields are subject to frequent destruction by floods.

Numerous water-control features, mostly check dams near the valley margins, were reported from a survey of Miller Canyon in the southeastern corner of the Zuni Reservation. Most of these features appear to be associated with the last prehistoric occupation of the canyon, contemporary with the Miller Ranch Ruin (complex B; Kintigh 1980: 44–45).

The only pueblo at which floodwater farming may not have been appropriate during complexes AB and B was Heshoda Yala:wa (Fig. 6.1). There were not many arroyos with large catchments within a kilometer or two of the pueblo (except across the Zuni River). About 2 km south, however, is one arroyo that drains a rather large area. The pueblo was close to both the Zuni River and Plumasano Wash, so that other types of floodwater farming may have been practiced there. For example, fields could have been located on the floodplains of these major drainages. An alternative interpretation is that the pueblo actually dates to a much later period. In Chapter 4, I noted the presence of ceramic data to support the interpretation of an early occupation (complexes B through D) and a much later occupation, during complex G or H. The site location fits better with the settlement pattern exhibited by sites dating to these later periods.

Ceramic Complex C
(A.D. 1250–1275)

In general, the locational data for complex C pueblos are consistent with a reliance on floodwater farming of the lower mesa slopes. However, the Mirabal Ruin, first occupied during complex C (Fig. 6.2), does not seem well placed for floodwater farming, as it is more than 2 km away from any likely spots for building check dams or contour terraces, and there are few arroyos in the vicinity. The presence of a lone ponderosa pine next to a blowout near the site and a basalt flow near the surface may indicate a hydrological situation in which groundwater is more directly accessible. Except for Heshoda Yala:wa and Mirabal, the pueblos occupied during complex C were topographically situated such that floodwater farming could have been possible, although at some of these locations the shortness of the frost-free season would have presented a problem for farming.

Ceramic Complex D
(A.D. 1275–1300)

During complex D (Fig. 6.3), the pueblos of Yellowhouse and Halona:wa South were built west of the focus of previous occupation. Yellowhouse was well situated for floodwater farming, at a place where two major side canyons enter the Zuni River Valley. Halona:wa South apparently was not located with this type of farming in mind, but irrigation from the river or floodwater farming of the broad Zuni River floodplain was probably possible. If the water table was sufficiently high, deep-rooted crops planted on the floodplain may have obtained groundwater directly.

During this same complex, the Cienega Site was built close to the Mirabal Ruin and was subject to the same locational considerations discussed above. At about the same time, North Atsinna was established on a mesa top along the southern edge of the El Morro Valley. Unlike the mesa-top locations of pueblos occupied in earlier periods, which had abundant possibilities for fields that could capture substantial amounts of slope wash, the amount of runoff available near North Atsinna was limited by the relatively small size of the mesa. Also, as shown in Figure 7.4, it is relatively far from any good agricultural soils. Finally, Upper Nutria Village was first occupied during complex D. Although floodwater farming was probably possible in the vicinity, waters from major springs were also available for irrigation.

Ceramic Complex DE
(A.D. 1300–1325)

The apparent diversification of agricultural strategies that was evident during complex D, particularly the possible use of irrigation from springs, is even clearer during complex DE (Fig. 6.4). Within this relatively short time, the three pueblos near the Pescado Springs were established very close together in locations well suited for spring-fed irrigation. Water from the springs probably also reached Lower Pescado Village, established during this complex about 2 km downstream. As long as it was not too deeply cut, the Rio Pescado may have been usable for irrigation. A stream fed by Muerto Spring runs within a few meters of Pueblo de los Muertos. Watson and others (1980: 207) report a low masonry wall following the slope contour on the stream bank adjacent to the pueblo, although they are unsure of its function. The inhabitants of Pueblo de los Muertos, like those of the Pescado Springs ruins and Upper Nutria Village, may have practiced some combination of spring irrigation and floodwater farming.

Halona:wa South continued its occupation into complex DE. The small pueblo of Achiya:Deyała was constructed at the bottom of a ridge close to the Zuni River, where a variety of floodwater farming techniques, or river irrigation, could have been used. The location, size, and architectural layout of Achiya:Deyała do not fit with the patterns for this complex and the possibility that it was a seasonal or temporary site must be considered.

The Kluckhohn Ruin, Yellowhouse, and the Ramah School House Ruin, all of which were well located for floodwater farming of mesa slopes, continued their occupations into this period. Cienega and Mirabal on the floor of the El Morro Valley also continued to be occupied. Atsinna, which was subject to the same considerations that applied to North Atsinna, was established during complex DE.

Ceramic Complexes E, F, and G
(A.D. 1325–1400)

The topographic situations of the pueblos occupied during complexes E (Fig. 6.5) and F (Fig. 6.6) are similar to those of sites occupied during the previous period. Only Heshot uła was added to the settlement distribution of complex DE. Heshot uła, like nearby Yellowhouse, is advantageously placed for floodwater farming of slopes. It is centrally located along the Rio Pescado at a point where three major side canyons enter the main river valley.

Ceramic Complex H
(A.D. 1400–1625)

A major shift in agricultural strategy is indicated by the distribution of pueblo locations in complex H (Fig. 6.7). It appears that there was an almost complete reliance on irrigation agriculture and a greater use of river irrigation of fields, as opposed to irrigation using springs. At Kechiba:wa and Hawikku spring water for irrigation was available from the Ojo Caliente springs. Mats'a:kya, Halona:wa North, Binna:wa, Hambassa:wa, Kwa'kin'a, Chalo:wa, and probably Kyaki:ma were situated in areas where river irrigation was feasible. In addition, at Kwa'kin'a and Chalo:wa slope wash could have been captured and used. At all of the locations near rivers, floodwater farming of the Zuni River floodplain (or Galestina Canyon, in the case of Kyaki:ma) could have been practiced. However, considering the apparent uniformity of the adaptation and the risks of floodwater farming of a river floodplain, it seems unlikely that this water-control strategy was the dominant one.

Settlement Location and the
Distribution of Natural Resources

In Chapter 7, I argued that an agriculturally based subsistence system could not succeed using only rain that fell directly on the fields. In the previous section I discussed, for each ceramic complex, the water-control technologies that, on the basis of available data, *could* have been employed in the areas surrounding the pueblos occupied during that period. There is, however, little direct information on prehistoric water control in the Zuni area during the late prehistoric period. However, we can further examine the ways in which site locations reflect the distribution of natural resources in the area.

Although the mix of hunted, gathered, and agricultural subsistence items may well have been significantly different in the late prehistoric period, agriculture was at the core of the historic Zuni subsistence system as it has been recorded. As noted above, the dominant crop at the time of Spanish contact was maize, and the prehistoric importance of maize is indicated by the large amounts of stored corn that were recovered from the burned rooms at the Scribe S Site. Because of this reliance on agriculture, because of the proportion of time and energy probably involved in agriculture as compared with hunting and the gathering of wild plants, and because the hunting and gathering must have occurred over a very dispersed area (Ferguson 1981b), the remainder of this discussion of settlement location and resource distribution revolves mainly around the environmental factors that are necessary for agriculture.

Catchment Analysis

Catchment analysis is one way of examining the relationship of a site to the resources in its surrounding area (its territory or catchment; Higgs and Vita-Finzi 1972). In broad terms, the catchment of a site is defined as the area from which the subsistence for the pueblo is obtained. Because of travel and transportation costs, in a sedentary agricultural system there is a limit to how far away fields may be if the producers are to maintain residence in a village. Chisolm (1968: 131) argues that beyond 1 km, travel time becomes a consideration, and 3 km to 4 km is the limit beyond which adjustments to the settlement system, such as the establishment of subsidary field houses or satellite villages, will be required. He further suggests that, in most cases, fields will be limited to a 1-km to 2-km radius around the site.

On the basis of this argument, we expect that *if* a pueblo is generally self-sufficient for the main subsistence items, and *if* the producers reside at the pueblo, then an area of productive agricultural fields sufficient to support the population will be found within a 1-km or 2-km radius of the pueblo. If the area surrounding the pueblo is not sufficiently productive to support its population, then one of the assumptions of the argument must have been violated. Stated in another way, given these assumptions, a pueblo's population will not exceed the productive potential of its catchment.

An interesting commentary relevant to this approach is given in the emergence myth from Hopi Shungo'povi (Wallis 1936: 13–14, as quoted by Bradfield 1971: 40):

Shungo'povi was built first [of the Hopi pueblos], and there the Hopi first made their abode. . . . After a while people were arriving continually. Soon the farms were too far away from the owners' homes. Shungo'povi was soon a big village. The man who knows how to make rain [i.e. the village Chief] said to his sister and brother of the Bear clan, "Go to Oraibi and live there." The man's sister had a husband. They went. His brother was the chief (the chief is always of Bear clan, and is succeeded by the son of his sister). He sent another sister and her husband, also a brother, to Walpi. He gave them land as he had done at Oraibi and marked off their respective tracts. He put up a stone to indicate the boundary line.

Some idea of the amount of area that must be cultivated using irrigation is derived from the 19th century Picuris data presented by Ford (1977, at the end of the previous chapter). At Picuris, about 0.40 ha of irrigated land per person was planted. When combined with the estimate of 1.3 persons per room in an occupied pueblo (a number derived by discounting the number of rooms in a pueblo by 35 percent for unoccupied rooms, and assuming that there were two people per occupied room), this suggests that 52 ha (0.52 square kilometer) of productive land would have to be planted for each 100 rooms in a pueblo; a 500-room pueblo would require 260 hectares; and a 1000-room pueblo, 520 hectares.

These figures imply that more than a third of a 1.5 km radius catchment (707 hectares) around a 500-room pueblo would have to be planted in order to support the population, and that almost three-fourths of the catchment would have to be planted in order to support a 1000-room pueblo. Clearly, it is most unlikely that such a large a fraction of a site's catchment will be irrigable, although for a site with 100 or 200 rooms, a 1.5 km radius catchment may be adequate (7 to 15 percent of the catchment would need to be cultivated). If a 3.0 km radius catchment size (2827 hectares) is used, 9 percent of the catchment would be required to support a 500-room pueblo, and 18 percent for a 1000-room pueblo. For pueblos that were supported by irrigation agriculture of their catchments and that were located on or adjacent to large areas of good, irrigable soils, these last computations do not appear to be unreasonable and may indicate that the catchment radius was on the order of 1.5 km for small sites and 3 km for larger sites.

To obtain similar figures for floodwater farming, we may use the information Bradfield (1971) has compiled for Hopi. As mentioned in the last chapter, he used Stephen's (1936) data concerning floodwater farming at Hopi in 1892 to obtain an estimate of 1.0 ha of cultivated floodwater fields per person. Bradfield (1971: 21, 39–40) also makes a detailed argument that indicates that floodwater fields must be located within 6.4 km (4 miles) of the village. While this figure is substantially larger than Chisolm's 4 km limit, it may be justified by the fact that floodwater fields require less care (and hence less travel) than fields cultivated using more intensive techniques.

Bradfield's figures indicate that 130 ha of fields would be necessary per 100 rooms. Thus, a 500-room pueblo would require 650 ha of fields and a 1000-room pueblo would require 1300 ha. Within a 6.4 km radius catchment (12,868 hectares) of a pueblo, 5 percent of the area would need to be cultivated to support a 500-room pueblo, and 10 percent to support a 1000-room pueblo. Hack (1942: 25) reports that due to the physiography, less than 3 percent of the Hopi country is farmed. Bradfield indicates that about 8 percent of the Oraibi Valley (4 square miles out of 52.5 square miles) had been cleared for fields at one time or another. These figures also appear reasonable, suggesting a catchment radius on the order of 6.4 km.

However, it must be recognized that other arguments can be made that would substantially alter these conclusions. The pueblos may not have been supplied primarily from their own catchments, or the reliance on hunted and gathered resources may be underestimated. Unfortunately, the degree of reliance on hunted and gathered resources cannot be determined using available data. Major interdependencies among these early pueblos with respect to primary subsistence needs seem unlikely, because at any one time almost all of them appear to have been exploiting environmental zones with similar agricultural potentials. Although there are historic references to the use of field houses, there is essentially no evidence for their use in the late prehistoric period.

Thus, the relevant catchment radius appears to be a function of the water-control technology employed. For some pueblos (for example, those using irrigation), a 3 km radius catchment may include the relevant agricultural resource area, while for others a larger catchment size must be used. However, an obvious lack of adequate resources within even a large catchment may be indicative of another subsistence orientation or the use of other locational criteria.

In order to evaluate the productivity of the immediate catchments of specific sites, it was necessary to determine a composite index of agricultural productivity for each soil

TABLE 8.1
Productivity of 1.5 km Radius Site Catchments

No.	Site	No. of Rooms	Elevation (meters)	Topographic Location	Productivity Index
1.	Spier 81	43	2060	Base of mesa	0.36
2.	Miller Ranch Ruin	60	2219	Ridge top	0.25
3.	Spier 61	122	2039	Base of mesa	0.38
4.	Upper Deracho Ruin	30	2103	Mesa terrace	0.34
5.	Vogt Ranch Ruin	39	2115	Base of mesa	0.36
6.	Kay Chee Ruin	255	2167	Ridge top	0.31
7.	Pettit Site	125	2134	Mesa top, base	0.32
8.	Pescado Canyon Ruin	723	2252	Mesa top	0.28
9.	Lower Deracho Ruin	609	2088	Base of mesa	0.34
10.	Scribe S Site	410	2231	Ridge top	0.44
11.	Heshoda Yala:wa	150	1875	Bluff top	0.78
12.	Box S Ruin	473	2106	Valley floor	0.22
13.	Shoemaker Ranch Ruin	17	2274	Mesa top	0.34
14.	Day Ranch Ruin	574	2091	Valley floor	0.36
15.	Lookout Site	300	2271	Mesa top	0.17
16.	Jack's Lake Ruin	245	2225	Base of mesa	0.38
17.	Archeotekopa II	1412	2256	Base of mesa	0.32
18.	Fort Site	216	2289	Mesa top	0.31
19.	Tinaja Ruin	163	2240	Butte top, base	0.13
20.	Kluckhohn Ruin	1142	2137	Base of mesa	0.32
21.	Mirabal Ruin	743	2198	Valley floor	0.56
22.	Yellowhouse	425	2012	Valley floor	0.54
23.	Ramah School House Ruin	186	2099	Valley floor	0.44
24.	North Atsinna Ruin	180	2268	Mesa top	0.21
25.	Upper Nutria Village	180	2079	Valley floor	0.48
26.	Halona:wa South	375	2050	Valley floor	0.78
27.	Cienega Site	500	2201	Valley floor	0.56
28.	Upper Pescado Ruin	405	2067	Valley floor	0.36
29.	Pueblo de los Muertos	880	2219	Base of mountain	0.44
30.	Atsinna	875	2265	Mesa top	0.21
31.	Achiya: Deya'la	5	1878	Ridge top	0.51
32.	Lower Pescado Village	420	2048	Valley floor	0.54
33.	Pescado West Ruin	445	2060	Valley floor	0.42
34.	Lower Pescado Ruin	180	2060	Valley floor	0.42
35.	Heshot u'la	85	2030	Valley floor	0.48
36.	Rainbow Spring Ruin	108	1935	Base of mesa	0.70
37.	Hambassa:wa	39	1892	Hill top	0.73
38.	Binna:wa	168	1911	Ridge top	0.78
39.	Hawikku	800	1899	Ridge top, slope	0.78
40.	Mats'a:kya	901	1932	Hill top, slope	0.78
41.	Kyaki:ma	250	1969	Base of mesa	0.43
42.	Kwa'kin'a	186	1887	Ridge top	0.73
43.	Chalo:wa	455	1868	Ridge top	0.78
44.	Kechiba:wa	824	1966	Mesa top	0.43
45.	Halona:wa North	200	1920	Valley floor	0.78

zone shown in Figure 7.4. In deriving this index, I assigned a weight to each irrigation class defined in Chapter 7. The weight was assigned somewhat arbitrarily as Class 1, 1.00; Class 2, 0.75; Class 3, 0.50; Class 4, 0.25; and Class 6, 0.00. For the zones of different irrigation potential (characterized by a mix of lands from different irrigation classes), the sum of this weighting, multiplied by the fraction of land in each irrigation class in that zone, gives a value of the relative agricultural potential for the zone. These values for the zones, which could range from 1.0 (100 percent class 1) to 0.0 (100 percent Class 6), are shown in the far right column of Table 7.6. Thus, zone 1–2, which is composed of 52 percent class 1 soils, 28 percent class 2 soils, 8 percent class 3

soils, 2 percent class 4 soils, and 10 percent class 6 soils has a composite value of 0.78:

$$0.78 = (0.52 \times 1.00) + (0.28 \times 0.75) + (0.08 \times 0.50) + (0.02 \times 0.25) + (0.10 \times 0.00)$$

In order to measure the catchment productivity for a specific site, I estimated the percentage of the land in each area of different irrigation potential within the catchment radius around the site to the nearest 12.5 percent (one-eighth). These percentages were then multiplied by the area's productivity index and summed to give a relative catchment productivity, a figure that for the study area ranges from 0.78 (100 percent of the catchment is in an area of 100 percent zone 1–2) to 0.07 (100 percent of the catchment is in soil association zone 6). The productivity figures for each site are given in Table 8.1.

In order to obtain an estimate of the productivity of the immediate area of the pueblo, an analysis of 1.5 km radius catchments was performed. This type of analysis was not done for catchment sizes expected under floodwater agriculture, because floodwater agriculture is as dependent on topographic suitability as it is on soil productivity. Because it was not possible to obtain the necessary environmental information to formulate a realistic productivity estimate for a floodwater farming catchment, no quantitative analysis directed toward this agricultural technology was attempted. Nonetheless, if the prehistoric pueblos had adjacent kitchen gardens, perhaps similar to the hand-watered waffle gardens observed historically at Zuni Pueblo, then one would still expect the pueblos to be located near small areas of productive lands. If this was the case, then the analysis of 1.5 km radius catchments may have some small utility for pueblos at which floodwater farming was used.

If the observed settlement patterns were relatively stable phenomena resulting from growth in place, with the budding off of new villages as the population's need exceeded the productivity of the pueblo's catchment, then a situation would be expected in which a pueblo's size was approximately proportional to its catchment productivity, and in which contemporaneous pueblos had nonoverlapping catchments. A brief examination of Figures 6.1 through 6.7 shows that reasonable catchment radii for pueblos (given the arguments presented above) did overlap substantially for some pueblos in each period except complex H. Figure 8.1 shows that even for the complex H pueblos, there was no relationship between pueblo size and catchment productivity.

For a situation in which the population size was stable or declining, the expectation would be that pueblos had non-overlapping catchments of sufficient size to support themselves, but that no particular relationship would be found between pueblo size and catchment productivity. If the pueblos were initially located to avoid conflict over agricultural lands and if there was no population growth, then competition among contemporaneous pueblos for the productive land would not be expected, and pueblo size would be limited only by agricultural productivity, not strictly determined by it. This interpretation is consistent with the observed complex H site distribution. The 1.5 km radius catchments are almost completely nonoverlapping (and somewhat larger catchments would not show substantial overlap), and the demographic data, presented in Chapter 6, indicate a stable or declining population through this period.

Another interpretation is that the assumptions behind the catchment analysis are incorrect because the pueblos were interdependent for subsistence goods and did not rely primarily on production from their own catchments for subsistence. In this regard, one suggestion that might be offered is that there existed central pueblos with satellite communities, perhaps something like the historic Zuni farming villages. The 19th century farming villages (large, masonry pueblos) were occupied mainly during the summer, but for the winter ceremonial season almost the entire population returned to the main pueblo. If they existed, the prehistoric

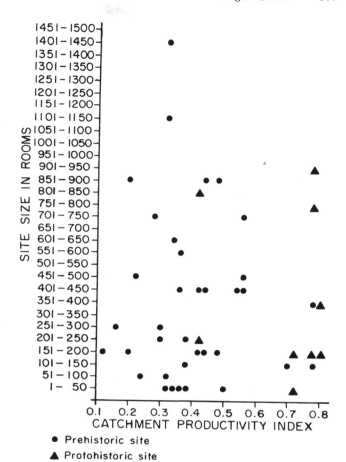

Figure 8.1. Scatter plot of Zuni site size by catchment productivity.

satellite communities might have been seasonally occupied like the historic Zuni farming villages. Alternatively, the satellites could have been permanently occupied. However, if there were such satellite communities, one might expect that in order to minimize transportation costs, there would have been widely spaced large pueblos surrounded by a number of satellite communities, or that the interdependent pueblos would occupy a diversity of environmental situations in order to minimize risk of crop failure due to climatic variation. Also, one might expect a fairly high ratio of small to large pueblos. The available data (Figs. 6.1–6.7, 6.10*b–h*, 7.4) do not seem to correspond to any of these expectations. Nonetheless, the possibility of seasonal occupation of some pueblos cannot be rejected.

Because of what is argued to be a reliance on floodwater farming in many pueblos occupied prior to complex H, the analysis of 1.5 km radius catchments is not expected to substantially aid our understanding of the earlier settlement patterns. Nonetheless, we might expect these pueblos to be located near productive lands for use in kitchen gardens. Furthermore, we might expect that relatively large catchments around the pueblos would not overlap to a large degree. In Figures 6.1 to 6.6 we do see substantial overlap in the catchments with 3 km to 6 km radii. In some cases, contemporaneous pueblos are only a kilometer or two apart,

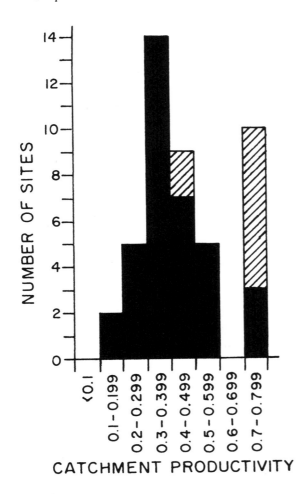

 Protohistoric site
Prehistoric site

Figure 8.2. Histogram of Zuni site productivity.

causing us to consider whether the prehistoric communities might have consisted of more than one architecturally distinct unit. No answer to this question can be suggested with the available data.

There does seem to be a relationship between agricultural productivity and site locations for both the prehistoric and protohistoric (complex H) pueblos (Fig. 8.2). Although in excess of half of the study area is covered with poor soils, few sites were located in areas of low productivity. The seven major exceptions (sites with a catchment productivity of less than 0.30) include Tinaja, Box S, and the Miller Ranch Ruin, as well as four of the five sites with the best defensive locations: Atsinna, North Atsinna, the Lookout Site, and Pescado Canyon (the other defensively located site, Shoemaker Ranch Ruin, is small and has a productivity of 0.34). Thirty-five of the sites are located in one of the four most productive soil associations and seven of the ten remaining sites are located within 2 km of one of these associations. It is interesting to note the absence of sites in the 8 km stretch of zone 2–3–6 soils along the Zuni River between Yellowhouse

and Matsa:kya (Fig. 7.4), which may be due to the presence of extensive basalt flows. Finally, the historic and protohistoric sites are *all* located in or directly adjacent to the relatively small zone of soils with the greatest irrigation potential of the entire study area.

Agricultural Technology Prior to the Protohistoric Period

Considering the evidence for floodwater farming around A.D. 1250 and suitability of the areas inhabited for this form of water control, it seems clear that floodwater farming of slopes was used extensively in the prehistoric period considered here. From about A.D. 1250 to 1375 (complexes C through F), the mean site elevation was over 2050 m (Table 6.2). The climatic analysis of Chapter 7 indicates that the growing season at higher elevations is considerably shorter than at the elevations around Zuni and the other protohistoric pueblos. Furthermore, it appears that the rainfall differential between the higher and lower elevations was probably not sufficient to have a major impact on agricultural success, because some form of water control had to be used. Thus, what was the economic advantage, if any, of the site locations occupied before the protohistoric period as compared with the lower Zuni River Valley?

A tentative answer is that riverine irrigation was *not* used extensively during that interval (complexes C through F), and that the eastern and central parts of the study area were utilized *because of* the availability of opportunities for floodwater farming that were not as plentiful at the lower elevations. Otherwise, it is difficult to understand why the lower elevations were not utilized.

Spring irrigation seems to have developed during this period and this technique was probably used in conjunction with floodwater farming. At these higher elevations, spring irrigation of the valley floors would have carried substantial risk of serious crop damage due to frost. However, the risk of frost damage at these same elevations was probably less in prudently placed floodwater fields on slopes, where eastern exposures would capture the early morning light and nighttime temperatures were moderated by cold air drainage off the mesas. (That same cold air would tend to settle on the valley floors where the irrigated fields would be located.) However, the experimentation with riverine irrigation that may have started at Halona:wa South around 1300 eventually culminated in the settlement pattern shift to the locations of the protohistoric towns and in a near complete reliance on riverine and spring irrigation.

Protohistoric Agricultural Technology

It seems that the protohistoric pueblos relied mainly on irrigation agriculture for their subsistence, and that their catchments were sufficiently productive to support their populations. The uniformity of the locations of the pueblos with respect to water resources, soils, and topography suggests that these factors influenced settlement location, and that similar subsistence strategies were used at all the pueblos.

Computation of nearest neighbor distances among these pueblos (the distance from each pueblo to the closest other contemporaneous pueblo) shows a much closer (indicated by a smaller mean nearest neighbor distance computed over all sites in a period) and more uniform spacing (indicated by a lower standard deviation of nearest neighbor distances) during the protohistoric period than at any other time (Table

TABLE 8.2
Nearest Neighbor Distances (in km) by Ceramic Complex

| | Ceramic Complex (A.D.) | | | | | | |
	End B 1250	End C 1275	End D 1300	End DE 1325	End E 1350	End F 1375	Mid H 1450
Mean nearest neighbor distance	8.4	6.7	6.2	5.3	5.9	10.7	3.6
Standard deviation	8.4	10.0	5.6	6.4	6.8	12.0	1.8
Number of sites	13	14	14	14	10	6	8

8.2). The excellent soils for irrigation, the proximity of the Zuni River or other major water sources, uniformity of the spacing of the pueblos, and the lack of overlap of the 1.5 km radius catchments appear to indicate an intensive use of the catchments surrounding these sites for irrigation agriculture.

Other Resources

Besides productive land and water, most other natural resources required were relatively widespread. Most sites are located near sources of building material, usually sandstone outcrops. On the average, the protohistoric sites are probably more distant from stone sources than sites dating earlier. Wood for fires and construction is widely available although, again, its availability is not quite as great for the protohistoric pueblos. Ponderosa pine logs for major construction projects had to be obtained from the higher elevations in the eastern part of the region. Pinyon, usable both as a food and fuel source, is widespread, although the degree to which the area might have been deforested cannot be estimated now. Sources for clay and the distribution of raw materials for chipped stone have not been adequately identified, although petrified wood is probably more common in the western part of the region, and jasper is more common in the east. Lithic materials such as obsidian must have been obtained either through trade or by expeditions to the sources, which lie outside the immediate area. Salt undoubtedly was obtained from Zuni Salt Lake, which is about 75 km south of Zuni. The distribution of animals of economic importance is largely dictated by the environmental zones described in Chapter 7. There is no obvious locational association of sites with these other natural resources, but their availability may have worked with other factors to influence settlement locations.

Conclusions

While the locations of natural resources, particularly water and suitable agricultural lands, do aid in an understanding of the settlement patterns, the distribution of the natural resources does not, by any means, explain all of the variability in settlement location. From an economic perspective, there are several pueblos whose locations do not make sense given the reconstruction presented here.

The most difficult site locations to understand are perhaps those of Jack's Lake and Archeotekopa II, occupied from about A.D. 1250 to 1300, during ceramic complexes C and D. Archeotekopa II is the largest site studied, with over 1400 rooms estimated. Both pueblos were at a high elevation (2256 m; 7400 feet) and were near the end of a narrow canyon with little bottomland nearby. No other natural resources are known to be accessible there that are not available elsewhere.

Pueblos that were located on mesa tops have character-

istically low productivities (Table 8.1) and some, notably Atsinna, North Atsinna, and the Lookout Site, were not even located particularly close to good agricultural soils (Fig. 7.4). In these cases, a defensive motive for the settlement location is suggested.

Cultural Determinants of Settlement Location

Warfare

Woodbury (1959) has discussed the ethnographic evidence that the Pueblo Indians were not the pacific tribes they are often argued or assumed to have been in prehistoric times. Rather, he states that warfare may have been a regular part of early historic and prehistoric Pueblo life, thus supporting a possible connection between warfare and settlement location.

Danson and Molde (1950) describe the late Pueblo III and early Pueblo IV (about A.D. 1300) site of Casa Malpais near Springerville, Arizona (about 125 km southwest of Zuni), which, they argue, was a fortified site located for defensibility. They suggest that the lack of sites in the area dating to that time, with the exception of two other defensible ones, may have been due to a period of prevalent warfare.

The case for warfare as an important explanatory variable for the El Morro Valley settlement pattern has been made most forcefully by LeBlanc (1978: 48). He believes warfare was a cause for the highly clustered arrangements of the complex C (Scribe S phase) pueblo communities and, later, was a cause for the shift to walled towns. Watson, LeBlanc, and Redman (1980: 216–217) evaluate the evidence for this hypothesis as "thin" but worthy of consideration. Supporting the argument, they list the shift to walled towns, the apparent concern for a secure nearby source of domestic water, and the fact that many of the rooms excavated at the Scribe S Site were burned and robbed of stone.

For present purposes, a defensible location is defined as one where access to the area was severely restricted by the physiography of the location. The defensibility of a pueblo was enhanced if possible attack routes could be monitored from within or near the pueblo. Defensibility was also increased by a permanent source of water in or near the pueblo. A defensible architectural configuration was one with a closed or nearly closed perimeter. An outside wall more than one story high added to the defense. Size also enhanced defensibility; presumably a large pueblo had more warriors than a small one.

Of the sites reviewed here, the following are considered defensible both in location and configuration: North Atsinna, Atsinna, the Lookout Site, and the Fort Site. Shoemaker Ranch Ruin has an excellent defensive position, but is divided into a number of room blocks on top of a mesa. However, there is a prehistoric wall around one of the upper terraces that may have been built for defensive purposes. The Pescado Canyon Ruin has a somewhat defensible location but the architectural configuration is not closed. The Pettit Site and Tinaja have room blocks both on the top and at the base of buttes on a valley floor, a configuration that also may be considered defensive.

These defensive pueblos have among the lowest productivity values in the study area (Table 8.1), reinforcing the argument for a noneconomic stimulus for their locations. They have a range of sizes and span complexes B through F, A.D. 1200 to 1375, in their occupation. At no time was a large proportion of the total population housed in these defensible pueblos and, in general, they are sufficiently far from other settlements that they would not have been particularly suitable as strongholds. The availability of domestic water sources for most of these sites is not well known because many springs may have dried up since prehistoric times. However, the Rainbow Spring Ruin, the Pescado Springs ruins, Pueblo de los Muertos, and the Cienega Site had springs in or adjacent to the ruins; Kechiba:wa and Atsinna had reservoirs; and Atsinna and North Atsinna had the permanent natural pool at the base of the mesa. As Watson and others (1980) have pointed out, almost all the pueblos in nondefensible locations that had "planned" layouts (Table 8.1) may be considered to have had defensive architectural configurations.

Jack's Lake Ruin and Archeotekopa II, at the end of a canyon near the top of a mesa, do not seem to be located defensively. Although the pueblos were remote from the valley floors, access to these sites is not restricted. They, like most contemporaneous large pueblos, had closed perimeters and high walls. As indicated above, the locations of these two sites remain unexplained and factors that are not illuminated by this analysis must have been operating in determining the locations of these two pueblos.

It appears that defensibility was the critical factor in the locations of only a few pueblos throughout the period from A.D. 1200 to 1400, although defensive considerations may have influenced the architecture of nearly all of them. Separate local groups may have responded differently to the possibility or actuality of warfare, some locating their pueblos defensively and some not.

Long-distance Trade

Advantageous placement of a trade route may be an important influence on settlement location. The historic Zuni and their predecessors did engage in long-distance trade (Riley 1975; Hart 1981), but little is known about the prehistoric trade. The known trade routes seem to have followed the valley bottoms. Thus, pueblos in the main valley, from Hawikku to Atsinna, were probably on a major trade route. Unfortunately, there is little reason to suspect that one location on this strip was any more advantageous than another. In any case, long-distance trade does not seem to help explain the locations of any of the pueblos, with the possible exception of Atsinna. It was on the major route from the Zuni area to Acoma and on to the Rio Grande, and the prominence afforded by its mesa-top location would have made it easy to locate.

The Apparent Settlement Gap

The demographic analysis (Chapter 6) reveals an almost discontinuous occupation of the Zuni area just prior to the protohistoric period. Figure 6.9 shows a dramatic drop in population at the end of ceramic complex F, about A.D. 1375, and a dramatic rise in population a short time later, at the start of complex H (about A.D. 1400). Such a situation seems intuitively suspect and deserves closer examination.

The identification of an apparent hiatus (or near absence of occupation) in the Zuni area just prior to the protohistoric period is not new. Spier (1917: 286, 303–305) noted the same problem and suggested that the ruins temporally connecting the two periods might be located along the Little Colorado River west of Zuni. Stimulated by the problem, he surveyed in the Little Colorado (Spier 1918) and White Mountain (Spier 1919) areas looking for evidence of pueblos dating to this gap. While Spier (1918: 338, 345) was not able to connect the two groups of ruins, he did suggest that the origin of the historic Zuni sites was to the west, in the northern Arizona "buffware" sites (Spier 1918: 341–345).

Woodbury (1956: 561, 1979: 469) does not see this hiatus but rather suggests that there was no break in cultural continuity with the historic villages. He believes the population moved from Atsinna and contemporaneous pueblos in the area more or less directly to the historic towns, and he indicates that this movement might have been due to an environmental change or population decline.

Based mainly on data from Spier (1917) and Hodge (published by Smith and others 1966), Watson and others (1980: 215–216) take a rather different position. They argue that there may be a temporal gap between the latest El Morro sites and the earliest levels of Binna:wa, but that the lack of sites for this period should not be characterized as a cultural break. They suggest that there is at least as large a gap between Binna:wa and Hawikku as there is between El Morro and Binna:wa. They postulate a sequence in which the El Morro Valley is abandoned early in the 1300s; soon thereafter Binna:wa and Kechiba:wa were occupied, and subsequently abandoned about the time the occupation of Mats'a:kya began near A.D. 1400. The occupation of Hawikku followed shortly after 1400.

This two-gap scenario appears to complicate the issue unnecessarily. From the analysis presented here, it appears that the argument of Watson and others suffers from: dating the abandonment of the El Morro Valley too early (as discussed in Chapter 5); an inadequate appreciation of the importance of the large sites outside the El Morro Valley (such as Heshot uła and the Pescado Springs sites) that date to the same period as the late El Morro Valley sites; and perhaps an unwarranted confidence in the reliability and comparability of Hodge's data (as noted in the Chapter 4 discussion of Hawikku, site 39). Their temporal placement of Kechiba:wa as contemporaneous with Binna:wa but preceding Mats'a:kya is at variance with both the archaeological and historical data.

Unfortunately, the data now available are not sufficient to resolve whether there actually was a hiatus in occupation, or whether this apparent gap is due to inadequate archaeological data or to problems with the analytical methods used. Several propositions concerning this question may be presented and evaluated.

1. There could have been a precipitous depopulation or abandonment of the entire area and subsequent reoccupation, all within a short time, as Spier believed. A modification of this proposition is that there was not a mass exodus but rather a severe depopulation, perhaps caused by disease, followed by a new migration into the area from some other region.

A migration out of the Zuni area in the late 1300s of the scale that seems to be indicated should be readily apparent in the destination area. It appears, without systematic investigation, that the relatively small number of large sites in the Southwest that were occupied at about A.D. 1400 had sufficient precursors in their immediate areas to more than account for their size, without a massive immigration (see Upham 1982). Furthermore, an exodus or other depopulation from the Zuni area, followed quickly by a movement into the area by a *different* cultural group or groups, is contradicted by what appears to be the considerable ceramic continuity from 1200 to 1600. Nonetheless, some interaction with Salado people from the south and west of Zuni around 1400 may be indicated, as discussed below.

If this hypothesized movement did take place, it still seems (as Spier suggested) that the area most likely to be involved is the Little Colorado area to the west of Zuni, which is part of the same general ceramic tradition as Zuni. However, investigations in this area show no evidence for a large influx of population at this time.

2. There was no hiatus in settlement of the area; instead, the protohistoric sites were occupied substantially earlier than was argued above. This implies that the early deposits at the major protohistoric sites have not been recovered, as Woodbury seems to suggest, or that we are underestimating the importance of the relatively small proportions of earlier wares found at these sites. If this were the case, there might have been a rather gradual decline in population from about A.D. 1300 to 1500, instead of the abrupt decline and increase about 1400.

Supporting this proposition is the fact that there is very little good stratigraphic data from these large and long-occupied sites. The length of occupation and depth of the archaeological deposits at such sites as Binna:wa (6.5 feet, 1.98 m), Mats'a:kya (5 feet, 1.52 m), and Hawikku (15 feet, 4.57 m, or more), indicate that even major early deposits could be deeply buried. With the exception of Hawikku, systematic testing has been restricted to small trenches in trash middens. Considering the sizes of the sites, it would be easy to miss evidence of substantial earlier deposits, and the several trenches dug by Spier at Halona:wa North (Zuni Pueblo) illustrate the extreme variance in assemblages that can be found in different trenches at the same site, lending credence to the possibility that the transitional period has simply not been located. However, the data that may be mustered to support this proposition are almost entirely negative and must be regarded as inconclusive.

3. At this time there was some kind of massive upset in the workings of cultural systems all over the Southwest. Substantial dislocations have been noted elsewhere at about this time and it appears that *something* also occurred at Zuni. Whatever happened to cause this shakeup in Southwestern settlement patterns would appear to be the result of processes operating at a regional level that cannot be examined by a study on this scale. A manifestation of this regional upset at Zuni might have been the movement to the protohistoric towns and an influx of some population, or at least increased interaction with other areas of the Southwest.

Supporting this proposition is the fact that in several areas of the Southwest, including the White Mountains and southern Arizona, as well as Zuni, it is clear that some dramatic (and not easily explained) changes occurred at this time (see Upham, 1982, for one interpretation of this phenomenon, which he calls the Pueblo IV collapse). Although in the Zuni area there is ceramic continuity, evidenced by the apparent production of several types *across* this gap, buff ware and black ware and intrusive Hopi and Salado types were newly introduced at this time. Zuni buff ware may be a result of Little Colorado (Hopi) influence and black ware is reminiscent of Hohokam plain wares. The mechanism producing that "influence" is not known, but it could be a result of much expanded trade or migration or both. In addition, cremation, long practiced in southern Arizona, first appears in Zuni at the protohistoric towns.

This social upheaval and the increased foreign "influences" might have resulted in rapid change in Zuni ceramic production. Considering the paucity of good stratigraphic data, what we see as the gap in the Zuni ceramic sequence might be simply an unusually rapid change in ceramic production that does not happen to be well illustrated in any of the few trenches available. Indeed, the difficulty in correlating the collections from the latest sites in the eastern part of the area to the early levels at Binna:wa, and the later levels from Binna:wa with the collections from Zuni and Mats'a:kya, might be construed as evidence for a rapid and somewhat discontinuous change in ceramic production at the different sites.

4. The gap identified in the ceramic sequence does not indicate a period of time, but rather is indicative of a failure of the analytical techniques, due to a violation of assumptions on which these methods rely. Of course, two of the fundamental assumptions in building a ceramic sequence are that ceramic change is more or less continuous and that it happens essentially contemporaneously in the area under consideration. A serious violation *in fact* of these assumptions could well result in an *apparent* gap in the sequence.

In ceramic terms, the apparent gap is the result of an inability to date a substantial amount of occupation to complex G and early complex H. In other words, few sites seem to date to the time when Kechipawan Polychrome was produced in the absence of Matsaki buff wares, and to the time when Matsaki buff wares and black ware were first produced. If Kechipawan Polychrome and the Matsaki buff wares were introduced essentially simultaneously, rather than sequentially, complex G would be eliminated and the gap would be narrowed considerably. The available data do not present strong reasons to reject this alternative reconstruction.

5. Upham (1982: 107–108) sees a collapse of a majority of the large settlements on the Plateau at that time, with the remaining settlements unable to accommodate the population of the abandoned centers. As a result, he argues, a large number of these people may have changed their subsistence strategy to a more mobile, hunting and gathering mode. However, if there was such a large hunting and gathering population in the Zuni area at the time, no evidence of it has been found. As noted earlier, a substantial amount of intensive survey has been done in the area. There is, by now, a large amount of negative evidence against a substantial dispersed population at that time.

The data are not adequate to choose among these five propositions. Although the first and fifth propositions cannot be rejected with a high level of confidence, there is what I consider to be considerable negative evidence against them. However, the second, third, and fourth propositions, all of which indicate that the gap is apparent rather than due to an actual hiatus in settlement, are by no means mutually exclusive; most likely, some combination of these three operated to produce the observed situation.

DIACHRONIC SYNTHESIS

In the following sections, changes in the late prehistoric Zuni area settlement patterns are interpreted by analyzing environmental change, technological evolution, and changing mechanisms of social integration. The two events specifically considered are the initial aggregation and movement of settlements within the eastern part of the study area, including the major influx and subsequent outflow of population from the El Morro Valley during this period, and the major settlement shift to the protohistoric towns.

Environmental Change

The Great Drought

Watson, LeBlanc, and Redman (1980: 214) and LeBlanc (1978: 49) advance an argument that the deteriorating climate in the late 1200s may have made the El Morro Valley more attractive for settlement than the areas of lower elevation to the west, resulting in the late 13th century population influx to the El Morro Valley. A reversal of this climatic deterioration at the beginning of the 14th century likewise led to what they see as an exodus to a lower elevation at that time, about 25 years later.

Their argument rests on the fact that areas of higher elevation, like the El Morro Valley, generally receive more rainfall than areas of lower elevation, but that the higher areas generally have dangerously shorter growing seasons. It is further argued that periods of depressed rainfall would be accompanied by lengthened growing seasons. Thus, in a time of climatic decline, the risk of agricultural failure at higher elevations is somewhat reduced (because of the longer growing season) while that risk in lower elevations (due to decreased rainfall) is increased, possibly tipping the balance in favor of the higher elevations. A reversal of this trend would again make the lower elevations more attractive and the higher elevations more risky for agriculture.

The climatic changes involved in this line of reasoning are the well-documented drought from about A.D. 1276 to 1302 and the wet period from 1303 until about 1340 (Table 7.4,

Fig. 7.2; Dean and Robinson 1977, 1978: 33). Modern data (Table 7.2) do show the dramatic difference in length of the growing season between the higher and lower elevations.

However, results presented in this study call into question other aspects of the argument presented by Watson, LeBlanc, and Redman. First of all, the El Morro Valley was clearly habitable both before and after the drought. Although Watson and her colleagues realize that there was a significant population in the El Morro area prior to the onset of the drought (at the Scribe S Site and elsewhere), contrary to their argument it appears that some of the El Morro Valley pueblos (Atsinna, Pueblo de los Muertos, and Cienega) were occupied for quite some time after the end of the drought—in fact, clear through the 40-year cooler and moister period that followed the drought (Fig. 7.2). (The occupation of Atsinna until at least A.D. 1349 is substantiated by a tree-ring date obtained in the course of this study.)

Second, the modern climatic data (Table 7.1) do not support the assumption of a large difference in rainfall associated with higher elevations. As indicated in Chapter 7, in order for agriculture to succeed, some kind of water-control technology had to be employed, both in the El Morro Valley and elsewhere in the study area. An amount of water equivalent to the rain falling on an area *several times* the size of the field must be captured in order to provide adequate moisture for corn. If this observation is correct, then it seems unlikely that the 10 percent or so difference in rainfall between Zuni and the El Morro Valley would make the higher elevations sufficiently attractive to stimulate a massive settlement shift.

Third, although my analysis does agree with the conclusion that there was a substantial population increase in the El Morro Valley area at about the time of the beginning of the drought (at the beginning of ceramic complex D, about A.D. 1275), the exact character of the settlement shift is not known, because for the time immediately before the drought the data are seriously incomplete. We do know that just prior to the drought, a number of small sites not considered here were occupied; however, it does not appear that these sites were at substantially lower elevations than the pueblos occupied after the onset of the drought. Most of this earlier occupation was not at the lower elevations near Zuni, as the argument of Watson and others implies, but at relatively high elevations in the central and eastern parts of the study area (Ferguson 1980).

The available data do confirm the *trends* in elevation suggested by Watson and others; but the magnitude of these changes is relatively small. Table 6.2 shows that, from the end of complex B (A.D. 1250) to the end of complex D (about A.D. 1300), the weighted mean of the site elevations rises only 18 m. That is, 25 years prior to the drought, the sites were only at slightly lower elevations than they were 50 years later at the end of the drought. In fact, from the beginning of the drought to the end of the drought, the average elevation dropped 17 m (assuming that the absolute dates we have associated with complex D are accurate). Furthermore, from the end of the drought (the end of complex D) to the end of the 40-year cool, wet period (sometime during association E), the weighted mean of the site elevations dropped only about 46 m. While most of these changes are generally in the right direction to support the climatic change argument, it is difficult to believe that this effect has much to do with differential rainfall, when the 10 percent difference in rainfall between Zuni and El Morro Monument is associated with a 237 m difference in elevation, and the changes discussed above are all less than 50 m.

The difference in rainfall between locations occupied before, during, and after the drought is probably slight, at most only a few percent. Considering the characteristic variability of the rainfall (plotted in Fig. 7.2), it seems most unlikely that such a small percentage difference between areas would be either perceptible or important.

These elevation changes are intriguing, nonetheless, returning us to a consideration of the length of the growing season. Although the drought was associated with increased temperatures, the magnitude of these differences is not known at present. Nonetheless, Tables 7.2 and 7.3 show that a difference in growing season of 37 days between Zuni and El Morro results from an average temperature differential of only 1.6° C. Thus, if the drought increased temperatures an average of even 1° C, it could have had a major impact on the growing season and dramatically decreased the risk of crop failure. This kind of environmental effect seems much more likely to stimulate a substantial settlement change than the change in rainfall.

From a cultural standpoint, a plausible scenario can be suggested. The drought-induced increase in temperature lengthened the growing season in the El Morro Valley. Long-time residents of the valley (for example, the population at the Scribe S Site) would have noticed and passed this information on to other groups in the area, who then moved to the El Morro Valley. However, two additional questions must be answered to complete this picture.

First, if it was not increased rainfall, what made the El Morro Valley more attractive than the areas previously inhabited by the people who moved there? The increase of population in the El Morro Valley was accompanied by a decline in the number of sites in the south-central portion of the study area. If a population movement is inferred from this, then the population was moving not so much to an area of higher elevation (as Watson and others suggest), as it was from a high area with narrow canyon floors to an area of similar elevation but with a broad valley floor against the Zuni Mountains. Although the economic advantage of this move is not certain, it may have involved either climatic conditions in the El Morro Valley that are not so much determined by elevation as they are by the topography of the Valley. Alternatively, there may have been a perceived lack of suitable nearby agricultural fields in those areas of narrow canyons to support the populations recently aggregated into large pueblos. Finally, it is possible that the drought had some unknown but important secondary effects, such as stimulating dust storms or increasing insect populations, that favored the El Morro area over others.

Second, why was there not an exodus from the El Morro Valley when there was change from an extreme drought to a 40-year period of cooler and damper climate in the early 1300s? Again, no well-substantiated answer can be presented, but two suggestions are offered. Through an evolution of subsistence technology and through an improved understanding of the local environment, an adaptation may have developed that continued to make the El Morro Valley viable in a way that was not possible using the subsistence strategies

of the mid–1200s. Alternatively, social mechanisms may have developed to lessen the consequences of the riskier environment of the area. For example, increased redistribution in the entire Zuni River Valley would mitigate the effects of crop failure in one area through redistribution from areas not affected.

In sum, the argument of Watson and others does not stand as stated, in the light of the additional climatic and archaeological data presented here. However, there is some indication that the environmental variation of the late 1200s and early 1300s did affect the settlement patterns of the area, probably due in part to the effect of the drought on temperature and hence on the length of the growing season.

Arroyo-cutting and Aggradation

The hydrological sequence presented by Euler and others (1979) indicates that all over the Colorado Plateau an episode of arroyo-cutting started at about A.D. 1300 and lasted until just before 1500. It would have taken some time for the arroyo-cutting, and the concomitant lowering of the water table, to affect subsistence pursuits in a serious way. Although increasingly eroded arroyos and streams would have adversely affected floodwater farming, particularly akchin farming (Hack 1942: 70–80) and floodplain and arroyo terrace and arroyo bottom farming, it also could have had serious consequences for riverine irrigation. Floodwater fields formed by contour terraces and check dams would probably have been somewhat less affected. Because of the lowering of the streams with respect to the fields, canals would have had to be longer to reach the fields, and an increased likelihood of floods, due to decreased ground cover and increased runoff, would make headgates and other diversion features more difficult to maintain. The aggradation period that started just before 1500 would have eventually reversed these processes.

Unfortunately, in the absence of detailed geomorphological work in the area, only qualitative generalizations can be made; the extent and importance of these effects cannot be determined. The onset of arroyo-cutting is indicated about A.D. 1300, near the beginning of ceramic complex DE, and the aggradation would have begun about 1500, during complex H.

In the synchronic reconstruction presented above, I have argued that irrigation from springs began in complexes D or DE (A.D. 1275–1325), and riverine irrigation may have begun at about the same time. Although I am not prepared to argue that there was a causal link, the use of spring irrigation may have been an adaptive response to the problems caused by increased arroyo-cutting. The timing of the introduction of this water-control technique corresponds approximately with the onset of arroyo-cutting. Experimentation with riverine irrigation, if it began at about the same time (near Halona:wa), may not have been seriously affected by the arroyo-cutting at that time.

During this period of arroyo-cutting, the settlements became increasingly associated with the major permanent streams of the area. During a period of arroyo-cutting, floodwater fields on the floodplains may be washed out more often because of an increased danger of flooding. This argues against attributing this trend in settlement location to an increasing reliance on floodwater agriculture on the stream banks or floodplains, and may support an argument for increasing irrigation from the streams. Although floods may damage water-control features, it might have been possible to put fields on river terraces that were sufficiently high to avoid the floods.

There is no obvious change in settlement patterns that can be associated with the period of aggradation that started just before 1500. However, if the subsistence system at that time relied largely on riverine irrigation, a period of aggradation probably only made this subsistence practice easier, and no settlement shift or technological response would necessarily be expected.

Precipitation Cycles and Other Climatic Variation

Even a brief examination of modern climatic records (Tables 7.1 and 7.2) is sufficient to point out the extreme variability of the local climate. Unfortunately, the effects of high-frequency variability on agricultural success are dramatic. Because they appear on the surface to be unpredictable, there must have been little hope of systematically formulating an adaptive response to a particular climatic episode.

Even when the dendrochronological data are aggregated and standardized into the decade departure values given in Table 7.4 and Figure 7.2, decades less than one standard deviation away from the normal value are the exception rather than the rule. During the 300-year period that is of interest here, the two most substantial deviations from this overall pattern of variability are the Great Drought of A.D. 1276 to 1302 and the four-decade, cool, moist period following the drought.

On the basis of present information, it seems both methodologically unwise and theoretically unlikely that direct correlations can be seen between changes in the settlement patterns and specific climatic episodes during this period (other than for the two deviations mentioned above). The methodological difficulty is that after the early 1300s, settlement changes cannot be dated in absolute terms, and the frequency of high-amplitude variations in the decade departure index considerably exceeds the resolution of the site dating methods. The theoretical objection is that with this large amount of climatic variability, it probably would have been unwise for the prehistoric populations to try to react to specific climatic episodes because, whatever the response, it was likely to backfire during the next climatic oscillation. The dendroclimatic record is testimony to the fact (undoubtedly understood by the prehistoric farmers) that the next oscillation would come, although its timing was completely unpredictable.

It seems clear that what was required to adapt to this variability were more generalized responses that minimized the deleterious effects of this variation. It seems likely, therefore, that the only climatic episodes that would have elicited specific cultural responses were those of extreme length and severity, such as the Great Drought.

Evolution of Agricultural Technology

Spring-fed Irrigation

No direct evidence is available to date the introduction of spring irrigation, although it may have begun in complex D,

and quite likely began by complex DE (near the time of the introduction of the Heshotauthla types about A.D. 1300). The rather sudden clustering of sites near springs during complex DE indicates their importance, so this innovation is tentatively dated during this complex. Nonetheless, it is recognized that the importance of the springs in these cases may have been only as a source of domestic water.

Riverine Irrigation

Dating the introduction of riverine irrigation is even more difficult. Although water-control technology in the area has not been widely discussed, the prevailing view has been that irrigation was introduced quite late, or perhaps even during historic times. The data presented here indicate that riverine irrigation was a dominant water-control method throughout the protohistoric period (complex H, after the introduction of Matsaki buff wares) and it suggests that riverine irrigation may have begun much earlier, perhaps as early as complex D.

Although the lower Zuni River floodplain can be irrigated, the irrigation potential of the area farther upstream of the historic town of Mats'a:kya is less certain. In the absence of direct evidence, in my opinion, the settlement pattern of complex H is indicative of a system making substantial, if not almost exclusive, use of spring and riverine irrigation.

All of these pueblos are located on or adjacent to soils with by far the greatest irrigation potential of the entire area (Fig. 7.4; Tables 7.6, 8.1). Furthermore, the gradient of the portion of the Zuni River that is occupied during this period is approximately half that of the upstream sections of the river and its major tributaries. The gradient of sections of the river downstream of Mats'a:kya ranges from 2.7 to 1.9 meters per kilometer. Upstream of Mats'a:kya, the gradient of measured sections of the river ranges from 3.6 to 6.3 meters per kilometer. A lower gradient probably would be advantageous for canal irrigation, because the ability to maintain headgates for the main canals would have been largely dependent on the swiftness of the stream (which is a function of the gradient) and the frequency of floods.

The presence of Salado polychromes at these protohistoric towns, and the knowledge 16th century Indians in southern Arizona had of the Zuni, as reported by early Spaniards in the area, indicate some communication between Zuni and central or southern Arizona, where riverine irrigation technology was well-developed and had been in use for centuries. Certainly the residents of the Zuni area had some knowledge of irrigation technology (whether or not it was used) well back into the prehistoric period. Finally, the early Spanish reports seem to indicate that irrigation was used prehistorically.

If it is accepted that the protohistoric towns used riverine irrigation, then we may ask how much earlier use of this technology began. Woodbury (1970: 4) proposed that:

> . . . the shift of settlements toward the Zuni River and its main tributaries, the Nutria and Pescado, may have coincided with the introduction of riverine irrigation, in contrast with the akchin farming that was probably widely practiced prior to this.

When integrated with the settlement sequence presented in Chapter 6, this statement suggests a beginning of irrigation in complex D (about A.D. 1275 to 1300) or perhaps even earlier.

Although riverine irrigation probably could have been used at a number of the early pueblos located on valley bottoms, such as Lower Deracho and the Day Ranch Ruin, the amount of irrigable land in this area is somewhat restricted by the narrowness of the valley floor. A similar labor investment in canal construction at Halona:wa South probably would have irrigated a vastly larger area. Furthermore, Halona:wa South is the first site to be occupied that seems unsuited for flood-water farming, and thus more strongly indicates the use of irrigation. The beginning of riverine irrigation may be tentatively dated to complex D, to the time of the start of occupation at Halona:wa South, although the resolution of this question must await further research.

The only evidence that argues against prehistoric riverine irrigation at this early date is the regional hydrology. It indicates that this development would have occurred near the beginning of an episode of arroyo-cutting, from about A.D. 1300 to 1500, which would make irrigation more difficult (although not necessarily impossible). However, the down-cutting might have been less severe downstream (that is, near Halona:wa), where the river would have flowed more slowly than in areas farther to the east.

SOCIAL INTEGRATION

In the mid–1200s, typical Zuni settlements had twenty or fewer rooms, while occasional pueblos had as many as 60 rooms (Ferguson 1980: 77–81). Within a short time (probably much less than 50 years) during the last part of the 13th century, the nature of the settlements was completely transformed. By the end of the century, the typical pueblo had from 200 to 725 rooms (Table 6.5). This transformation was followed by a century characterized by an incredible amount of construction, movement, and abandonment of large pueblos. Between the mid–1200s and the late 1300s or early 1400s, 28 large pueblos with over 13,000 rooms were built and abandoned, all within a relatively small area. In dramatic contrast, the protohistoric settlement pattern established by about A.D. 1400 appears to have been extremely stable, remaining largely intact into the 17th century.

Also, between A.D. 1250 and 1400, it appears that the subsistence system was largely transformed from one in which floodwater farming was dominant to one dependent on irrigation agriculture. This technological change was accompanied by a shift in the locus of settlement from a diversity of environmental settings at higher elevations in the eastern part of the study area to environmentally uniform locations along the lower part of the Zuni River Valley.

Such dramatic changes in these aspects of the cultural system must have been accompanied by important changes in social organization and integration. Most obviously, stronger mechanisms of social control must have been required to integrate the communities with many hundreds of people that were the norm in the late 1200s than were required in communities with no more than a few dozen people occupied almost exclusively only 20 or 30 years earlier.

Many of the changes in settlement pattern that are observed during the period of interest here may reflect the social instability of the earlier large sites and the evolution to the more stable protohistoric and historic Zuni social institutions.

It would be unwise to assume that ethnographic information concerning Zuni social organization is applicable to the period in prehistory prior to A.D. 1400, because those very social institutions may well have been developed during this time.

It is assumed that the mid–13th century sedentary inhabitants of the Zuni area had a form of social organization that Sahlins (1968) would consider tribal. He considers a tribe to be a "body of people of common derivation and custom, in possession and control of their own extensive territory" (Sahlins 1968: vii–viii). He characterizes tribes as primitive segmentary societies, "a cultural formation, at once structurally decentralized and functionally generalized" (Sahlins 1968: viii).

The tribe builds itself up from within, the smaller community segments joined in groups of higher order, yet just where it becomes greatest the structure becomes weakest: the tribe as such is the most tenuous of arrangements, without even a semblance of collective organization. . . . Its economics, its politics, its religion are not conducted by different institutions specially designed for the purpose but coincidentally by the same kinship and local groups: the lineage and clan segments of the tribe, the households and villages, which thus appear as versatile organizations in charge of the entire social life (Sahlins 1968: viii).

Sahlins (1968: 5) notes that tribes lack a sovereign political authority to keep peace through force; rather they depend on various tribal institutions to maintain control.

Gellner (1969: 41–45), attributing the general notion to Evans-Pritchard, describes the way in which social integration is maintained in an ideal segmentary society (one that has no important social ties that crosscut the hierarchical arrangements of the social segments). Cohesion of any social segment at any level of the hierarchy is maintained by an inherent threat from *outside* that segment, that is, from a structurally opposed segmentary group of the tribe. If a conflict should arise, there are always segmentary groups that can be activated by the parties to the conflict whose opposition will tend to balance each other.

Because of the lack of central authority (Titiev 1944: 68), and because lower-order segments of the tribe (the households and lineages) are the most strongly integrated units, with increasingly inclusive units having weaker and weaker internal ties, tribes have a built-in tendency toward factionalism. This tendency may be mediated in various ways such as by organizations whose membership crosscuts the primary segments and by the maintenance of reciprocal obligations, notably including the exchange of marriage partners among members of different segmentary groups.

Before adding observations concerning the specific organizational characteristics of the ethnographic Pueblos, we may examine the consequences of this basic tribal model in the light of the settlement patterns illuminated above.

The small pueblos characteristic of the early and mid–13th century probably were composed of low-order portions of the segmentary hierarchy. Residential units (small pueblos) included only one or a few households and, as such, would have had a relatively high degree of internal cohesion. Various contemporaneous living groups in an area were probably linked through the more encompassing tribal structure. In particular, ceremonial duties and reciprocal obligations may have tied together inhabitants of the various pueblos. In the absence of strong competition for scarce resources such as arable land, there would have been comparatively little need for strong integrative mechanisms for groups larger than the residential units. As long as adequate land was available, competition within a community may have been resolved by the budding-off of new villages to open areas. Competition between villages could have been minimized simply by locating new villages at a sufficient distance from existing ones to avoid conflict.

In many places in the area there was apparently a relatively sudden aggregation of 20 to 50, or perhaps even more, of these small villages (or portions thereof) into a single physical structure, a large pueblo, apparently without any intervening occupation of villages of intermediate size. If the picture of tribal structure presented here is at all applicable in this case, the new large communities undoubtedly were faced with serious problems of social integration.

In earlier periods, small settlements had room to spread out along a strip of a valley margin suitable for floodwater agriculture in such a way that the primary fields of any community were close to the pueblo (as seems to have been the case in Miller Canyon). However, in a large pueblo, competition for the most attractive land near the pueblo seems inevitable. This, and other sorts of conflicts that might have had minor impact on a spatially dispersed social group must have required better resolution mechanisms in the compact community of a large pueblo. Furthermore, if these stronger mechanisms of social integration were not required in the dispersed case, there is little reason to believe that they existed all along, perhaps dormant, but ready to deal with this vastly larger community.

On the other hand, the planned architectural layout of many of the earliest large sites, and the likelihood that major portions of them were built in a single episode (see the description of Pueblo de los Muertos, site 29, in Chapter 4), clearly indicate that the cooperation of a rather large number of people was achieved at least occasionally. Nonetheless, I suggest that once constituted, these pueblos had insufficiently developed mechanisms of social integration and, as a result, conflicts bred factions, and eventually broke apart the communities.

Consequently, the tremendous amount of construction, movement, and abandonment that is observable in the late 13th and 14th century settlement patterns is argued to be, in large part, the product of a repeating process of division and recombination of social groups into large pueblos. Of course, I am not suggesting that this is the only process that operated to produce the late prehistoric settlement sequence. That there is an environmental-technological component to these changes in village location is clearly evidenced by the long-term trends elucidated above.

Although in the long run these general trends are relatively clearcut, a substantial component of the new construction does not appear to be in the direction of the environmental-technological trends, suggesting other causes for the relocation. Often, these constructions appear to be in environmental situations similar to those only recently abandoned. Witness,

for example, the abandonment of Lower Deracho in complex C and the construction of the Day Ranch Ruin, less than one kilometer distant, during complex D.

An example of the kind of community fission suggested here occurred in relatively recent times at the Hopi village of Oraibi, described in detail by Titiev (1944: 69–95). The conflict began in 1880 as the result of a change of opinion of the village chief concerning the Americans. Over the next 26 years the two factions became more and more antagonistic. (Bradfield, 1971, proposes an economic rather than philosophical interpretation of this event, based on the loss of about one-third of Oraibi's prime agricultural land between 1901 and 1906.) In any event, in 1906 there was a showdown in which the two groups had what amounted to a tug-of-war, or more precisely, a push-of-war, to determine which faction would have to leave the village. The losing faction did depart and, as a result, one new village (Hotevilla) was established immediately and another (Bakavi) was established the next year. The village split fairly evenly, with 324 in one group and 298 in the other. In accord with our expectations for a segmentary society, while the division tended to be along clan lines, many clans were split; however, households showed more cohesion. Titiev's data indicate that of the 131 households for which information was available, only 22 households divided on this critical issue.

In contrast to the 13th and 14th century cases, the proto-historic settlement system apparently has been relatively stable. This difference, in large part, may be explained by two factors. First, during the period considered by this study, more effective mechanisms of social integration may have been developed. Second, a change in the subsistence system to a reliance on irrigation produced a situation that was less likely to precipitate conflicts and, at the same time, required more cooperation.

The Zuni, and other Pueblo groups, have developed elaborate ways of maintaining social control:

> The type of social integration among the western Pueblos follows a common pattern, although there are considerable differences in village size and dispersal at present. In all the villages the kinship system is a primary integrating factor, kinship being widely extended within the tribe and, through the clan organization, to other tribes as well. The Hopi, with their emphasis upon the clan system, have developed little in the way of centralization of control. Zuni, on the other hand, has developed a strong central hierarchy, which holds this large village together; the clans have less importance and fewer functions than among the Hopi, and the phratry organization is obsolescent (Eggan 1950: 303–304).

Speaking of Zuni, Kroeber adds:

> The clans, the fraternities, the priesthoods, the kivas, in a measure the gaming parties, are all dividing agencies. If they coincided, the rifts in the social structure would be deep; by countering each other they cause segmentations which produce an almost marvelous complexity, but can never break the national entity apart (Kroeber 1917: 183, cited in Eggan 1950: 304).

Turning again to the archaeological data, Adams (1981: 323) believes that the katchina cult reached Hopi and Zuni (from the Casas Grandes area) during the 1300s. This cult may well have had significance with respect to social integration, as Titiev (1944: 66) indicates that the Hopi katchinas help regulate village working parties.

Settlement pattern data derived from archaeological survey has a limited potential to illuminate the details of prehistoric mechanisms of social interaction; indeed, these aspects of society are difficult to probe archaeologically, even with well-controlled excavations. Nonetheless, the site-size histograms presented in Figure 6.10 do suggest some intriguing possibilities.

First, the two very large composite round and square pueblos appeared in the early stages of the population aggregation. After a short period they disappeared, and pueblos of that size were never constructed again. In light of the argument presented above, this early experimentation with very large pueblos may have been unsuccessful and the attempt to maintain communities of this size was abandoned.

Second, as observed in Chapter 6, during complexes B, C, and D, the range in size of the pueblos occupied shows no convincing modalities. However, in complexes DE, E, and F, clear modalities are present at about 180, 425, and 875 rooms, although the smallest of these modes almost disappears after complex DE. The existence of the modalities in itself is interesting, because it suggests that the cultural processes that formed the communities changed over time, such that the later communities appear in more or less uniform sizes. This uniformity is also reflected in a lowered standard deviation of site sizes during complexes DE and E (Table 6.5), by more standardized architectural plans (Table 6.6), and by a decreasing diversity of topographic settings utilized (Table 6.3) during these periods.

This uniformity suggests an increased level of integration over the entire area. Perhaps the most obvious way in which these site-size modalities could arise would be for the social segments of different levels of inclusiveness to have modalities in their size that, when they are combined in a pueblo, result in proportional modalities in the pueblos housing them.

Interestingly, site-size modalities are approximately in the proportions 2, 4, and 8, with 6 conspicuously absent. Certainly no definite conclusions may be drawn, but this result seems more suggestive of a dual form of organization, characteristic of the eastern Pueblos (Ortiz 1969), than of the clan and phratry systems of the western Pueblos. In a clan or phratry system, one would expect divisions along clan or phratry lines, but even if these units were of more or less equal size, one would not expect the divisions so consistently divided into these size modes. However, in a dual system, nested and cross-cutting pairs of groups are formed that more likely would result in the observed pattern of size modes.

"At Zuni there are references in the mythology to a dual grouping of clans associated with summer and winter and some seasonal distinctions in terms of calendar and ceremonial activity" (Eggan 1950: 302). However, Eggan (1950: 316) also notes that "The dual principle of organization is the simplest form of segmentary organization, beyond the band or village, and operates most effectively in relatively small groups."

Although a great deal more research is required to examine this proposition more carefully, it is conceivable that the changing patterns of site size shown in the histograms are reflecting an evolution of segmentary social organization from a system based primarily on households or small villages to a system of dual organization, and then, in the protohistoric times when the modalities again disappear, to the ethnographically known, clan-based system.

According to this interpretation, the large amount of construction and abandonment in the late 13th and 14th centuries is a product of the lack of adequate mechanisms of social integration, resulting in the repeated fission and recombination of pueblos. Modalities in site size that appear during this time may be an indication of the development of new institutions of social integration and control. Over time, it appears that a more stable social organization evolved, as evidenced by the apparently stable protohistoric settlement system and by the complex social structure that is known for ethnographic Zuni.

Appendix
PERCENTAGES OF CERAMIC TYPES AND WARES BY SITE

Percentages of Ceramic Types and Wares by Site

No.	Site	Collection type	Collector	Excavation level	Sample size	Red Mesa Black-on-white	Puerco Black-on-white	Reserve Black-on-white	Tularosa Black-on-white	Pinedale Black-on-white	Unidentified white ware	Puerco Black-on-red	Wingate types	St. Johns matte types	St. Johns subglaze types	St. Johns glaze types	Springerville Polychrome	Pinedale Polychrome	Heshotauthla types	Unidentified red ware	Kwakina Polychrome	Salado polychromes	Pinnawa Glaze-on-white	Pinnawa Red-on-white	Kechipawan Polychrome	Unidentified cream ware	Matsaki types	Unidentified buff ware	Hopi buff ware	Corrugated gray ware	Corrugated buff ware	Black ware	Hawikuh types	Zuni polychromes	Historic plain red	Unidentified ware
1.	Spier 81	D	K		32		3	19			9		31	19	9					16										9						
		Q	K		219		3	1	13		4		5	7	7					16										44	14					2
2.	Miller Ranch Ruin	D	K		101		10	2	12		7	9	28	14						3										35	1					
		Q	K		101		1		14		13	5	18	8						6										40						
3.	Spier 61	Q	Z		182		2	1	13		7	1	16	12		1		1		9										40						
4.	Upper Deracho Ruin	D	K		19				16				21	32						5										26						
5.	Vogt Ranch Ruin	D	K		27				7		19	4	11	11						11										37						
6.	Kay Chee Ruin	D	S		29			3	34		3		10	21									3	3						17	3					
7.	Pettit Site	D	K		5									60						20										20						
8.	Pescado Canyon Ruin	D	Z		12				50					33		8				8																
		Q	Z		63			3			5			13	22					8										38						11
9.	Lower Deracho Ruin	D	K		30		3	17			3		13	20						20										23						
		Q	K		96		2	2			1		2	6		1				13										73						
10.	Scribe S Site	E	C		219	0	1	16	6		2		18	43						13																
		Q	C		239	0	0	14			10	2	35	14		0				23																
11.	Heshoda Yala:wa	D	K		106			8		1	6	3		5	2				3	20	4	1		1			1	5		11		5		24		2
		D	S		39	3	8		10		5	18		3	3				10	8	23		3							8						1
		Q	K		90			9		1	9		18	1						11	1									43	6					1
		Q	S		306		6	3	4		7	1	5	3	1					10	1	0								58	0					1
12.	Box S Ruin	D	C, S		186		1	1	24	5	9		3	39		1				14										3						
		E	S		134		1	13		1	8	1	3	16		1		1		7	1									40						6
13.	Shoemaker Ranch Ruin	D	K		210			0	27	2	7	1	9	20		0	2	0		11	1									16						
		Q	K		42				10		2	7	12	14						7										48						
14.	Day Ranch Ruin	D	K, S		131		2	2	21	8	2	1	3	31		3	1	1		5	1									18						2
		E	S		548		1	3		3	7		5	12		1		0		10	0									57	0					1
		Q	K		12		8				8			17																67						
15.	Lookout Site	D	C, S		371		2	1	22	0	0		11	41		1	2		5	1	6		2	1			2			2						1
		E	S		598				7		5		8	21	1	0				15	0	0								43	0					
16.	Jack's Lake Ruin	D	K		98			1	19	1	3		16	21		5	1		2	15	3									11						
		Q	K		236			0	5		7		3	8		2	0			18	0									57	0					
17.	Archeotekopa II	D	K, S		199			3	19	1	4		10	28		8	4	1	1	7	5		1							7	2					2
		E	S		491			1	14	1	2	0	6	18		1	1	0	0	8	1									43	2					1
		Q	K		176			1		2	3		7	13		4	1		1	36	2									26	5					2
18.	Fort Site	D	S		36			3	31	3				44					6	3																6
19.	Tinaja Ruin	E	C	0	144				6		5	2		40	1				1	37	3															2
		E	C	4	153				18		8		7	35	2				5	24																
20.	Kluckhohn Ruin	D	S		111			1	25				4	36		4	1		5	8	2	1								14						
21.	Mirabal Ruin	D	C		87			2	1		7	1	11	66		2	1	1		7																
		E	C	1	130			1			5	4	8	45		2				28	5	1														2
		E	C	8	51			2	4		16		4	55						10																10
22.	Yellowhouse	D	K		203		4	2	14		12		6	7			1		5	12	2								0	23	9	0				3
		Q	S		195		1	2	13	1	4		3	7					4	18	1									42	4					
23.	Ramah School House Ruin	D	S		27				7		15			22		7			7	4										37						5
24.	North Atsinna Ruin	E	C		210				4	0	3		7	32		0	1		5	40	2															5
25.	Upper Nutria Village	D	Z		8			25	25					38					13																	
		Q	K		36						11			8						3									39	22		6		3	6	3
26.	Halona:wa South	E	S		223	0	4	8			4	1	2	13		1	0	0	3	7	1						1			49	0					3
		E	Z		299		1	3		1	4	0	5	12		0	1		5	18	2					1		1	1	38		1		4		2
27.	Cienega Site	D	S		59			3						22		5			29	2	29	2					2			5						
		E	C	1	86			2			5			26		2			59	1	3	1														2
		E	C	10	129				2	2	4		15	40					34	2																2

Percents

No.	Site	Collection type	Collector	Excavation level	Sample size	Red Mesa Black-on-white	Puerco Black-on-white	Reserve Black-on-white	Tularosa Black-on-white	Pinedale Black-on-white	Unidentified white ware	Puerco Black-on-red	Wingate types	St. Johns matte types	St. Johns subglaze types	St. Johns glaze types	Springerville Polychrome	Pinedale Polychrome	Heshotauthla types	Unidentified red ware	Kwakina Polychrome	Salado polychromes	Pinnawa Glaze-on-white	Pinnawa Red-on-white	Kechipawan Polychrome	Unidentified cream ware	Matsaki types	Unidentified buff ware	Hopi buff ware	Corrugated gray ware	Corrugated buff ware	Black ware	Hawikuh types	Zuni polychromes	Historic plain red	Unidentified ware
28.	Upper Pescado Ruin	Q	K		51			6					6						12		4								37	35					
29.	Pueblo de los Muertos	Q	Z		908	0		1	15	3	10		6	18	2	0	1	12	29	2			0													1
		E	C	2	185				2	3			4	9			1	1	43	29	4		3			1										2
		E	C	7	33				3				12	33					6	33	4		3			1										2
		E	C	11	48					4	6		10	40	4				31	2						3.										3
30.	Atsinna	E	C		272	0			2	2	4		6	2					43	35	4		0													2
																																			1
31.	Achiya:Deyała	Q	K		35			3			17		6						17	6	14		3			3	6			26						
32.	Lower Pescado Village	D	K		221	0	1		13	1	2		6						17	6	14		3			3	6			26						
33.	Pescado West Ruin	Q	K		42	2		5			10		5						14	26	2						1		12	9	0	6	2	0	
		Q	K		75	1			3										15	16	3				1				35	27					
34.	Lower Pescado Ruin	Q	Z		733			0	8	1	3		4	15	2			2	23	33	6		0			0	0									
		Q	K		70			4											10	14			1						39	31		1	0		1
		Q	Z		600	0	0				5		4	1	3	1			24	49	10		3													
35.	Heshot uła	D	K,S		285	1	4		11	4	9		4	16	2	0			21	5	4		0				2	0		8	8					1
		Q	K		48	2		2	10	10									13	2	2								44	15					
		Q	S		76	3	1	1			11			1		1			5	9			1	1						54	11					
36.	Rainbow Spring Ruin	Q	K		56			2	2		7	2							13	38	18	2							18						
		Q	S		127											1			6	28	8	3	6			12				28		8				1
37.	Hambassa:wa	D	K		116	1	1			4									6	4	11	1	7	1	1	3	5	1	1	8				18	12	15
		Q	K		99					1									6	3		6		4	4		6		27				11	4	19
38.	Binna:wa	D	K		220		1	1	3	0	3		3	7			0	0	17	16	11		3		1	3	4	12	5	4		6	27		11	4	19
		E	S	D	175			1		1	1								2	11	1		3		1	9	2		7	12	47					3
		E	S	H	752	2		0		8			0	1					4	22	2	3	1	1	3	5	2	1	13		30					1
		E	S	K	328	2				2			0	1					7	23		4	1	2	3	1		14		35					2
		E	S	M	117	1				6									16	38			1		2	3		18	1	12					
39.	Hawikku	Q	K		197	1				3			1	1					2	18	3	2	1	1	8		5	2	45					1
		D	K		170	4		2			1								7	8	3	2	3	2	1	29	11	1	2	1	8	5	5	5	
40.	Mats'a:kya	Q	K		268				2		0								5	1	1	1	0	12	13	1	0	55	1	5	5	2	
		D	K		200	2			1	2			1	6		1	3	1	38	15	1	3	1	24	2		2						
		E	S	A	105								1	1	1	1	2	1	1	2	18	10				57	1		1	3			
		E	S	D	266	1							7	2	0	2			1	2	7	4	0	3	67				1	2			
		E	S	G	217						1			6			0	4	2	1	1	6	14	55					1				
		E	S	I	101						6								4	5	3	1	1	1	44	36							
41.	Kyaki:ma	Q	K		84	1			6										10					13	23	4		37				4	
		D	K,S		120	3		2		4		1		2					8	17	8	1	6	2	3	3	15	2	3	2	18				2
		E	S		89									3	1	1			11	3		1	8	3	7	57						2
42.	Kwa'kin'a	Q	K		44	2													7	5				16	20	2	5	32		2		9	
		Q	S		161	2	1			1	6		2		2				2	9	2	1	3	1	9	6	1	4	45		1		2	
		D	K		115			1	2	1	2		1	4					13	5	5		5	1	1	29	5	1	1	7	5	3	4	3
43.	Chalo:wa	Q	K		151	1		1											9	1	1			1	11	8		8	1	42	1		7	8
		D	K		59					2									12	2		3		44	10	3	2	15	2				5
		E	S	B	27			4	4										4	15	4					11	59					
		E	S	C	48	2		6		4									19	15				2	4	2	10	29				4
44.	Kechiba:wa	Q	K,S		294	1	0	1		7	1	1	1	0					2	4	1	1	1	6	5	7	0	61				
		D	K		162	2	7		1			5	1	3					2	7	6	4	4	1	2	27	9	2	9	2	1	6
		E	S		25			4		8									4	4					24	12		44				
45.	Halona:wa North	Q	K		376	1			3				1						0	9	1		1		0	15	17	4	43	1	0	4
		Q	S		249	0	0		0		1		0	0					1	9			0	0	12	7	1	1	48	5	0	4	8
		E	S	A	219	0				0		0	0							11					0	0	0	63		22		6
		E	S	G	55			2											2	9		2			4	4	2	49	5	9		13
		E	S	I	87	1	1		2		3	2							14	6		6	1	1	10	3		13	32	1		2
		E	S	M	61					8									15	18								48	8			3

Collection Type: D, Diagnostic; E, Excavated; Q, Quantitative.
Collector: C, CARP; K, Kintigh; S, Spier; Z, ZAP.

REFERENCES

Adams, E. Charles
  1981 The view from the Hopi mesas. In "The protohistoric period in the North American Southwest," edited by David R. Wilcox and W. Bruce Masse. *Arizona State University, Anthropological Research Paper* 24: 321–335. Tempe: Arizona State University.

Altschul, Jeffrey H.
  1978 The development of the Chacoan interaction sphere. *Journal of Anthropological Research* 34(1): 109–146.

Ammerman, Albert J.
  1981 Surveys and archaeological research. *Annual Review of Anthropology* 10: 63–88.

Amsden, Theodore
  1934a Report on archaeological survey at El Morro National Monument from January 15 to February 15, 1934. Ms. on file, Zuni Archaeology Program, Zuni, New Mexico.
  1934b Final report of archaeological survey at El Morro National Monument from Feb. 15 to April 1. Ms. on file, Zuni Archaeology Program, Zuni, New Mexico.

Bandelier, Adolph F.
  1890a Final report of investigations among the Indians of the southwestern United States, carried on mainly in the years from 1880 to 1885 (Pt. I). *Papers of the Archaeological Institute of America, American Series* 3.
  1890b Hemenway Southwestern Archaeological Expedition: contributions to the history of the southwestern portion of the United States. *Papers of the Archaeological Institute of America, American Series* 5.
  1892a Final report of investigations among the Indians of the southwestern United States, carried on mainly in the years from 1880 to 1885 (Pt. II). *Papers of the Archaeological Institute of America, American Series* 4.
  1892b Hemenway Southwestern Archaeological Expedition. I, An outline of the documentary history of the Zuni tribe. *Journal of American Ethnology and Archaeology* 3: 1–115.
  1981 *The Discovery of New Mexico by the Franciscan Monk, Friar Marcos de Niza in 1539*, edited and translated by Madeleine Turrell Rodack. Tucson: University of Arizona Press.

Banteah, Terry
  1979 Archaeology monitoring program: Pescado Springs pipeline project, phase I, Zuni Indian Reservation, McKinley County, New Mexico. Ms. on file, Zuni Archaeology Program, Zuni, New Mexico.

Binford, Lewis R.
  1967 Smudge pits and hide smoking: the use of analogy in archaeological reasoning. *American Antiquity* 32: 1–12.

Blaney, Harry F., and Wayne D. Criddle
  1962 Determining consumptive use and irrigation water requirements. *United States Department of Agriculture, Technical Bulletin* 1275.

Blaney, Harry F., and Karl Harris
  1951 *Consumptive Use and Irrigation Requirements of Crops in Arizona*. Washington: United States Department of Agriculture, Soil Conservation Service.

Bohrer, Vorsila L.
  1960 Zuni agriculture. *El Palacio* 67: 181–202.

Bordne, Erich F., and J. L. McGuinness
  1973 Some procedures for calculating potential evapotranspiration. *Professional Geographer* 25(1): 22–28.

Bradfield, Maitland
  1971 The changing pattern of Hopi agriculture. *Royal Anthropological Institute of Great Britain and Ireland, Occasional Paper* 30.

Breternitz, David A.
  1966 An appraisal of tree-ring dated pottery in the Southwest. *Anthropological Papers of the University of Arizona* 10. Tucson: University of Arizona Press.

Bushnell, G. H. S.
  1955 Some Pueblo IV pottery types from Kechipaun, New Mexico, U.S.A. *Anais do XXXI Congresso Internacional de Americanistas, São Paulo* 2: 657–665. São Paulo: Editora Anhembi.

Carlson, Roy L.
  1970 White Mountain Redware: a pottery tradition of east-central Arizona and western New Mexico. *Anthropological Papers of the University of Arizona* 19. Tucson: University of Arizona Press.

Casselberry, S. E.
  1974 Further refinement of formulae for determining population from floor area. *World Archaeology* 6: 117–122.

Castañeda, Pedro
  1966 *The Journey of Coronado*. Readex Microprint.

Caywood, Louis R.
  1972 *The Restored Mission of Nuestra Señora de Guadalupe de Zuni, Zuni, New Mexico*. St. Michael's, Arizona: St. Michael's Press.

Chisolm, Michael
  1968 *Rural Settlement and Land Use: an Essay in Location*, 2nd ed. Chicago: Aldine.

Colton, Harold S.
  1946 The Sinagua. A summary of the archaeology of the region of Flagstaff, Arizona. *Museum of Northern Arizona, Bulletin* 22. Flagstaff: Museum of Northern Arizona.

Colton, Harold S., and Lyndon L. Hargrave
  1937 Handbook of northern Arizona pottery wares. *Museum of Northern Arizona, Bulletin* 11. Flagstaff: Museum of Northern Arizona.

Crampton, C. Gregory
  1977 *The Zunis of Cibola*. Salt Lake City: University of Utah Press.

Crown, Patricia L.
  1981 The ceramic assemblage. In "Prehistory of the St. Johns area, east-central Arizona: the TEP St. Johns project," by Deborah A. Westfall. *Arizona State Museum Archaeological Series* 153: 233–290. Tucson: Arizona State Museum.

Cushing, Frank H.
  1886 A study of Pueblo pottery as illustrative of Zuni cultural growth. In *Fourth Annual Report of the Bureau of American Ethnology, 1882–1883*, pp. 467–521.
  1920 Zuni breadstuff. *Museum of the American Indian, Heye Foundation, Indian Notes and Monographs* 8. New York: Museum of the American Indian. (Reprinted 1974; orig-

Cushing, Frank H. (continued)
  inally published in 1884 in the Indianapolis *Millstone* 9,
  numbers 1–12 and in 1885, *Millstone* 10, numbers 1–4,
  6–8.)
Danson, Edward, and Harold Molde
  1950 Casa Malpais, a fortified pueblo site at Springerville,
  Arizona. *Plateau* 22(4): 61–67.
Dean, Jeffrey S.
  1970 Aspects of Tsegi Phase social organization: a trial reconstruction. In *Reconstructing Prehistoric Pueblo Societies*,
  edited by William A. Longacre, pp. 140–174. Albuquerque: University of New Mexico Press.
Dean, Jeffrey S., and William J. Robinson
  1977 *Dendroclimatic Variability in the American Southwest,*
  A.D. 680 to 1970. Tucson: Laboratory of Tree-Ring Research, University of Arizona.
  1978 *Expanded Tree-ring Chronologies for the Southwestern
  United States* (Chronology Series III). Tucson: Laboratory
  of Tree-Ring Research, University of Arizona.
Dodge, William A., and T. J. Ferguson
  1976 Archaeological clearance investigations: the Pescado
  Springs pipeline archaeological survey and mapping
  project, Zuni Indian Reservation, McKinley County,
  New Mexico. Ms. on file, Zuni Archaeology Program,
  Zuni, New Mexico.
Eggan, Fred
  1950 *Social Organization of the Western Pueblos*. Chicago:
  University of Chicago Press.
Eggan, Fred, and T. N. Pandey
  1979 Zuni history, 1850–1970. In *Handbook of North American
  Indians* 9, *Southwest*, edited by A. Ortiz, pp. 474–481.
  Washington: Smithsonian Institution.
Euler, Robert C., and George J. Gumerman (editors)
  1978 *Investigations of the Southwestern Anthropological Re-
  search Group: the proceedings of the 1976 conference.*
  Flagstaff: Museum of Northern Arizona.
Euler, Robert C., George J. Gumerman, Thor N. V. Karlstrom,
Jeffrey S. Dean, and Richard H. Hevley
  1979 The Colorado Plateaus: cultural dynamics and paleo-
  environment. *Science* 205: 1089–1101.
Ferguson, T. J.
  1980 *Zuni Settlement and Land Use: an Archaeological Perspective.* Prepared for the Pueblo of Zuni, Zuni Indian
  Tribe v. United States, Docket No. 161–79L, before
  United States Court of Claims.
  1981a The emergence of modern Zuni culture and society: a
  summary of Zuni tribal history—A.D. 1450 to 1700. In
  "The Protohistoric Period in the North American Southwest," edited by David R. Wilcox and W. Bruce Masse.
  Arizona State University, Anthropological Research Paper
  24: 336–353. Tempe: Arizona State University.
  1981b Rebuttal report. In *Rebuttal Reports of Plaintiff Zuni In-
  dian Tribe.* Prepared for the Pueblo of Zuni, Zuni Indian
  Tribe v. United States, Docket No. 161–79L, before
  United States Court of Claims.
Ferguson, T. J., and Barbara J. Mills
  1982 Archaeological Investigations at Zuni Pueblo, New Mexico, 1977–1980. *Zuni Archaeology Program Report* 183.
  Zuni: Zuni Archaeology Program.
Ferguson, T. J., William A. Dodge, and Barbara J. Mills
  1977 Archaeological investigations at Kyaki:ma, Zuni Indian
  Reservation, McKinley County, New Mexico. Ms. on
  file, Zuni Archaeology Program, Zuni, New Mexico.
Fewkes, J. Walter
  1891 Reconnoissance of ruins in or near the Zuni Reservation.
  Journal of American Ethnology and Archaeology 1: 92–
  132.
  1909 Ancient Zuni pottery. In *Putnam Anniversary Volume:
  Anthropological Essays Presented to Frederic Ward Putnam in Honor of his Seventieth Birthday, April 6, 1909,*
  edited by Franz Boas and others, pp. 43–82. New York:
  G. E. Stechert and Son.

Ford, Richard I.
  1977 The technology of irrigation in a New Mexico pueblo. In
  "Material Culture: Styles, Organization and Dynamics of
  Technology," edited by Heather Lechtman and Robert
  Merrill. *Proceedings of the American Ethnological Society
  1975.*
Gellner, Ernest
  1969 *Saints of the Atlas.* Chicago: University of Chicago Press.
Gladwin, Harold Sterling
  1957 *The History of the Ancient Southwest.* Portland, Maine:
  Bond Wheelwright.
Grebinger, Paul
  1973 Prehistoric social organization in Chaco Canyon, New
  Mexico: an alternative reconstruction. *The Kiva* 39: 3–23.
Green, Jesse (editor)
  1979 *Selected Writings of Frank Hamilton Cushing.* Lincoln:
  University of Nebraska Press.
Hack, John T.
  1942 The changing physical environment of the Hopi Indians of
  Arizona. (Reports of the Awatovi Expedition 1.) *Papers
  of the Peabody Museum of American Archaeology and
  Ethnology* 35(1). Cambridge: Harvard University.
Harlow, Francis H.
  1973 *Matte-paint Pottery of the Tewa, Keres and Zuni Pueblos.*
  Santa Fe: Museum of New Mexico.
Hart, E. Richard
  1980 *Boundaries of Zuni Land: with Emphasis on Details Relat-
  ing to Incidents Occurring 1846–1946* (Vol. I). Prepared
  for the Pueblo of Zuni, Zuni Indian Tribe v. United States,
  Docket No. 161–79L, before United States Court of
  Claims.
  1981 Zuni trade. In *Rebuttal Reports of Plaintiff Zuni Indian
  Tribe.* Prepared for the Pueblo of Zuni, Zuni Indian Tribe
  v. United States, Docket No. 161–79L, before United
  States Court of Claims.
Haury, Emil W.
  1945 The excavation of Los Muertos and neighboring ruins in
  the Salt River Valley. *Papers of the Peabody Museum of
  American Archaeology and Ethnology* 24(1). Cambridge:
  Harvard University.
Higgs, E. S., and C. Vita-Finzi
  1972 Prehistoric economies: a territorial approach. In *Papers in
  Economic Prehistory: Studies by Members and Associates
  of the British Academy Major Research Project in the
  Early History of Agriculture,* edited by E. S. Higgs, pp.
  27–36. London: Cambridge University Press.
Hill, James N.
  1970 Broken K Pueblo: prehistoric social organization in the
  American Southwest. *Anthropological Papers of the Uni-
  versity of Arizona* 18. Tucson: University of Arizona
  Press.
Hodge, Frederick W.
  1888 Letters to F. H. Cushing concerning the excavations at
  Heshot uɬa, dated October 28, November 6, and November
  15, 1888. Ms. on file, Zuni Archaeology Program, Zuni
  New Mexico.
  1918a Excavations at Hawikuh, New Mexico. In "Explorations
  and Field Work of the Smithsonian Institution in 1917."
  Smithsonian Miscellaneous Collections 68(12): 61–72.
  1918b Excavations at the Zuni pueblo of Hawikuh in 1917. *Art
  and Archaeology* 7(9): 367–379.
  1920a The age of the Zuni pueblo of Kechipauan. *Museum of the
  American Indian, Heye Foundation, Indian Notes and
  Monographs* 3(2): 41–60. New York: Museum of the
  American Indian.
  1920b Hawikuh bonework. *Museum of the American Indian,
  Heye Foundation, Indian Notes and Monographs* 3(3):
  61–151. New York: Museum of the American Indian.
  1921a Turquoise work at Hawikuh, New Mexico. *Museum of the
  American Indian, Heye Foundation, Leaflets* 2. New
  York: Museum of the American Indian.

1921b Work at Hawikuh. *El Palacio* 11(9): 118.

1922 Recent excavations at Hawikuh. *El Palacio* 12(1): 1–16.

1923 Circular kivas near Hawikuh, New Mexico. *Contributions from the Museum of the American Indian* 7(1): 1–37. New York: Museum of the American Indian.

1924a Pottery of Hawikuh. *Museum of the American Indian, Heye Foundation, Indian Notes* 1(1): 8–15. New York: Museum of the American Indian.

1924b Excavations at Kechipauan, New Mexico. *Museum of the American Indian, Heye Foundation, Indian Notes* 1(1): 35–36. New York: Museum of the American Indian.

1924c Snake-pens at Hawikuh, New Mexico. *Museum of the American Indian, Heye Foundation, Indian Notes* 1(3): 111–119. New York: Museum of the American Indian.

1926 The six cities of Cibola, 1581–1680. *New Mexico Historical Review* 1(4): 478–488.

1937 *History of Hawikuh, New Mexico, One of the So-Called Cities of Cibola.* Los Angeles: Southwest Museum.

1952 Turkeys at Hawikuh. *Masterkey* 26(1): 13–14.

Holmes, Barbara E., and Andrew P. Fowler
1980 *The Alternate Dams Survey: an Archaeological Sample Survey and Evaluation of the Burned Timber and Coalmine Dams, Zuni Indian Reservation, New Mexico.* Zuni: Zuni Archaeology Program.

Hrdlička, Aleš
1931 Catalogue of human crania in the United States National Museum Collections. *United States National Museum, Proceedings* 78, Art. 2, pp. 1–95.

Hunter-Anderson, Rosalind L.
1978 An archaeological survey of the Yellowhouse Dam area. Ms. on file, Office of Contract Archaeology, University of New Mexico, Albuquerque.

Judd, Neil M.
1964 The architecture of Pueblo Bonito. *Smithsonian Miscellaneous Collections* 147: 1.

Kaemlein, Wilma R.
1967 *An Inventory of Southwestern Indian Specimens in European Museums.* Tucson: Arizona State Museum.

Kidder, Alfred V.
1962 *An Introduction to the Study of Southwestern Archaeology with a Preliminary Account of the Excavations at Pecos.* New Haven: Yale University Press. Original edition, 1924.

Kintigh, Keith W.
1980 An archaeological clearance survey of Miller Canyon and the southeast boundary fence line, Zuni Indian Reservation, McKinley County, New Mexico. Ms. on file, Zuni Archaeology Program, Zuni, New Mexico.

1982a An outline for a chronology of Zuni ruins, revisited: sixty-five years of repeated analysis and collection. In "The Research Potential of Anthropological Museum Collections," edited by Anne-Marie Cantwell, James B. Griffin, and Nan A. Rothschild. *Annals of the New York Academy of Sciences* 376: 467–487.

1982b *Settlement Patterns in Late Zuni Prehistory.* Doctoral dissertation, University of Michigan. Ann Arbor: University Microfilms (82–24983).

Kroeber, A. L.
1916 Zuni potsherds. *Anthropological Papers of the American Museum of Natural History* 18: 1–37. New York: American Museum of Natural History.

1917 Zuni kin and clan. *Anthropological Papers of the American Museum of Natural History* 18: 39–205. New York: American Museum of Natural History.

Lange, Charles H., and Carroll L. Riley (editors)
1970 *The Southwestern Journals of Adolph F. Bandelier, 1880–1884.* Albuquerque: University of New Mexico Press.

LeBlanc, Steven A.
1975 Micro-seriation: a method for fine chronological dif-
ferentiation. *American Antiquity* 40: 22–38.

1976 Temporal and ceramic relationships between some late PIII sites in the Zuni area. *Plateau* 48: 75–83.

1978 Settlement patterns in the El Morro Valley, New Mexico. In *Investigations of the Southwestern Anthropological Research Group: An Experiment in Archaeological Cooperation,* edited by Robert C. Euler and George J. Gumerman, pp. 45–51. Flagstaff: Museum of Northern Arizona.

Linthicum, B. Lynn
1980 Pettit Site Masonry: A Study in Intrasite Social Integration. Master's thesis, Department of Anthropology, Wake Forest University, Winston-Salem.

Lowe, Charles H.
1964 *Arizona's Natural Environment.* Tucson: University of Arizona Press.

Maker, H. J., H. E. Bullock, Jr., and J. U. Anderson
1974 Soil associations and land classification for irrigation, McKinley County. *New Mexico State University Agricultural Experiment Station, Research Report* 262. Las Cruces: New Mexico State University.

Maker, H. J., L. W. Hacker, and J. U. Anderson
1974 Soil associations and land classification for irrigation, Valencia County. *New Mexico State University Agricultural Experiment Station, Research Report* 267. Las Cruces: New Mexico State University.

Marquardt, William H.
1974 *A Temporal Perspective on Late Prehistoric Societies in the Western Cibola Area: Factor Analytic Approaches to Short-term Chronological Investigation.* Doctoral dissertation, Washington University, St. Louis. Ann Arbor: University Microfilms.

Marshall, Michael P., John R. Stein, Richard W. Loose, and Judith E. Novotny
1979 *Anasazi Communities of the San Juan Basin.* Public Service Company of New Mexico and the Historic Preservation Bureau, Planning Division, Department of Finance and Administration of the State of New Mexico.

Martin, Paul S., and Fred Plog
1973 *The Archaeology of Arizona: A Study of the Southwest Region.* Garden City, New York: Natural History Press.

McGregor, John C.
1965 *Southwestern Archaeology.* Urbana: University of Illinois Press.

Mills, Barbara
1979 Archaeological clearance investigation, Ondelacy reseeding project, Upper Pescado drainage, McKinley County, Zuni Indian Reservation. Ms. on file, Zuni Archaeology Program, Zuni, New Mexico.

Mindeleff, Victor
1891 A study of Pueblo architecture: Tusayan and Cibola. In *Eighth Annual Report of the Bureau of Ethnology, 1886–7,* pp. 3–228.

National Weather Service
1908-1981 *Climatological Data, New Mexico.* Washington: United States Department of Commerce, National Oceanic and Atmospheric Administration.

Orr, Brennon R.
1982 Water resources of the Zuni tribal lands, McKinley and Cibola Counties, New Mexico. *U.S. Geological Survey Open-File Report* 82–1013.

Ortiz, Alfonso
1969 *The Tewa World: Space, Time, Being, and Becoming in a Pueblo Society.* Chicago: University of Chicago Press.

Pandey, Triloki Nath
1972 Anthropologists at Zuni. *Proceedings of the American Philosophical Society* 116: 321–337. Philadelphia: American Philosophical Society.

Riley, Carroll L.
1975 The road to Hawikuh: trade and trade routes to Cibola-Zuni during late prehistoric and early historic times. *The Kiva* 41: 137–159.

Roberts, Frank H. H., Jr.
1931 The ruins at Kiatuthlanna, eastern Arizona. *Bureau of American Ethnology Bulletin* 100.
1932 Village of the Great Kivas on the Zuni Reservation, New Mexico. *Bureau of American Ethnology Bulletin* 111.

Roberts, John M.
1956 Zuni Daily Life. *University of Nebraska, Laboratory of Anthropology, Monograph* 2. Lincoln: University of Nebraska.

Robertson, Ben P.
1980 Archaeological survey for a buried telephone cable in Zuni Pueblo for Universal Telephone Company of the SW, Zuni Indian Reservation, McKinley County, New Mexico. Ms. on file, Zuni Archaeology Program, Zuni, New Mexico.

Robertson, Linda Butler
1983 *Achiya: Dekyap'bowa: Alliance and Polity in the Development of Cibola*. Doctoral dissertation, Brown University, Providence. Ann Arbor: University Microfilms (83–26026).

Rodack, Madeleine Turrell
1981 Fray Marcos de Niza and the search for Cibola. In *The Discovery of New Mexico by the Franciscan Monk, Friar Marcos de Niza in 1539*, by Adolph F. Bandelier, edited and translated by Madeleine Turrell Rodack, pp. 27–39. Tucson: University of Arizona Press.

Romancito, Anders
1980 Archaeological test excavations near Binna:wa: ditch and dike project, Zuni Indian Reservation, McKinley County, New Mexico. Ms. on file, Zuni Archaeology Program, Zuni, New Mexico.

Rose, Martin R., Jeffrey S. Dean, and William J. Robinson
1981 The past climate of Arroyo Hondo, New Mexico, reconstructed from tree rings. *Arroyo Hondo Archaeological Series* 4. Santa Fe: School of American Research Press.

Rowe, John Howland
1962 Alfred Lewis Kroeber, 1876–1960. *American Antiquity* 27: 395–415.

Sahlins, Marshall D.
1968 *Tribesmen*. Englewood Cliffs, New Jersey: Prentice-Hall.

Schreiber, Katharina J.
1979a Archaeological testing of site NM:12:K3:122 for proposed road improvement along Z–2 west of Zuni Pueblo, Zuni Indian Reservation. Ms. on file, Zuni Archaeology Program, Zuni, New Mexico.
1979b The environment of the Zuni study area. Ms. on file, Zuni Archaeology Program, Zuni, New Mexico.

Simpson, James H.
1850 Journal of a military reconnaissance from Santa Fe, New Mexico, to the Navajo country, made with troops under command of Brevet Lieutenant Colonel John M. Washington, Chief of the Ninth Military Department, and Governor of New Mexico, in 1849. U.S. 31st Cong., 1st Sess., Sen. Ex. Doc 64, pp. 55–168. Union Office, Washington.
1964 *Navajo Expedition: Journal of a Military Reconnaissance from Santa Fe, New Mexico, to the Navajo Country made in 1849 by Lieutenant James H. Simpson*, edited by Frank McNitt. Norman: University of Oklahoma Press.

Skinner, Elizabeth Jo
1981 *A Systematic Analysis of Chipped Stone Industries from the El Morro Valley, New Mexico*. Doctoral dissertation, Washington University, St. Louis. Ann Arbor: University Microfilms (82–23816).

Smith, Watson
1971 Painted ceramics of the western mound at Awatovi. (Reports of the Awatovi Expedition 8.) *Papers of the Peabody Museum of American Archaeology and Ethnology* 38. Cambridge: Harvard University.

Smith, Watson, Richard B. Woodbury, and Nathalie F. S. Woodbury
1966 The excavation of Hawikuh by Frederick Webb Hodge: report of the Hendricks-Hodge expedition. *Contributions from the Museum of the American Indian, Heye Foundation* 20. New York: Museum of the American Indian.

Spier, Leslie
1917 An outline for a chronology of Zuni ruins. *Anthropological Papers of the American Museum of Natural History* 18: 205–331. New York: American Museum of Natural History.
1918 Notes on some Little Colorado ruins. *Anthropological Papers of the American Museum of Natural History* 18: 333–362. New York: American Museum of Natural History.
1919 Ruins in the White Mountains, Arizona. *Anthropological Papers of the American Museum of Natural History* 18: 363–387. New York: American Museum of Natural History.

Stephen, Alexander M.
1936 Hopi journal of Alexander M. Stephen, edited by Elsie Clews Parsons. *Columbia University Contributions to Anthropology* 23. New York: Columbia University.

Steponaitis, Vincas P.
1981 Settlement hierarchies and political complexity in non-market societies: the Formative Period of the Valley of Mexico. *American Anthropologist* 83: 320–363.

Stevenson, Matilda Coxe
1904 The Zuni Indians: their mythology, esoteric fraternities, and ceremonies. In *Twenty-third Annual Report of the Bureau of American Ethnology, 1901–2*, pp. 3–634.
1915 Ethnobotany of the Zuni Indians. *Thirtieth Annual Report of the Bureau of American Ethnology, 1908–1909*, pp. 31–102.

Steward, Julian H.
1942 The direct historical approach to archaeology. *American Antiquity* 7: 337–343.

Taylor, Walter W.
1963 Leslie Spier, 1893–1961. *American Antiquity* 28: 379–381.

Titiev, Mischa
1944 Old Oraibi: a study of the Hopi Indians of Third Mesa. *Papers of the Peabody Museum of American Archaeology and Ethnology* 22(1). Cambridge: Harvard University.

Tuggle, H. David, and J. Jefferson Reid
1982 Cross-dating Cibola White Wares. In "Cholla Project Archaeology, Volume 5, Ceramic Studies," edited by J. Jefferson Reid. *Arizona State Museum Archaeological Series* 161: 8–17. Tucson: Arizona State Museum.

Upham, Steadman
1982 *Politics and Power: A History of the Western Pueblo*. New York: Academic Press.

Vivian, R. Gwinn
1970 An inquiry into prehistoric social organization in Chaco Canyon, New Mexico. In *Reconstructing Prehistoric Pueblo Societies*, edited by William A. Longacre, pp. 59–83. Albuquerque: University of New Mexico Press.
1974 Conservation and diversion: water-control systems in the Anasazi Southwest. In "Irrigation's Impact on Society," edited by Theodore E. Downing and McGuire Gibson. *Anthropological Papers of the University of Arizona* 25. Tucson: University of Arizona Press.

Wallis, D. W.
1936 Folk tales from Shungo'povi. *Journal of American Folklore* 49: 1–68.

Watson, Patty Jo, Steven A. LeBlanc, and Charles L. Redman
1980 Aspects of Zuni prehistory: preliminary report on excavations and survey in the El Morro Valley of New Mexico. *Journal of Field Archaeology* 7: 201–218.

Whipple, A. W.
1856 Report of explorations for a railway route, near the 25th parallel of north latitude, from the Mississippi River to the Pacific Ocean. In *U.S. War Department, Reports of Explorations and Surveys to Ascertain the Most Practicable and Economical Route for a Railroad from the Mississippi River to the Pacific Ocean*, Pt. I, III. Washington: A. O. P. Nicholson.

Wiessner, Polly
1974 A functional estimator of population from floor area. *American Antiquity* 39: 343–350.

Wilcox, David R.
1981 Changing perspectives on the protohistoric pueblos, A.D. 1450–1700. In "The Protohistoric Period in the North American Southwest, A.D. 1450–1700," edited by David R. Wilcox and W. Bruce Masse. *Arizona State University, Anthropological Research Paper* 24: 378–409. Tempe: Arizona State University.

Willey, Gordon R.
1953 Prehistoric settlement patterns in the Viru Valley, Peru. *Bureau of American Ethnology Bulletin* 155.

Willey, Gordon R., and Jeremy A. Sabloff
1974 *A History of American Archaeology.* San Francisco: W. H. Freeman.

Winship, George Parker
1896 The Coronado expedition, 1540–1542. In *Fourteenth Annual Report of the Bureau of American Ethnology, 1892–93,* pp. 329–613.

Wittfogel, Karl A., and Esther S. Goldfrank
1943 Some aspects of Pueblo mythology and society. *Journal of American Folklore* 56: 17–30.

Woodbury, Richard B.
1954a Columbia University archaeological fieldwork, 1952–1953. *Southwestern Lore* 19: 11.
1954b Archaeological field work conducted in the summer of 1953 by the Department of Anthropology, Columbia University. Ms. on file, Zuni Archaeology Program, Zuni, New Mexico.
1954c Preliminary report on archaeological investigations at El Morro National Monument in the summer of 1954. Ms. on file, Zuni Archaeology Program, Zuni, New Mexico.
1955 Preliminary report on archaeological investigations at El Morro National Monument, New Mexico, during the summer of 1955. Ms. on file, Zuni Archaeology Program, Zuni, New Mexico.
1956 The antecedents of Zuni culture. *Transactions of the New York Academy of Sciences,* series 2, 18: 557–563.
1959 A reconsideration of pueblo warfare in the southwestern United States. *Actas del XXXIII Congreso Internacional de Americanistas* 2: 124–133. San Jose, Costa Rica.
1961a Climatic changes and prehistoric agriculture in the southwestern United States. *Annals of the New York Academy of Sciences* 95: 705–709.
1961b Prehistoric agriculture at Point of Pines, Arizona. *Memoirs of the Society for American Archaeology* 17.
1970 Symposium on prehistoric southwestern water control systems: the Zuni area. Paper presented at the 1970 Pecos Conference, Santa Fe.
1979 Zuni prehistory and history to 1850. In *Handbook of North American Indians* 9, *Southwest,* edited by A. Ortiz, pp. 467–473. Washington: Smithsonian Institution.

Woodbury, Richard B., and Nathalie F. S. Woodbury
1956 Zuni prehistory and El Morro National Monument. *Southwestern Lore* 21: 56–60.
1966 Decorated pottery of the Zuni area. Appendix II of The Excavation of Hawikuh by Frederick Webb Hodge: report of the Hendricks-Hodge expedition, by Watson Smith, Richard B. Woodbury, and Nathalie F. S. Woodbury. *Contributions from the Museum of the American Indian, Heye Foundation* 20: 302–336. New York: Museum of the American Indian.

Zier, Christian J.
1976 Excavations near Zuni, New Mexico: 1973. *Museum of Northern Arizona Research Paper* 2. Flagstaff: Museum of Northern Arizona.

INDEX

The pottery found in each site described in Chapter 4 is listed in the Appendix; the discussions of ceramic types discussed elsewhere in the text are indexed alphabetically by type name. The sources of the ceramic collections from those sites are also listed in the Appendix and are not indexed.

Abandonment, 1, 5–6, 111. *See also* Population growth and decline
Acenntelowa. *See* Achiya:Deyała
Achiya:Deyała, 11, 21–23, 52, 66, 73, 75, 80–81, 84, 104, 106, 121
Acoma, 7, 33, 110
Adamana Polychrome, 10
Adams, E. Charles, 97, 117
Aggregation, ix, 1, 83, 112
Agricultural productivity. *See* Catchment analysis
Agriculture, ix, 1, 52, 96–104, 108–109, 112.
    See also Ak chin; Dams; Floodwater farming; Growing season; Hopi agriculture; Irrigation; Sand dune agriculture; Terraces; Waffle gardens; Zuni agriculture
Ak chin, 101, 113–114
American Museum of Natural History, x, 3, 9
Ammerman, Albert J., 77
Amsden, Theodore, 33, 44, 51
Ancestral Zuni Village, 33, 36, 45, 49, 51, 54, 55
Anderson, J. U. *See* Maker, H. J.
Antenna Hill, 35
Archaeological Institute of America, 3
Archeotekopa I. *See* Jack's Lake Ruin
Archeotekopa II, 17, 22–23, 37–39, 73, 75, 78–79, 81, 84, 106, 109–110, 120
Architectural planning, 88–89, 109–110, 116
Architecture, 3, 21–70
Arizona State Museum, x, 4, 24
Arizona State University, x, 4, 9
Arroyo bottom farming, 52, 101–103
Arroyo cutting. *See* Hydrology
Ashiwi Polychrome, 10
Atsinna, x, 4, 22–23, 45, 51–52, 71–73, 75, 80–82, 84, 101, 104, 106, 108–110, 112, 121

Bandelier, Adolf F., 3, 5–6, 33–34, 43–46, 49, 51, 54–55, 58–59, 63–65, 68–69, 74, 86
Banteah, Terry, x, 55
Binford, Lewis R., 2
Binna:wa, 18–19, 22–23, 58–59, 64–65, 68, 73, 75, 81, 83–84, 86, 104, 106, 110–111, 121
Black Rock. *See* Zuni weather station
Black ware, 10, 14–15, 18–20, 72, 111
Blaney, Harry F., 99
Blind Canyon Draw, 34
Bohrer, Vorsila L., 96–97
Bordne, Erich F., 99
Bosson Wash, 26
Box S Ruin, 16–17, 22–23, 33–34, 73, 75, 77–79, 81, 84, 106, 108, 120
Bradfield, Maitland, 98, 102, 104, 116
Breternitz, David A., 14–15, 17
Buff ware, 10, 20, 72
Bullock, H. E., Jr. *See* Maker, H. J.
Bureau of American Ethnology, 3
Bureau of Ethnology. *See* Bureau of American Ethnology

Burial
    cremation, 60, 68
    inhumation, 60, 68
Bushnell, G. H. S., 68–69

Cambridge University Museum of Archaeology and Ethnology, 68–69
Candelaria Ruin. *See* Pueblo de los Muertos
Carlson, Roy L., 7–8, 10, 14–17
CARP. *See* Cibola Archaeological Research Project
Casa Malpais, 109
Casselberry, S. E., 21
Casteñeda, Pedro, 6, 74
Catchment analysis, 105–108
Caywood, Louis R., 4, 69–70
Cebolla Creek, 35, 44
Cebollita. *See* Kluckhohn Ruin
Ceramic chronology, ix, 3, 9, 12–20
Ceramic collections, 8–10, 12–13, 19–20, 24.
    See also individual site descriptions
Ceramic complexes, 1, 12–20, 24
    A, 16
    AB, 16–17, 77–78, 83–85, 87–89, 103
    B, 16, 77–78, 83–89, 103
    C, 16–17, 77–78, 83–89, 103, 108, 112
    D, 17, 77, 79, 81, 83–89, 104, 108, 112–115
    DE, 17, 80–81, 83–89, 104, 108, 112–114
    E, 17–18, 80–81, 83–89, 104, 108
    F, 18, 81–89, 104, 108, 110
    G, 18, 81, 83, 86, 104, 111
    H, 18–19, 81–89, 104, 107–108, 110, 114
    I, 19
    J, 19
Ceramic group, 12
Ceramics. *See by type name*
Chacoan system, 5
Chalo:wa, 22–23, 66–68, 73–75, 81, 83–84, 104, 106, 121
Chalowe. *See* Chalo:wa
Check dam. *See* Dams
Chisolm, Michael, 105
Chyan-a-hue, 68–69
Cibola, 3, 5–7. *See also* Zuni area
Cibola Archaeological Research Project, x, 4, 6, 8–9, 11, 19–20, 24, 31, 40, 42, 48, 50–51, 72
Cibola White Ware, 14, 17
Cienega Site, 22–23, 36, 42, 48–49, 52, 71–73, 75, 79–82, 84, 90, 104, 106, 110, 112, 120
Circular Kivas Near Hawikuh, 59–61
Clan, 116
Climate, 1, 92–96
Climatic change, 5, 112–114
Climatic reconstruction, 1, 93–97
Colorado Plateau, 90, 112–113
Colton, Harold S., 10, 12, 14
Columbia University, 24
Complex. *See* Ceramic complexes

Continental Divide, 7
Contour terrace. *See* Terraces, agricultural
Corn, 96–99, 104
Corn Mountain. *See* Dowa Yalanne
Coronado, Francisco, 6, 59, 96
Corrugated buff ware, 10, 15, 17–19
Corrugated gray ware, 10, 15–20
Crampton, Gregory, 5, 90
Cremation, 60, 68
Criddle, Wayne D. *See* Blaney, Harry F.
Crockett Ruin. *See* Fort Site
Crown, Patricia L., 17
Cushing, Frank H., 3, 9, 11, 45, 47, 55, 64, 66, 96–98, 101

Dams, 28, 97, 101–103. *See also* Reservoirs
Danson, Edward, 109
Davis, Mrs. Paul, ix
Day Ranch Ruin, 16–17, 22–23, 35, 73, 75–76, 78–79, 81, 84, 106, 115–116, 120
Dean, Jeffrey S., x, 21, 94, 96
Decade departure index, 94
Defensibility, ix, 5, 51, 79, 109–110. *See also* Warfare
Demography. *See* Population growth and decline
Dendrochronology. *See* Tree-ring dates
Dendroclimatology. *See* Climatic reconstruction
Dobyns, Henry, 5
Dodge, William A., 49, 54–55
Dowa Yalanne, 63, 65, 90
Dowa Yalanne Spring, 91
Drought, 5, 94, 96–97, 112–114
Dual organization, 117

Eggan, Fred, 24, 46, 53, 64–65, 69, 116–117
El Morro (Inscription Rock), 4, 31, 42, 44–45, 48, 51, 81
El Morro Airport weather station, 92–95, 98–99
El Morro National Monument, 4, 7, 31, 44–45, 51. *See also* Atsinna; North Atsinna
El Morro National Monument weather station, 92–95
El Morro Valley, 3–8, 11, 13, 16, 19, 21, 31, 36, 41–42, 45, 48, 50–52, 71–74, 79, 81, 83, 90, 100, 102, 104, 109–110, 112–113
Elevation, 5, 83–85, 89–90, 92–93, 102, 108, 112–113
Environment, ix, 24, 90–102, 116. *See also* Climate; Elevation; Fauna; Flora; Growing season; Rainfall; Topography
Escavada Black-on-white. *See* Puerco Black-on-white
Estevan, 6, 59, 64
Ethnographic analogy, 2
Euler, Robert C., 94–95, 113

Factionalism, ix
Farming villages, 107. *See also* Lower Pescado Village; Ojo Caliente; Upper Nutria Village